On Board

ON BOARD

My Life in the Navy, Government, and Business

PAUL R. IGNATIUS

Naval Institute Press
Annapolis, Maryland

Naval Institute Press
291 Wood Road
Annapolis, MD 21402

Library of Congress Cataloging-in-Publication Data

Ignatius, Paul R.
    On board : my life in the Navy, government, and business / Paul R. Ignatius.
        p. cm.
    Includes bibliographical references.
    ISBN 1-59114-381-0 (alk. paper)
    1. Ignatius, Paul R. 2. United States. Dept. of the Navy—Biography. 3. Cabinet
officers—United States—Biography. 4. United States. Navy—Officers—Biography.
5. Businessmen—United States—Biography. I. Title.
    E840.5.I38A3 2006
    359.0092—dc22

                                                              2005028642

Printed in the United States of America on acid-free paper ∞
13 12 11 10 09 08 07 06   9 8 7 6 5 4 3 2
First printing

For Nancy

And yet a spirit still, and bright / With something of angelic light.

William Wordsworth, "She Was a Phantom of Delight"

Contents

Preface

IN THE LATE 1920S AND EARLY 1930S, MY FATHER RENTED AN apartment for a couple of weeks each summer at the beach in Ocean Park, California. There was a roller coaster named the Highboy at the nearby amusement pier that enticed riders with a continuous, sing-song recording: "It's a High, Smooth, Fast, Safe-Sane, Sen-Say-Shun-Al Ride." I rode the Highboy whenever I had a dime, and I hung around for a long time listening to the mesmerizing, mechanical voice.

Now I am in my middle eighties wondering where the time has gone and how it all adds up. I think about the family I came from, my wife and kids, the people who helped me along the way, and the unexpected, improbable turns of events. I've had a sensational ride—fast, smooth for the most part, and, thanks to good fortune, safe and sane. I'd like to take the ride again if I could.

If I can't, I can at least recount the highs and lows and the momentum, starting slowly in California and accelerating rapidly in Washington, D.C. There are two parts to my story. I covered the first part—growing up in California and serving in the U.S. Navy in World War II—in a privately published book, *Now I Know in Part.* I described my Armenian heritage, how my grandfather was compelled to leave his ancestral home because he had written some poems about freedom and liberty, and then, after spending twenty years in England, why he decided to move with his wife and children, including my mother, to Glendale, California, in 1911. I talked about my proud and forceful father, a businessman and leader of the Armenian community in Southern California, who said one day that "America is lucky to have me" in response to my sister's comment that he was lucky to have come to America.

I decided to write this memoir because I had worked in several fields—government, large and small business, nonprofit enterprises, and community organizations—and thought that a recounting of these various activities, what they meant and how they differed, might be of interest. I also wanted to say something about critical events of the twentieth century that I knew at first hand. I was a teenager during the Great Depression of the 1930s; a naval officer in the Second World War; a Defense Department consultant during the Cold War and the Korean War; a senior government official in the Vietnam War; a reluctant participant in the Pentagon Papers case; a major player in the air traffic controllers' strike, the deregulation of the airlines, and the energy crisis of the 1970s. I was also the parent of four college-age children during the troubled and tumultuous 1960s and '70s.

I also wanted to understand more about myself. When I was young, I wanted to be a creative person—an actor, a writer, a movie director. I was probably influenced by the example of some of my parents' friends, such as the writer William Saroyan and the stage and screen director Rouben Mamoulian. I acted in school plays and with little theater groups, played bit parts in several movies, and tried, unsuccessfully, to write screenplays. My parents, to their great credit, let me do what I wanted. They didn't object when I decided to quit college for a term and go on the bum as an aspiring writer in Carmel, California, and when I left college once again to work as a locomotive fireman, shoveling three tons of coal a day to stoke a steam engine's boiler, for the Santa Fe railroad in Winslow, Arizona. They were patient as I stumbled to adulthood, always encouraging me to believe that I would amount to something some day, though they weren't quite sure what.

Like so many young men, my adolescence came to an end with my wartime service. It took me awhile before I understood why we needed to fight the fascist enemies. I was influenced strongly in this by my mother's pacifist views and the antiwar poems she encouraged me to read. I came to realize in combat against the Japanese that there were values worth fighting for, even if it meant giving up one's life. I came out of the U.S. Navy in 1946 ready to take my place in the world of adults.

In college I had read an article by Dean Acheson, who served in both the Roosevelt and Truman administrations and became Truman's secretary of state, praising the virtues of public service. I made up my mind that I would serve in the government if an opportunity arose. My hopes were realized when I was invited to join President John F. Kennedy's administration as an assistant secretary of the Army, and I continued to serve until the end of President Lyndon B. Johnson's administration eight years later, in a succession of high-level Pentagon positions: undersecretary of the Army, assistant secretary of defense, and secretary of the Navy. In this period, while I worked long hours, my wife, Nancy Weiser Ignatius, bore the major responsibility for raising our four children, somehow managing at the same time to earn a master's degree in international relations at American University. I have dedicated the book to her with lines from William Wordsworth.

———

Many people in addition to my wife have helped me in this endeavor. My journalist son, David, read early drafts and encouraged me in many thoughtful ways throughout the entire effort. My other journalist son, Adi, carefully read each chapter and spotted places that needed correction. My daughters, Sarah and Amy, gave me good advice on certain sections. The staff members of the Air Transport Association helped me to recall details of my time there as the association's president. My former and longtime secretary, Sally Moser, made the finished copies of the manuscript before her death in 2005. Several individuals—Robert McNamara, Robert Pursley, Bob Pierpoint, Albert Beveridge, Worth Bagley, Paul Gorman—read selected chapters and gave me useful comments. Patricia Haas, a senior editor at Alfred Knopf, offered some good advice. Finally, I could not have been better served than by the staff at Naval Institute Press. The editorial director, Mark Gatlin, guided the effort along with Linda O'Doughda, the managing editor. Most important, they assigned a gifted and experienced editor, John Raymond, who, with his able assistant Katy Meigs, made innumerable suggestions for improving the clarity and verifying the accuracy of the text. I am grateful for their devoted efforts. Any factual errors, arising from faulty memory or other causes, are my responsibility.

———————

Now, back to that roller-coaster recording. The mechanical voice says at the end, "You'll Enjoy It!" I enjoyed the sensational ride and I hope you will enjoy reading about it.

Paul R. Ignatius
Washington, D.C.
2005

ON BOARD

One

A Life on the Ocean Wave

My service as a lieutenant in the u.s. navy in world war ii was a transforming experience that left me with a sense of confidence that I could handle responsibilities of increasing importance.

I entered the U.S. Navy through the unusual route of the Harvard Business School. In early January 1942, several weeks after the Japanese attack on Pearl Harbor, I was in my last semester at the University of Southern California. Harry Hague, my best friend in high school and at USC, told me that an assistant dean from Harvard would be interviewing applicants for a special program. The regular master of business administration program was being modified to emphasize industrial administration and war production. Anyone accepted would be obligated to apply immediately for a commission in the Army or Navy but could return to Harvard when the war ended to complete the requirements for a master of business administration degree. Hague said he was going to meet with the visiting dean and I said I would go along with him. After a lengthy interview, a great deal of thought, and several conversations with my father, I applied, hoping my excellent record at USC would help me gain admission. I was accepted and awarded a scholarship that paid part of my tuition. I arrived at Harvard in May, took the naval physical in June, and was commissioned as an

1

ensign in naval ordnance in August. Hague was also accepted and was commissioned in the Navy Supply Corps.

During World War II, the Harvard Business School became virtually a military academy. The Navy established its premier educational program for Supply Corps officers there. Another school, for Army Air Forces officers, taught advanced statistical analysis techniques and attracted such people as Robert McNamara, a future secretary of defense, and Charles "Tex" Thornton, who led the group of "whiz kids" (which included McNamara) that modernized management at Ford Motor Company after the war. Some faculty members took leave to join war administration agencies in Washington, and others were commissioned as Navy or Army officers to teach military courses at the school. A special program was launched for businessmen from companies whose products were no longer produced after the shift to war production. They were trained to be industrial managers in an effort that became, after the war, Harvard's famed Advanced Management Program.

Ordnance and Supply Corps officers were issued naval uniforms and required to attend Navy classes as well as demanding courses with case studies on war mobilization issues. I decided to take a voluntary course in navigation taught by a Harvard professor who was an accomplished sailor. Some of my classmates were called to active duty after only a few weeks, and others remained for longer periods, as I did. It all depended on the scheduling at the training centers we would shortly attend. Meanwhile, the Navy thought our rigorous education, grappling with challenging case studies, would make us more valuable officers.

The Harvard curriculum was extremely demanding, far more so than my classes at USC. There were no lectures and almost no text material. Instead, there were several case studies each day drawn from actual experience that set forth issues and problems for analysis, discussion, and decision. The instructor's role was to stimulate a comprehensive and penetrating discussion of the situation—the facts, uncertainties, recognized or unrecognized assumptions, human implications, and risk assessment. A student had to defend his recommended course of action against the opposing views of other students, as well as cross-examination from the instructor, a sometimes withering, palm-sweating experience.

Because of the war, many new cases on the vast war effort were being developed. One, for example, required a survey of six midwestern cities as potential sites for an ammunition plant. Data had to be assembled on water supply, electric power, the transportation network, labor requirements and availabilities, and so forth. Then each of us had to decide which site to recommend and to prepare a lengthy report setting forth the reasons. Another case asked whether corporate salaries should be capped at $25,000 for the war's duration, with the discussion covering a multitude of considerations involving equity, morale, incentives, administrative difficulties, and philosophical leanings. In all instances, the student was placed in the position of the accountable person, the one who had to make a decision. There were no right or wrong answers, only a reasoned defense of a chosen course of action. Some students, notably engineers, had difficulty with the approach, having been trained in disciplines in which precise answers to specific problems—e.g., how much weight can this bridge truss bear?—were needed. But the further along I progressed, the more I was persuaded that the case method was the best way to foster the development of sound business judgment.

My full-time Navy duty began in May 1943 when I reported for eight weeks of basic training at Fort Schuyler, New York. My required naval courses at Harvard and the navigation course gave me a leg up on some of my classmates. Still, I was a long way from the real thing.

The training staff filled our heads with naval science and our arms with vaccines to ward off the three Terrible Ts—typhoid, tetanus, and typhus. We were roused at 0600 and given nine minutes to wash and dress in sweat suits for a half hour of calisthenics. Then, after a shave, shower, and breakfast, we had a long day of drills on navigation, communication, gunnery, ordnance, and seamanship—enough material for a full year crammed into two months. We learned a little bit about a lot of things, enough to ask sensible questions in unfamiliar surroundings. We also got into great physical shape with daily exercise periods and miles of marching.

On most weekends, from Saturday noon to Sunday evening, we were free for liberty in New York. We wore our summer whites to dances on the roof of the Hotel Astor, went to the theater on half-price servicemen's tickets, and visited the familiar landmarks. We also logged a lot of time in bars and hotels, sampling their beer and whiskey. One night, I met up with a fraternity brother from USC, Lt. Bill Tanner, a naval aviator who had fought in the Solomons and other campaigns and had been shot down. On another weekend, I went into the Brooks Brothers store on Madison Avenue and bought a blue uniform. The salesman let me charge the $62 purchase, no questions asked, and I became a lifelong customer.

Schuyler was basic training—basically boring, something to endure and be done with. At the end of the course I got orders to the General Ordnance School at the Navy Yard in Washington, D.C., for six weeks of intensive training in naval guns, torpedoes, and ammunition. The Navy manufactured some of its ordnance in shops in the yard, giving us first-hand experience with the weapons along with the classroom instruction. Despite the oppressive August heat and humidity, we began each day with calisthenics on the parade ground in our khaki uniforms. Then we spent the rest of the day in our soggy clothes in rooms with no air conditioning.

Much of the course material prepared us for duty at naval ordnance manufacturing plants or ammunition depots, but I hoped to get orders to a ship. Because of my months of inactive duty while Bill Tanner and others bore the burden, I was anxious to make up for lost time with a challenging assignment and asked to be transferred from ordnance to the submarine service. My commanding officer recommended me, as did the medical officer after an arduous physical examination, but my application was returned after a week with the comment "subject officer does not have sufficient engineering background." If I was going to sea, it would be on, not under, the water. My CO said my best chance would be to request orders to the Aviation Ordnance School in Jacksonville, Florida, and hope it would lead to an aircraft carrier assignment.

On October 1, I began a twelve-week course at Jacksonville on aircraft bombs, fuses, rockets, and bomb-disposal procedures, all in preparation for arming aircraft at sea for fighter and bombing missions. Among the operational and training units at Jax was a torpedo plane squadron where I found my Hoover High School classmate Bob Reilly. I flew with Bob on simulated combat missions in the bombardier's seat of the three-place TBF, the Grumman Avenger, and became familiar with the demands on naval aviators and the tactics of torpedo and bombing runs.

An hour or two away, at Camp Blanding, there was a large Army basic training center commanded by my uncle, Col. Vaughn Jamgochian, who had been a reserve officer all those years when he worked at my grandfather's soap factory in Los Angeles. I visited him and his family one weekend in my Navy khaki uniform with the customary black shoes that naval officers wore. A young bootblack outside the camp stared at my shoes in disbelief and said, "You the first soldier I ever seen with black shoes."

Toward the end of the course, I heard about an opportunity that might get me an assignment to an aircraft carrier. The Navy was going to assign a few ordnance officers to temporary duty on subchasers to prepare them for standing deck watches on carriers. I applied for the experimental program and was one of two officers selected. My ship was a small patrol boat, 110 feet in length, that conducted antisubmarine searches in the Atlantic out of Mayport, Florida, near the Jacksonville Naval Air Station. We had search gear on board, two 20-mm guns, a couple of machine guns, and depth charges for attacking submarines. But our real responsibility, if we located a Nazi sub, was to report its position to a larger ship or aircraft squadron better equipped to make the kill.

On the several patrols we made in January and February, I learned how to stand deck watches under way. Our ship made frequent contacts with dolphins and an occasional whale, but we never sighted an enemy submarine. I prepared a report for the Bureau of Ordnance on the program, analyzing the situation as we were taught to do at the business school, and got a favorable comment from the bureau. More important to me was an accompanying recommendation for assignment to an aircraft carrier.

In March 1944 I reported to VC-80, a composite squadron of sixteen Wildcat fighters and twelve Grumman TBF Avenger torpedo
bombers, destined for duty on an escort aircraft carrier, or CVE. Called
"jeeps" or "baby flattops," the carriers were being built in large numbers to support landings in the rapidly expanding war against the Japanese, and for escorting troop and supply ships in the North Atlantic.
The squadron had begun training in Washington and Oregon and was
now at a remote naval air station in Holtville, California, near the Mex-
ican border, forty miles from the Salton Sea. With clear skies and vast
desert spaces, it was an ideal place for gunnery and bombing practice.

By this time, I knew a lot about bombs and the fuses that ignited
them. From my flights with Reilly at Jacksonville, I was at home around
naval aircraft and aviators, particularly those who flew the Grumman
Avenger. The Navy used it for torpedo runs and for "glide bombing,"
where the bomb was released from an angle of attack less steep than
those of the Navy's dive-bombers.

The TBF was also capable of horizontal bombing, the special
province of the Army Air Forces. For this purpose, the squadron was
equipped with the famous Norden bombsight, a secret weapon said to
be so accurate "you could drop a bomb down a pickle barrel."

All of the squadron's torpedo bombers were equipped with these
sights, and the training syllabus required the pilots to make several
horizontal bombing runs over the target area in the Salton Sea. The
only problem was that the Navy had supplied planes, pilots, bomb-
sights, and inert practice bombs, but no bombardiers. The squadron
commander thought it highly unlikely that we would ever need to do
any horizontal bombing but knew it would be unwise to ignore the syllabus. With my cursory knowledge of the Norden sight from course
work at Jacksonville and my flights in torpedo bombers with Reilly, I
was pressed into service as VC-80's amateur bombardier, and made
several flights with our pilots.

The most memorable one was with Ens. Bob Crandall, a hot pilot
who had wanted to fly fighters but had to settle for the slower and less
agile bombers. We took off for the training area to drop 500-pound
practice bombs into the Salton Sea below. We flew a straight, level

course, releasing the bomb when the Norden sight said the time was right with every expectation it would land directly on target. With one bomb remaining, Crandall got fired up and told the radioman and me that he was going to dive it. He pushed the TBF over into a steep and rapidly accelerating dive, released the bomb, and began to level out when the aircraft's only engine quit! To land safely Crandall would have to clear the water and lose altitude gradually for a wheels-up landing on the desert floor, without slowing down so much that the plane would go into a dangerous and perhaps fatal spin. He performed with great skill. We hit the ground hard; the plane was badly damaged but no one was hurt. Our skipper, Lt. Cdr. H. K. Stubbs, gave us three days' leave. He also told me with a smile that he was sure I must have lost the leather flight jacket I had been wearing, and if it ever happened to show up, I could go ahead and keep it. With an aviator's flight jacket, I felt I was now a full member of the squadron.

After several weeks in the desert, we were ordered to North Island, the Navy's huge aircraft base in the San Diego area, for carrier landing practice before going into combat. When I reported in, the billeting officer said there were no more rooms in the bachelor officers quarters and asked whether I would mind staying at the Del Coronado, the famous old Victorian hotel where the Navy had taken over a number of rooms for the duration of the war. I said everyone was giving up something for the war effort. My roommate was Lt. (jg) David Conroy, a torpedo pilot who had completed a tour in the Aleutians before assignment to VC-80. He was a thoughtful person with a marvelous sense of humor. We both returned to Harvard after the war—he to the law school and I to the business school—and resumed our friendship. Meanwhile, we made the most of our two-week stay at the Coronado, playing tennis one day with the vacationing Gary Cooper and eating dinner at a local restaurant that claimed to have invented the Caesar salad. The only serious note was a couple of days spent at a fire-fighting school where we learned to extinguish oil fires in confined spaces.

We went to sea again for night landing practice, far more exacting than daytime operations, and came through with no one hurt and only one plane damaged. We were ready to sail for Pearl Harbor and meet up with the carrier that would be our new home. On arrival, we learned that our ship had been delayed, and we were bedded down for two weeks at the Kaneohe Naval Air Station, across the island from Pearl. Since there was little to do but wait, we played tennis at Kaneohe and swam at Waikiki Beach. One of the bomber pilots and I got to the doubles finals of the Kaneohe tennis tournament. Our trophies—large salad bowls made of monkeypod wood—were presented to us by former tennis champion Bobby Riggs, now a chief petty officer.

The Battle of Leyte Gulf

Word came that our ship would be the USS *Manila Bay,* CVE-61, an escort carrier built by the Henry Kaiser shipyards and that had seen action in the Marshall Islands and New Guinea campaigns. The ship had returned to the United States for routine overhaul and to discharge its squadron. She returned to Pearl Harbor with a new commanding officer, Capt. Fitzhugh Lee, a member of a distinguished military family who later became a vice admiral. We loaded our planes and gear aboard and went to sea for qualification flights under the watchful eye of Captain Lee and our carrier division commander, Rear Adm. Felix B. Stump.

On September 15 we departed Pearl Harbor with battle plans for the invasion of Yap, a small island in the Palau group. Yap was one of the "stepping stones" in the island-by-island strategy leading to the major objective, the reconquest of the Philippines. While we were under way, a decision was made to bypass Yap because it was no longer necessary to secure it before the Philippine invasion. We were ordered to Manus, an island in the Admiralty group where the Navy had built a large base after the New Guinea campaign to prepare for the Philippine assault. Our overall boss was Gen. Douglas MacArthur, and we were called "MacArthur's Navy," but in fact were part of the Seventh Fleet commanded by Vice Adm. Thomas Kinkaid. The modern battleships of the *Iowa* class and the fast carriers making up the Third

Fleet, the most powerful in the world, were commanded by Adm. William F. Halsey. Halsey's superior was Adm. Chester Nimitz, the Pacific Fleet commander headquartered in Hawaii. The separate commands proved to be a serious problem as the battle for the Philippines unfolded.

In early October, we sailed in company with a heavy bombardment group as part of a seven-hundred ship armada for Leyte Gulf where our troops were scheduled to land on October 20. On D-day minus three, when we were supposed to begin bombing and strafing the Leyte beaches, we were hit by a typhoon, the first of several we were to encounter over a period of months, but we escaped without serious damage to our ship or aircraft. The ship rolled heavily and its steel plates snapped with reverberating roars as the high seas and wind pounded us. You can fight back at an enemy but you are powerless when nature turns violent.

The winds subsided and air operations began on the following day. We got our first kill—a Japanese plane shot down by Commander Stubbs and his wingman. My ordnance men loaded and reloaded the planes from first light until dusk, bringing the bombs and rockets from the magazines below to the planes on the flight deck. Modern carriers have special elevators for this purpose, but on a CVE it was time-consuming, exhausting work.

The first U.S. troops poured ashore on D-day while thousands of others waited their turn on the hundreds of ships and landing craft in Leyte Gulf. General MacArthur was poised for the dramatic moment when he would wade ashore and announce his return to the Philippines. And then, the unexpected happened. The Japanese fleet made its long-delayed appearance. What ensued was the greatest naval battle of World War II and a shining hour for the escort carriers and their accompanying destroyers.

The Japanese plan was called Sho, or Victory Operation, an attempt to win a decisive battle and thwart the Philippine landing, in the belief that the Japanese homeland could not be saved if those islands were recaptured. There were three main phases to the battle. First, a southern force under Vice Adm. Shoji Nishimura with two battleships, one heavy cruiser, and four destroyers, augmented by other ships steaming from the home islands, would sail through Surigao Strait at the southern end of Leyte and into the gulf to attack the vulnerable troop ships waiting to disgorge their soldiers. The central force, under Vice Adm. Takeo Kurita, had five battleships, including the *Yamato* and *Musashi,* the largest in the world, ten heavy cruisers, two light cruisers, and fifteen destroyers. This powerful force would sail through San Bernardino Strait at the northern end of Leyte and proceed to Leyte Gulf to deliver the knockout blow. A third force, under Vice Adm. Jisaburo Ozawa, with aircraft carriers, a battleship, and light cruisers, would head south from the Japanese Inland Sea. Ozawa's carriers had far fewer aircraft and pilots than normal, but their mission was not to attack but to lure Halsey's Third Fleet away from the battle zone.

On October 23, two U.S. submarines, the *Darter* and *Dace,* discovered Kurita's force and sank several of his ships. The next day, Admiral Halsey's Third Fleet aircraft made repeated strikes on Kurita, knocking out additional ships and damaging others. The *Musashi* was badly damaged and withdrawn from the fight. On the basis of optimistic reports from his pilots, Halsey believed that Kurita had been routed, and he headed north to intercept Ozawa's carrier force on October 24.

During the night of October 24–25, the Japanese southern force was soundly defeated at Surigao Strait by Rear Adm. Jesse B. Oldendorf, commanding the battleships, cruisers, and destroyers that had bombarded the landing beaches at Leyte. Oldendorf's battleships included the *California* and *West Virginia,* both sunk at Pearl Harbor but raised from the mud and sent to sea again, and the *Maryland* and *Pennsylvania,* both heavily damaged in the Pearl Harbor attack.

With Halsey heading north, San Bernardino Strait was left unguarded. A Halsey message to his battle line commander, Vice Adm. Willis A. Lee, to form Task Force 34 was interpreted by Adm. Thomas Kinkaid and others to mean that Halsey had detached his heavy ships to guard the strait, when in fact they were racing north with him. Admiral Nimitz sent a remarkable message to Halsey: "Where, repeat where, is Task Force 34? The world wonders." Halsey was infuriated and is said to have slammed his hat on the deck in anger. At dawn on the twenty-fifth Kurita and his ships, still a formidable force, sailed through the strait. There was nothing to stop them but the Taffies—the three groups of baby flattops and destroyers with radio call letters Taffy 1, Taffy 2, and Taffy 3. These ships had one 5-inch gun each compared to the Japanese 16- and 18-inch guns, and their aircraft and pilots were intended to support landings, not fight a major fleet.

Taffy 3, the northernmost group, came under attack around 0700. Its commander, Rear Adm. Clifton Sprague, broadcast an urgent message in plain language asking for help from anyone who could provide it. Taffy 1's ships were 130 miles away. In between the two carrier groups was Taffy 2, our group under Admiral Stump, consisting of the *Manila Bay* and six other CVEs, and a screening force of eight destroyers and destroyer escorts. Within ten minutes of Sprague's call for help, Taffy 2 launched aircraft in improvised strikes against the enemy fleet.

We had been alerted by Admiral Stump shortly before midnight to be ready to launch torpedoes on short notice against the Japanese ships crippled by Oldendorf at Surigao Strait. Readying torpedoes is a time-consuming task, but by working through the night, my ordnance men prepared the weapons for launch and rigged the Avenger's bomb bays to receive them. Thus, no time was lost when Stump ordered an attack. The ordnance men set records in the frantic effort to attack Kurita before he sank all of us. All the time spent at school and in drills was paying off.

Admiral Stump ordered his ships "to get the hell out of here" sometime around eight in the morning, and we headed south, away from Kurita, at our best speed of 17½ knots. We continued our air strikes while we fled, loading aircraft with whatever weapons we had, including depth charges for underwater targets, not surface ships. On our third strike of the day, the bombers were dangerously launched into a crosswind, since turning into the wind, the normal procedure for getting heavily loaded planes into the air, would have headed us toward Kurita.

Taffy 2's continuing strikes were intended to help Taffy 3, under relentless attack from Kurita. Two of Taffy 3's carriers, the *St. Lo* and *Gambier Bay*, were sunk. Destroyers *Hoel* and *Johnson* and destroyer escort *Samuel B. Roberts* were also sunk after laying down smoke to protect the carriers and attacking the overwhelmingly superior Japanese force at close range with guns and torpedoes. It was one of the most heroic actions of the war. Some of the armor-piercing shells went through the thin hulls of the jeep carriers and exploded in the water. Kurita assumed, quite wrongly, that he was facing major units with proper armor at the waterline, not the jerry-built CVEs.

Though Taffy 3's destroyers and airmen from both Taffy 3 and Taffy 2 continued to press the attack, there appeared to be no way to save the U.S. ships from annihilation. The rapidly advancing Japanese were closing in on our group, making 25 knots through the water to our 17½. I could see their shells landing astern of us, and the masts of their ships on the horizon. But at 0925, Admiral Kurita surprisingly broke off the attack, reversed course, and headed north.

Captain Lee shouted from the bridge to all who could hear that now was the time to go after them, and we continued our air strikes. Kurita sped toward San Bernardino Strait hoping to escape with the remainder of his fleet intact. Though he did not know it, Vice Adm. John S. McCain (grandfather of the Arizona senator), was heading at flank speed to engage Kurita from Palau where his ships, part of Halsey's Third Fleet, had been refueling.

Admiral Sprague, the Taffy 3 commander, said later that the failure of the enemy to completely wipe out his force "can be attributed to our successful smoke screens, our torpedo counter attacks, continuous harassment of the enemy by bomb, torpedo, and strafing air attacks, and the definite partiality of Almighty God."

With Taffy 3 particularly in mind, but also the other carrier groups, in his official history of the battle, *Leyte*, Samuel Eliot Morison wrote: "In no engagement in its entire history has the United States Navy shown more gallantry, guts, and gumption than in those morning hours between 0730 and 0930 off Samar." And C. Vann Woodward said in his account, *The Battle for Leyte Gulf*, "With due credit assigned to those forces [Third Fleet], it remains clear that the chief credit belongs to the CVE groups of the Seventh Fleet, to the sacrificial attack of the small screening vessels of the Northern Group, and to the air squadrons of all groups."

All of us had been so busy arming and launching aircraft that no one had much time to worry. As we saw the shells landing astern of us, I thought we would end up in the water. When Lee shouted from the bridge and over the ship's announcing system that we had been saved by Kurita's decision to reverse course, nobody could believe our good luck. We had tried to prevent his escape, but Kurita made it through San Bernardino Strait before nightfall.

According to Morison, Taffy 2 launched 117 Avengers and 87 Wildcats, dropped 49 torpedoes and 76 tons of bombs, and fired 276 rockets and thousands of rounds of ammunition during the battle. The *Manila Bay*'s torpedoes hit major ships, running true to their targets. Overall, the Japanese lost twenty-six ships in the Battle of Leyte Gulf, against six U.S. ships, all but one of them belonging to Taffy 3. Throughout the battle Captain Lee spurred us on, kept us informed, and afterward saw to it that the aircrews got the recognition they deserved.

Why Kurita turned around when he was fighting a vastly weaker force has been the subject of much speculation and inquiry. Many explanations have been offered: his ships had been allowed to operate individually, and he needed to regroup to regain control; he thought he was fighting a more powerful force than in fact was the case; he thought his destroyers would run out of fuel chasing the fleeing U.S. CVEs; he wanted to get safely through San Bernardino Strait before dark; the escort carriers put up an unexpectedly fierce attack, and he suspected that additional U.S. forces were on the way to the battle; his fleet, though damaged, represented the main force remaining to defend the homeland, and he didn't want to lose it in the Philippines. Had Kurita continued his attack, he would have knocked out the Taffy 2 ships and then entered Leyte Gulf and laid waste to the transports unloading troops. Admiral Oldendorf's force of old battleships could have helped, but his ships had expended most of their ammunition bombarding the Leyte beaches and in the previous night's engagement with the

Japanese southern force. We were lucky and grateful and immensely proud of our ship and its captain. Many of our pilots received medals for valor and superior airmanship, and Lee was awarded the Navy Cross. The ships of Taffy 3 won the Presidential Unit Citation, and the *Manila Bay* was later awarded the Navy Unit Commendation for Leyte Gulf and other actions.

After Leyte, we were ordered to Manus for rest and replenishment of the ship. Taffy 1's ships to the south of us were not so lucky. They came under heavy attack from a new weapon, the suicide planes flown by Japanese kamikaze pilots. The CVEs *Sangamon* and *Suwanee* suffered eighty-five killed and many more missing and wounded.

We spent three weeks at Manus. Although it wasn't as pleasant as Hawaii, we read letters from home and had a drink or two at the so-called Officers Club. When Felix Stump landed from his admiral's barge while a group of us were ashore, our air combat intelligence officer, Johnny Cross, a former Harvard yell leader, called out "Regular Cheer for Taffy 2!" Stump gave us one of those icy "we are not amused" stares.

Our main job at Manus was to replace the ammunition expended at Leyte. The *Mount Hood,* a large Navy ammunition ship, was anchored at Manus. We took our turn with the other ships getting the ammo and then loading it aboard the *Manila Bay,* which was about a half mile from the *Mount Hood.* Suddenly, we heard a tremendous roar and saw the sky light up with brilliant flashes, followed by huge clouds of black smoke. The *Mount Hood* had exploded with a force so great that she disappeared. We never knew for sure what caused the disaster—faulty ammunition or someone's carelessness—but there were 45 known dead, 327 missing, and hundreds more injured.

The Mindoro Operation

After getting over the shock of the *Mount Hood* tragedy, we turned our minds to the effort to reconquer the Philippines. The master plan called for the occupation of Mindoro Island to establish a staging base and airfield for the main objective, the island of Luzon, where the capital, Manila, was located. To reach Mindoro, it was necessary to pass through Surigao Strait into the inner seas that were surrounded by Japanese airfields on the nearby islands of the Philippine group. Air support for the Mindoro operation was supposed to be provided by Air Force planes from Leyte, but rain had slowed construction of the airfields. Naval aviation was the only alternative, but there was a great deal of anxiety about operating aircraft carriers in landlocked seas surrounded by Japanese airfields. Of particular concern were the kamikazes, after their aggressive attacks on Taffy 1's CVEs. The fast carriers operating with Halsey's Third Fleet were clearly unsuited for sailing in such close quarters, so a "Slow Carrier Task Force," in Captain Lee's phrase, was assembled. It included old battleships and cruisers, transports for carrying the assault troops, and the accompanying aircraft in the *Manila Bay* and six other CVEs with their destroyer screen. The mission was to protect the assault force from air attack en route to Mindoro and to support the landings with bombing and strafing runs. The officer in tactical command was our own Felix B. Stump.

Under cover of darkness on the night of December 12, we successfully traversed the narrow Surigao Strait, aided by the light from small bonfires set by Filipinos working with us onshore. The morning of December 13 began quietly, but at 0900 a Japanese plane spotted us and alerted nearby kamikaze units. Several hours later a suicide plane crashed into the cruiser *Nashville*, causing a number of explosions and killing 133 officers and men. Fighter planes from *Manila Bay* and the other CVEs were busy attacking the incoming enemy planes, and two of them were splashed by a *Manila Bay* pilot. Pilots from *Ommaney Bay* were particularly effective, intercepting a large raid in the late afternoon. But some planes got through and hit one of our destroyers, with a toll of 14 dead and 24 wounded. A second kamikaze headed for the *Manila Bay*, but it was shot down by our gunners 1,400 yards from the ship.

On December 15 the Army troops went ashore on Mindoro, encountering little opposition. But the air attacks on the ships continued. Kamikaze raids on the destroyer *Ralph Talbot* and the carriers *Marcus Island* and *Natoma Bay* were stopped by antiaircraft gunners.

The attacks continued, and this time the *Marcus Island* was hit and suffered casualties. Gunners from the *Manila Bay* and from screening destroyers accounted for one of the attackers, and another was stopped by gunfire from the *Natoma Bay*. Overall, the *Manila Bay* accounted for five suicide planes, some getting as close as three hundred yards.

The escort carriers had expected to retire after the troops had landed, with air cover to be provided by land-based planes from Leyte. Bad weather upset this plan and we were ordered to remain on station for another day. When it was all over, Adm. Arthur Struble, the officer in charge of the operation, said, "This group is the first combat team to consist of escort carriers with old battleships, cruisers, and destroyers. Beyond any possibility of doubt, the babies proved themselves equal of any." Admiral Stump was less effusive: "Without detracting from the CVE's excellent performance, it must be realized that we were lucky."

A Time Out

After the operation we were supposed to go to Palau. There we would have to ride at anchor because there were no facilities ashore. With Christmas just a few days away, Stump thought we deserved better and arranged for us to go to Manus instead, a miserable place but at least it offered a chance to get off the ship. While the decision was being made, we encountered another typhoon, but it was mild in our area compared to its effect on Third Fleet ships to the north of us. There, three destroyers capsized in the turbulent wind and seas with heavy loss of life. Again, nature enraged was the most formidable enemy.

The good news—and the bad news—was that we got to spend Christmas at Manus. If ever there was a place to dream of a white Christmas, Manus was that place. It had none of the breathtaking scenery of the Polynesian islands, and the women's teeth were red from chewing betel nuts. We tried our best to enjoy ourselves but everyone wished he were home. I thought of my extended family, the whole bunch of uncles and cousins and aunts, eating turkey and plum pudding at my grandfather's house.

During our stay at Manus, I began to stand deck watches after being transferred from the squadron to the ship's company, in response to orders from the Bureau of Ordnance. To my surprise, I grew to like the change. I still kept in touch with my pilot friends but made new friends among the ship's officers, like Roger Lapham, the supply officer, and Alexander Delancey, the chief engineer. Roger, an elegant sort, had gone to Harvard. His father had been head of the American Hawaiian Steamship Company and was then the mayor of San Francisco. Although Delancey had only a limited formal education before joining the merchant marines, he was a savvy engineer and we were lucky to have him. Many of the baby flattops had trouble with their engine shafts, but ours on the *Manila Bay* worked perfectly. One day I asked Delancey why this was, and he said, "Because I don't use the goddamn oil the Bureau says to use."

I asked if he had ever thought of writing a letter to the Bureau of Ships to explain why a different oil worked better, and he looked at me in disbelief. "I don't want to get into no boh-luminous correspondence with the Bureau," he said.

Unless we were running air operations, which kept me fully occupied with rearming duties, I stood deck watches under way when we returned to sea. A proud moment came when I was declared to be qualified as an Officer of the Deck. The OOD has the immediate responsibility for the ship, and at night when most of the seven hundred officers and men were asleep, including the captain, a young officer has a measure of responsibility unequalled in civilian life. Knowing when to act on your own and when to awaken the captain was only one of many circumstances that helped to develop good judgment.

Lingayen Gulf

Douglas MacArthur couldn't wait to reconquer Luzon, the main Philippine island where he had been evacuated after the fall of Manila and where American troops had been held prisoner on Corregidor. The Luzon landings were scheduled to begin on January 9, 1945, at Lingayen Gulf, north of Manila in the South China Sea. We were part of the assault group, and our carrier division commander once again was Admiral Stump. His group included five other CVEs and a screening force of seven destroyers. We sailed from Manus on December 27 through what was by now familiar territory—Surigao Strait, the inland seas, Mindoro—on our way to Lingayen. On January 3, CVE *Makin Island* came under kamikaze attack, but the suicide airplane was shot down before it could crash into the ship. We stayed at General Quarters throughout the day and again on January 4, but nothing much happened. Then a Japanese plane suddenly appeared and struck the *Ommaney Bay*, near us in the formation. The suicide plane carried two bombs that exploded when it hit the ship, causing a fire that ignited ammunition and gasoline stowed below deck. The sky was filled with plumes of smoke, not as terrible as those from the explosion of the *Mount Hood* but persistent and ominous against the darkening sky. The crew did their best to contain the raging flames, but they were unequal to the task. The ship was abandoned. Ninety-five men were killed or missing and sixty-five wounded. At 2000 one of our destroyers was ordered to fire a torpedo into the burning vessel and send it to the bottom.

The awful arithmetic of the kamikaze initiative—one airplane lost and a whole ship destroyed—was evident to us as we talked about the tragedy of the *Ommaney Bay*. We knew the attacks would continue and that we might well be the next target. Captain Lee interrogated the damage control officer from the *Ommaney Bay*, who had been rescued from the water and brought aboard our ship, about the fires and why they had not been extinguished. He learned that events had moved so rapidly after the suicide plane hit that there was no time to sound the sprinkler alarm. Lee immediately had a special alarm installed on the bridge so that he could sound the alarm if he concluded that his ship was about to be hit. Then water would be pouring from the sprinklers before the kamikaze struck, and with luck the fires would not get out of hand.

Throughout the day on January 5, the kamikazes pressed the attack, sometimes appearing singly and at other times in formations of ten or more. We watched them trying to fly through the heavy antiaircraft fire from our 20-mm Oerliken guns and 40-mm twin Bofors. I remember seeing aircraft wings and parts of the fuselage falling into the sea, and entire planes exploding in a single fireball.

At around 1700 hours outside the very Manila Bay for which our ship had been named, our turn came. Two kamikazes came flying directly toward our ship, one low over the water and the other at a higher altitude diving straight down. I was on the flight deck at the time overseeing the loading of torpedoes for a strike on some Japanese ships thought to be in the area.

The puffs of black smoke from the antiaircraft guns and the bright ribbons of tracer fire filled the sky. When it looked as though the planes would get through, I jumped from the flight deck onto a catwalk several feet below and took cover in a small compartment under the deck. One of the planes crashed into the bridge, destroying our radars and navigation gear, and exploded in the water.

The other hit the flight deck forward of where I had taken cover and crashed through to the hangar deck where the suicide plane and the bombs it carried exploded.

On the bridge Captain Lee had seen the inevitable result, ducked to avoid machine-gun fire from the attacking planes, and sounded the sprinkler alarm, which had been installed only a few hours earlier. Lee was hit in the back by debris from the explosion but his injuries did not put him out of action. On the hangar deck, two of our Grumman Avengers caught fire and fires raged in the surrounding spaces. But the alarm system had started the sprinklers ahead of time and the hangar was flooded with water.

Remembering the fires on the *Ommaney Bay* from the exploding bombs and aviation gasoline, I thought the torpedoes in the planes on deck might overheat and explode. I got permission from the air officer to throw them overboard as a precautionary measure. My chief petty officer and several of his men did the work quickly. It seemed like the right thing to do under the circumstances, but I had a moment's hesitation when I recalled that our instructor in ordnance school had told us how expensive torpedoes were and to look after them with the greatest care.

The fires on the hangar deck and in other parts of the ship were gradually coming under control. Our internal communications system had been knocked out and Lee shouted orders from the bridge with the help of a megaphone. Our planes that had been airborne landed on other carriers. When the fires were finally extinguished, the damage control crew went to work with emergency repairs to the flight deck and the radio communications equipment. Our radio call sign was "Circus" and Lee radioed Admiral Stump: "Circus performance interrupted for a while. Have two rings operating, expect to have third ring operating soon." Within twenty-four hours we resumed flight operations. Because our radars had been destroyed, we couldn't "see," so the other ships guided us on at night and nobody ran into anybody else.

Although Captain Lee's foresight and some uncommonly good luck enabled us to save the ship from the *Ommaney Bay*'s fate, the kamikaze pilots' desperate attack took a heartbreaking human toll. Fourteen of our shipmates were killed in the attack and many others injured. The dead were buried at sea according to naval tradition in ceremonies back aft on the fantail of the ship with the chaplain presiding. When we began to clean up the hangar deck and put things in order, we came upon a surprising object. It was the wallet of the kamikaze pilot who crashed into our ship and killed and injured our men. We had nothing but hate for him until we looked inside the wallet. In it was a photograph of the young Japanese man in his pilot's uniform. Next to him was an older couple, a man and woman standing proudly, presumably his parents. It looked very much like the photographs our own pilots kept in their wallets showing them on the day when the gold wings of a naval aviator were pinned on their uniforms, with proud parents and family standing by. The enemy suddenly had a human face. I had a momentary feeling of compassion for him and for his parents, despite the grave damage he had caused and the lives he had taken.

Though the attacks on the ships continued, the Lingayen Gulf landings went off on schedule and thousands of soldiers went ashore to reclaim the island of Luzon and Manila, its capital. For the next two weeks, under difficult conditions, we operated with a full complement of aircraft and did not retire from the scene until land-based planes were ready to take over.

Many of our aircraft had been damaged in the attack, and those that could not be repaired were replaced by ones from other carriers, including planes from the *Ommaney Bay* that were in the air when their ship was hit. Our flight deck was bumpy from the hasty repairs, and our elevator to the hangar deck had a bulge. But the ice cream machine was working again and we even gave a few gallons of the stuff to a destroyer that came alongside. Praise the Lord and pass the vanilla fudge!

Two tragic incidents marred our final days at Lingayen Gulf. One of our senior pilots walked into a whirling propeller on the flight deck and was hospitalized for over a year while surgeons tried to restore the use of his arm and shoulder. The tragedy had a happy ending when he married the faithful nurse who had attended him during his long ordeal. Another senior pilot, on a crowded deck before launch, was struck in the head by a whirling propeller and died instantly. We buried him at sea in an unforgettably sad and solemn ceremony. Commander Stubbs asked me to draft a letter from him to the pilot's wife. What do you say in a letter like that? He had flown boldly against the enemy and on our last day on station had walked into a propeller. What should you tell her to help ease the pain of her loss? I couldn't bring myself to write the truth of what happened. I said her husband had distinguished himself as a Navy pilot and had been lost in operations against the enemy. Stubbs sent the letter as drafted.

Stateside Repairs and Changes

Many members of the squadron and of the ship's company received medals for heroism, and Fitzhugh Lee got a second Navy Cross for keeping his ship in the fight. We received orders to sail to San Diego for repairs, and everyone was rewarded with twenty-one days of leave.

Captain Lee was detached and reassigned to Pacific Fleet headquarters, and we waited anxiously to see who would replace him. It would be a hard act to follow. Lee had everything—brains, bearing, courage, vision, and a cultivated mind. Roger Lapham found him reading Proust one day in the original French and expressed surprise. "You Harvard boys have got a lot to learn about the Naval Academy," Lee told him.

VC-80, the squadron I had joined so many months ago in the California desert, was detached, and a new squadron would join the ship when we returned to Pearl Harbor after the repairs were done. I had many close friends in VC-80 and feared I would never see them again. (As it turned out, the squadron got together every so often, and I attended two of the reunions. The brave young pilots were old men by then, some with hearing aids and others with canes to help them get about. Flying for the Navy in a war against tyranny had been the high point of their lives. They talked about their flying days with humor and deep feeling, and for a moment they were young aviators again.)

It took two months for the shipyard workers in San Diego to repair all the damage the two kamikaze planes had caused. With little to do, we had a lot of time off, which I spent happily in San Diego and with my family in Glendale. My folks fussed over me, particularly my mother. She had never been able to accept the idea of war and worried about me so much that her health suffered. One of my first cousins, who had been close to my family and to me, had been killed flying a bomber over Germany, and she had taken this very hard. I urged her not to worry, but it never did any good. Her overwhelming concern made me feel uncomfortable, and I tried to tell her this without hurting her feelings.

Our new skipper was Captain Leon Johnson, a tall, quiet Southerner, not as imposing a figure as Lee but a person of dignity and inner strength. We sailed for Pearl Harbor in May 1945 to pick up the new squadron and qualify the pilots for shipboard operation in the waters around Hawaii. En route we learned that the war in Europe had ended and that the formidable Eighth U.S. Air Force would be redeployed to the Pacific to help speed our victory against the Japanese. None of us thought victory was close at hand. The enemy was fighting with fierce determination to hold onto each of the islands we invaded, and we knew they would be even more resolute defending their home islands. The growing use of kamikaze pilots was a measure of their desperation and their determination.

The Last Battles

I was a lieutenant (jg) now, my khakis were faded, and my metal insignia had become nicely tarnished from the salt air. Many new officers had joined us in San Diego and they stood out because they wore the new gray uniform, the "Greyhound bus driver's uniform," that the Navy, stupidly we thought, had adopted.

One of the new officers was assigned as my assistant and eventual replacement. We now had fifty-seven enlisted men and four chief petty officers in the ordnance department. I continued to stand deck watches under way and developed a comfortable relationship with the new captain. He kidded me one day when I gave an order to the helm to come to new course "one-three-oh." "Don't say 'oh,'" Captain Johnson said in his Southern accent, "it sounds like 'foh.' Say, 'zee-roh.'"

We were heading for the western Pacific in the last weeks of May while the Okinawa campaign, which had begun in April, continued at a furious pace. Okinawa was a bloody experience on land, where many thousands died, and at sea, where the Navy suffered dreadful losses of men and ships to relentless kamikaze action. We arrived in time to participate in the final phase of the campaign, from June 9 to June 20.

Our assignment, in company with other jeep carriers and destroyers, was to neutralize Sakishima Gunto, a string of islands between Okinawa and Formosa (Taiwan) where the Japanese had built airfields. The fields were heavily defended, and our pilots met severe antiaircraft fire. Any plane we could hit on the ground or knock out in the air was one less to attack our troops in Okinawa or our ships at sea. We ran several missions each day—"milk runs"—and fortunately never came under attack ourselves. We were, nevertheless, taken out of action, not by the Japanese but by an explosion of the hydraulic catapult that launched our aircraft. No one was hurt, but the ship was slightly damaged and the catapult was a total loss. We were ordered to Guam for repairs.

It took several weeks to rebuild the catapult, time for us to enjoy life ashore. Guam was now the headquarters of the Pacific Fleet commander, Admiral Nimitz, whose flag flew atop a building on what the Navy called CinCPac (Commander-in-Chief, U.S. Pacific Fleet) hill. Captain Lee had been on Nimitz's staff for a couple of months and invited Roger Lapham and me to lunch one day, and to a ceremony where he was officially awarded his second Navy Cross. Lee was handling public information for the fleet, and had helped the *New York Times* prepare a four-column story on the *Manila Bay*'s exploits at Leyte and Lingayen. Through Lee, I met several war correspondents from *Time*, *Life*, and major newspapers, and struck up a pleasant relationship with W. H. Lawrence of the *New York Times*.

Bill Lawrence was an old-fashioned reporter, tough-talking, smart, experienced, and fond of drink. He had been a correspondent in Moscow and Washington, D.C., traveled with President Roosevelt to the Casablanca conference, flown in a couple of raids over Tokyo, and spent seventy days at the front with the troops on Okinawa. One day Bill got a wire from his editor in New York that said, simply: "Spaatz has it." Spaatz was Gen. Carl Spaatz, the senior air force commander coming to the Pacific War, and "it" turned out to be a case of Scotch whisky aboard Spaatz's plane. Bill shared it with Roger and me at picnics on the island and at a memorable dance with real women—Navy nurses at a base hospital. *Life* covered the dance with one of its "Life Goes to a Party" features, and we hoped to see our pictures in the popular magazine not looking too blotto from Bill's booze. Unfortunately, or perhaps fortunately, the story never ran.

I had a portable typewriter with me and wrote a lot of letters home. My parents kept all these letters and in one of them I said

> Here's something big. I just heard that the Japs have offered peace terms. From what I understand, the only condition is that we do not invade their homeland. This strikes me as one of the most astute propaganda moves they could have conceived. They

know that we are tired of the war at home. They know that if we continue now it would appear that we are the aggressors. They realize that tremendous pressure will be brought on Truman, Nimitz, Marshall, King, and the rest of the leaders. But don't you see that we cannot fall for this bait. We must invade their home-land or else accept peace terms with no strings attached. We all want the war to end, particularly those of us out here who will have to fight the balance of it. But if we should give in to the Japs, we would have gained nothing.

Aleutian Waters

The conference at Yalta, where Roosevelt, Churchill, and Stalin met early in February 1945 to plan the final phases of the war, didn't affect the *Manila Bay* until July. We were ordered to Eniwetok in the Marshall Islands to "winterize" the ship and then sail to Adak in the Aleutian chain. From there, we would escort convoys carrying war materiel to the Soviet Union, which had agreed at Yalta to join the war in the Pacific. I'm not sure I knew just what it meant to "winterize" the ship—I secretly hoped it didn't mean that Delancey would have to use a different oil for his driveshafts—but we got winterized and all hands were issued cold weather clothing. Meanwhile, we swam and snorkeled in the incredible coral beds surrounding the atoll, and had an occa-sional beer at the recreation center the Navy had built after the fight-ing ended on Kwajalein and Eniwetok.

Around the first of August, I was promoted to lieutenant—a two-striper in Navy lingo—and got a raise of $18 a month, bringing me to almost $200. I put a hundred of it into a savings bank and paid off some of my debts to Harvard. Occasionally I sent a check to my sister who had transferred from UCLA to Wellesley College. The Navy took care of all our needs and there was no problem in salting away money every payday.

With my lieutenant's bars shining brightly, we set sail for a few practice launches and then headed north for the Aleutians. On several occasions during the trip, our admiral ordered rearming drills, requiring us to bring the heavy bombs from the magazines below and hang them on the planes on the flight deck. My men complained about the arduous work, telling me they had proved themselves fighting the enemy. I explained that we had to make sure the new men understood their jobs and why we needed to remain ready at all times. During one of these drills, a bomb dropped on its nose and damaged the fuse that ignites it. The captain cleared the deck while I removed the broken fuse, using what I had learned from bomb-disposal training at Jacksonville. I had to perform this delicate task on an earlier occasion when a plane landed hard and several small incendiary bombs fell onto the deck.

On August 6, we got our first intimation that the war might be over sooner than we had thought. The *Enola Gay* had dropped a new, secret, and overpowering weapon on Hiroshima. Three days later, on August 9, a second atomic bomb was dropped, this time on Nagasaki. The Japanese initiated surrender discussions the following day. The Soviet Union had entered the war against the Japanese only five days before it was over, and we were sailing to Adak to run convoys that were no longer needed.

We heard that a *New York Times* reporter named Lawrence had flown on the plane that dropped the Nagasaki bomb and had written about it in his paper. My God, I thought, Bill Lawrence! He had been in Guam, near Tinian where the plane took off, and must have persuaded somebody, maybe his whisky supplier, General Spaatz, to let him go along for the historic ride. Only later did I learn that the *Times* had two reporters with the same-sounding name, my friend Bill and another Bill, William L. Laurence.

We sat around Adak for a week or so. It was a cold, dreary place with unsettling winds called williwaws. Clearly it was no place to fly, and we were glad to be riding at anchor and not running flight operations.

Witness to Surrender

Soon we got the exciting news that we would be joining Vice Adm. Frank Fletcher's North Pacific Fleet to patrol off Japan and participate in the surrender proceedings. We headed for the northern Japanese island of Hokkaido where there was a fine naval base at Ominato. Admiral Fletcher accepted the surrender of the local commanders and entered the bay in impressive fashion. I wrote a letter to my parents describing the situation:

It is incredible to be here. I can well imagine the humiliation of the Japanese people. Can you imagine us being able to see off the coast of Santa Monica a powerful fleet, launching scores of planes, to fly over Los Angeles, Glendale, and Pasadena? The Japs have been reduced to impotence. I think they realized after Midway that they had bitten off much more than they could chew. I have had access to a large amount of translated enemy publications, and these show how really weak in material the Japs were. Their early landings were midget things compared to our later gigantic amphibious assaults. They knew that in early 1942 we had nothing out here, and with their precious and limited resources, coupled with the surprise element, they hoped to knock us out quickly. They estimated our resources excellently, but they erred tremendously in their judgment of our power to come back fighting with new ships, planes, and a new Army.

Admiral Fletcher steamed into the bay today with regal pomp and splendor. His ships were in battle formation, and overhead throughout the day, he had a large flight of planes in parade formation. Their purpose was solely to make the Admiral's entrance impressive. It made me think of the conquerors of old, whose armies having sacked a city, triumphantly entered in the wake of buglers, bowmen, and lackeys of varying degrees of importance. The parade of air power announced the entrance of this modern conqueror. It is difficult to comprehend this concept of the conqueror, but that is just what we are. We have won and from now on they do what we tell them to do.

I realize now and, I think in many ways only now, that it is worthwhile to fight, and if necessary, even die for one's own country. I don't think I could stand to be in the Jap's position at this moment. I don't see how the Japs can bear the shame and humiliation. And

they are a far more fanatical people than we are. As countries go,
we in America are a reasonable group, I think. Yet, I wonder if we
could passively accept the will of the conqueror.

Admiral Fletcher learned from the Japanese commanders that
there was a prisoner-of-war camp in northern Hokkaido. We loaded
our planes with food, clothes, medical supplies, and cigarettes and
made repeated drops on the camp below. The pilots said they saw the
men cheering and waving their arms in joy. The camp was called Bibai
and held British, Australian, Chinese, and a lesser number of American
prisoners.

On September 12, we ended our patrols and entered Mutsu Bay
where the Ominato naval base was located. The channel had been swept,
but there were still a lot of mines in the water. Our destroyers blew them
up when they were sighted. There were also many Japanese airplanes at
the Hokkaido airfields—all potential kamikaze attackers—but the Japanese commanders had forbidden any offensive action. We anchored the
ship and hoped to go ashore, but the opportunity never came.

Troopship Home

All the talk now was about getting out of the Navy and returning to
civilian life. A point system was announced that permitted those with
the longest service to get out first, and several of my *Manila Bay*
friends were preparing to leave. All the available troop transports were
called upon to bring the boys home, but the demand was greater than
the supply and other ships were pressed into service, one of them the
Manila Bay.

We sailed to Pearl Harbor to be converted into a troopship. Our aircraft and ammunition were put ashore and our gasoline storage tanks
drained. The squadron waved good-bye and the rest of us watched
the yard workers weld double bunks to the hangar deck and make
other changes to accommodate a load of a thousand or more returning
servicemen.

The proud days of the *Manila Bay* were over. We were just a ferry-boat now, hauling passengers in cramped quarters. My friend Roger Lapham left the ship for San Francisco, along with other veterans of the fight against the Japanese. I expected to be detached because the last thing a ferryboat needed was an aviation ordnance officer. Captain Johnson had other ideas. He wanted me to be responsible for our new mission, handling the troops we carried home. He said the position of troop officer called for someone of higher rank, but he was confident I could do the job. I had hoped for shore duty in the States but was pleased at the captain's show of confidence in me and said yes.

We picked up a thousand or so Army men at a Pacific atoll and sailed for San Francisco. They included both black and white soldiers, and in those faraway days, when the military was still segregated, there were latent fears about racial conflicts between men living and eating in close quarters. Everyone got along just fine. We bedded them down on the hangar, exercised them on the flight deck, and fed them in shifts in the mess halls. It was a lot of work, like running a summer camp for kids or managing an overcrowded hotel.

I never look at the Golden Gate Bridge on trips to San Francisco without remembering the great joy of entering the bay on our return to the United States. Lapham had stationed a friend to stand on the bridge and bounce tennis balls off the flight deck as we passed through. Roger himself was on hand across the bay to greet us when we arrived. His father, the mayor, had arranged a festive welcome party for us at the Civic Center with enough food and drink for the whole Pacific Fleet. I consumed some of the former and more than my share of the latter. Somehow, I was able to get myself to the St. Francis Hotel where my brother, who was a medical intern in San Francisco, met me. He made a quick diagnosis and decided that heavy Italian food laced with olive oil was what his patient needed. We drove to Vanessi's in North Beach and before too long I recognized that the person next to me was, in fact, my brother speaking a language, English, that I was able to understand and use haltingly myself. I was grateful to my brother and to Vanessi's, and dined there for many years afterward until it closed its doors.

We returned to sea after our delightful stay in San Francisco to pick up another load of returning servicemen. En route to Pearl Harbor we received word that a Pan American Clipper plane was down in the water. We were told to search for it, and sometime after midnight found it floating on the sea. At first light the next morning, November 4, we put whaleboats alongside and picked up the crewmembers—the plane had been deadheading to San Francisco so there were no passengers aboard. Our boatswain mates then undertook the difficult job of taking the huge four-engine plane under tow for the remaining seven hundred miles to Hawaii.

The towing line parted soon after we got under way, and the captain thought it unwise to attempt to attach a second line. We reported the situation and were instructed to stand by the plane until an ocean-going tugboat arrived. We sat adrift on the ocean for eighteen hours, all engines stopped, waiting for the tug. When it arrived, the tug captain took over responsibility, and we resumed our journey. On November 8, Pan American threw a big party for us at the Moana Hotel on Waikiki Beach.

The servicemen waiting to go home were at the dock in Saipan when we arrived, as well as a commander who, to my amazement, had been ordered to replace me as troop officer. I was furious and spoke immediately to Captain Johnson, telling him something like "this is a helluva way to run a Navy to send some old guy to replace a young officer doing a good job."

The usually friendly Leon Johnson stared coldly at me and said, "Simmer down, Ignatius!" He continued in a quiet tone of voice and told me I had done an excellent job and fulfilled the confidence he had in me. He said the troop officer billet rated a full commander. "Your job," he said sternly, "is to help this new officer in every way you can so I don't lose my confidence in you."

I wasn't happy about the situation, but this was the Navy and you had to go with the system. We went to work, the new troop officer and I, taking aboard fifteen hundred men and looking out for them on the voyage home, this time to San Pedro. I spent a day or two at home and then it was back again, on the first of December, to pick up another load.

Over and Out

Throughout my time on the *Manila Bay*, I corresponded with my best friend from school and college, Lt. Harry Hague, the supply officer at a naval hospital on Guadalcanal. One day he got the welcome news that twenty Navy nurses would soon be arriving at the hospital for extended duty. Hague began to think about new supplies he should order, and immediately thought about sanitary napkins. He made some calculations—number of days per month, number of months per year, multiplied by twenty, that sort of thing—and came up with the quantity to order. He received the number of boxes he ordered, but in quantities of a gross, 144 dozen, not a dozen. Hague wrote to me that the island of Guadalcanal almost sank under the weight of the stuff. Contests were held to find innovative uses. Basketball teams discovered they made excellent knee guards, and everyone said they were great for washing jeeps.

Hague and I had a mutual friend, Sterling Livingston, who had gone, as we had, to Hoover High, USC, and Harvard Business School. Livingston, several years older than the two of us, was now a Navy commander and had taught at the Navy Supply Corps School at Harvard. From Harvard, the Navy ordered him to Washington to prepare a new and expanded version of the Supply Corps Manual of Regulations. Hague had been asked to join his staff. He wrote to me that Livingston needed a line officer to represent the user's point of view, and that I could have the job if I wished.

I informed Captain Johnson and he said to go ahead and take it, but from a personal standpoint he hoped I would stay with the ship. He then said he would recommend me for a spot promotion to the rank of lieutenant commander. I thanked him but said I was ready for something different and Washington sounded interesting. The orders came and I was detached from the ship on December 12, 1945.

Leaving the ship was an emotional experience, far more intense than leaving a school or moving to another city. A ship was so many things—a home, a place of work, and a neighborhood where you and your friends lived. Everyone's safety depended on the safety of the ship. In combat, the goal was to defeat the enemy, but it was necessary also to protect and defend the ship. Most of us were motivated less by hatred of the enemy than by wanting to do our part, not letting shipmates down. The award of the Navy Unit Commendation to the *Manila Bay*—to each one of us and all of us together in the ship—was the most appropriate award, because it recognized that what was done was done by all of us for one another.

What the Navy truly meant to me pretty much disappeared when I left the *Manila Bay*. The job in Washington was office work. I went to my desk in the morning and left it at night. The work was important in its own way, but the professionals were the experienced Supply Corps officers, and I was a supernumerary. The evenings, on the other hand, were great fun. My good friend Bill Lawrence had been transferred to the *Times* Washington bureau, and we dined and drank around the town, sometimes with interesting sources for the stories he was writing. After two months, our small staff was transferred to New York for the final printing of the manual and production of its associated training films.

My work in New York was more demanding. We had contracts with layout firms, printers, and film producers, and I was supposed to keep in touch with all of them and make sure that problems were identified and quickly solved. Delays were serious matters because we had to complete the project before our entire staff disappeared into civilian life.

On July 28, 1946, after the New York work had been completed, I was separated from the naval service in Los Angeles. Almost four years had gone by from when I was commissioned in August 1942. I spent a month at my parents' house and then left for Boston to complete my studies for the master's degree in business administration at Harvard.

My Navy life had come to an end. The *Manila Bay*'s life was also coming to an end. Launched on July 10, 1943, she was decommissioned three years later, on July 31, 1946. For several years, she lay quietly at anchor at an eastern seaport alongside other ships that had been quickly thrown together to meet a wartime need and now were not worth keeping. I read one day in 1959 that she had been sold for scrap to a Japanese steel mill and was being towed across the Pacific. It was an ironic ending that seemed to capture what had gone before and what lay ahead. The Japanese had said that one of the reasons for making war on the United States was the embargo we imposed on shipments of petroleum products and other vital materials, including scrap for making steel. Now we were friends again. They needed scrap for industrial production and got it from a ship they had tried so hard to kill.

We had come full circle and all that remained was the memories.

Two

Bound East for Boston

"THERE'S A GIRL IN MY CLASS I THINK YOU WOULD LIKE TO MEET."

"Maybe so," I said to my sister. "Look at this shirt, Miggs. You think I should wear it or put it away with this other stuff in the trunk?"

"Her name is Nancy Weiser," Miggs continued, paying no attention to the shirt. "She's from Holyoke, Massachusetts. Her mother went to Mt. Holyoke but she went to Wellesley."

"That's down the road a piece."

"She's a philosophy major."

The trunk was getting full. It was an old black steamer trunk that belonged to my parents, bound in wood, with solid brass fittings like the brass buttons on my Navy uniforms. After almost four years of wearing Navy blue or khaki, it was now time to see if my old tweed jacket and gray flannel trousers were still wearable, or whether I would have to spend a big chunk of my final Navy paycheck on civilian clothes. I loved the Navy and looked lovingly at the pile of clothes in the trunk—blue and white jackets, the green uniform I wore as a member of an air squadron, my dress cap with a blue cover for winter and white one for summer, and my baseball cap, its naval emblem still affixed, heavily tarnished from my months at sea on the aircraft carrier *Manila Bay*.

In a few weeks I would be leaving my parents' house where I had stayed since my separation from the Navy in July 1946 and heading for Boston to complete my studies for the MBA degree at Harvard Business School. My sister, Helen Mary, whom everyone called Miggs, would also be traveling eastward for her final year of college. She had spent her first two years at UCLA and, after only a year at Wellesley, had been elected to Phi Beta Kappa. A pianist of near concert-stage perfection, she was now more interested in writing and hoped to end up in New York as a writer or editor.

Living at home for a brief period was both a pleasant and unsettling experience. I slept in my old bed next to my brother Joe's in the bedroom where the two of us had grown up in Glendale. My parents made a fuss over me, cooking favorite foods for dinner and inquiring about my wartime experiences. They hoped I would return to Glendale after Harvard and said I could live with them until I had a place of my own. It was a generous gesture but the last thing I wanted. I had no real idea what I was going to do, but I was quite certain that whatever it was, it wouldn't be in Glendale. It had been a fine place for a boy, with good schools, good friends, and an affectionate extended family of grandparents, uncles, aunts, and cousins. But it had always seemed to be an unexciting provincial place, more so now that I had seen New York, Boston, and the world of the Navy.

Falling in Love with Nancy

Late in August 1946, I left for Boston. Some of my classmates from the earlier period at the business school, before I left for naval duty, had also returned. We were an older, wiser crowd now. In fact, the faculty came to believe that its postwar classes were the best they had ever seen. Though most of us had been in the Army or the Navy rather than in business, we had been officers, responsible for the welfare of others, for meeting objectives, for reconciling differences in policies and personnel matters, and for accepting a measure of risk in decisions where all the facts could not be known. In short, administrators in the business school mold. The case studies were no longer academic exercises. They were recognizable real-life situations, illuminated by the knowledge and experience we brought to bear. The school was so impressed with the performance of the postwar classes that it modified its admission policies to favor applicants who had a year or two of experience over those coming directly from college.

I had been back in Boston for only a few weeks when Miggs called to say that her friend Nancy Weiser was lonely and would welcome some company. She had been confined to the Wellesley campus for three weeks because she had returned to the school one night after 10 PM without prior written permission. On Friday evening, after borrowing a car from my friend Harry Hague, I drove to Wellesley to meet Nan for the first time. She was trim, about average in height, and was wearing a wraparound skirt tied together with a large gold safety pin. Miggs introduced us and then disappeared. Nan and I went to the Well, a place on campus for sandwiches and refreshments, and had a brownie and ice cream. Our conversation for the most part was perfunctory. Later, she told my sister that I seemed awfully old. I told Miggs that I was glad to meet her friend but that she wasn't anyone special, just another good-looking blonde.

I must have been more impressed with her than I had led my sister to believe because I called her for a date when her confinement was over. I surprised both Nan and myself by taking her to dinner at Locke Ober's, Boston's best restaurant. We had a fairly good time, nothing special, and talked more about the food than about ourselves.

The next date was different. Arthur Miller was trying out his new play, "All My Sons," in Boston before its New York opening. It was about a businessman who sold faulty parts to airplane manufacturers that led to the death of aviators in combat. It was an intense, emotional drama, directed by Elia Kazan, whom I had known briefly in California. There were powerful scenes between the father and the son, and of the wife's refusal to acknowledge her husband's guilt. After the play we went to a bar near the theater. We discussed the play in depth and compared our reactions to its moral implications. I had never talked so easily, so intimately with a girl at any time during my four years at USC. I knew that I wanted to see more of Nan, and I hoped that she wanted to see more of me.

We continued to see one another, and then something occurred that brought us close together. My sister had an emotional breakdown. There were no parents on hand to take charge of the situation, and the full responsibility fell on me and on her best friend, Nancy Weiser. I telephoned my father in California, but he refused, almost defiantly, to believe what I was telling him. I said Miggs had to go to a place I had located on the North Shore of Boston where people would know how to treat her problems. I added that it would be expensive.

Over a period of a month or so, Nan and I visited my sister during the course of her treatment. She made encouraging and steady progress. The school term was almost over and she returned to Glendale rather than remaining at Wellesley. At a later point, she was given an opportunity to take her final exams, and though unable to attend the graduation ceremony, she was included as a member of the class of 1947 along with Nan and her many friends.

My sister's misfortune permitted me to see qualities in Nan that might not have been so apparent without our shared responsibility. She faced the situation squarely with me and helped immensely. And she saw in me characteristics of steadiness and calmness that made her think that I might be a dependable companion for life. It was a maturing experience for both of us.

We got quite serious one night while we talked in her dorm after seeing a movie. She said her mother wanted her to return to Holyoke after graduation, join the Junior League, and take her place in the traditional New England community like the other daughters of the owners and executives of the town's factories. Nan, on the other hand, wanted to work in New York and live in Greenwich Village. But she knew this would disappoint her parents and wasn't sure what to do. "You could always marry me," I said in the best Harvard Business School tradition of seeking a way out of irreconcilable alternatives.

"Yes, I could," said Nan, and thought we had become engaged at that moment. But I, concentrating on problem solving rather than proposing, promptly forgot my words.

In her final semester at Wellesley, Nan's father had loaned her an automobile that he seldom used. One weekend she invited me to join her on a visit to her parents' house where her mother was sick with the flu and needed some help. During the drive, I noticed that she was coughing and sneezing, and by the time we arrived she was almost as sick as her mother. The task of preparing meals and looking after the two sick women fell to her father, Richard Mather Weiser, and me. He was a reserved, soft-spoken man, a descendent of Cotton Mather, the formidable Congregational minister who figured prominently in the Salem witchcraft trials of the seventeenth century. No two people were more different than Mr. Weiser and me, but somehow we found things to talk about as we washed and dried the dishes, and each of us ended up thinking that the other was a pretty good guy.

In June I went with Nan's parents to her graduation at Wellesley. The speaker was Secretary of Defense James Forrestal. My father joined me for my graduation a few days later (my mother was ill and had to stay in California). At the festivities in Harvard Yard the leading speaker was Gen. George Catlett Marshall, then secretary of state, and he delivered the "Marshall Plan" speech that became the basis for the European recovery program after the devastation of World War II. I did not perceive the full implications of what Marshall was saying in his understated way, and was gratified to learn some time later that neither did James Bryant Conant, the president of Harvard.

Research Assistant

I had become a research assistant at the Harvard Business School several months earlier after completing my MBA requirements in February. Several of my classmates did the same thing: Paul Lawrence and Abe Zalesnik, both of whom later became full professors; my study mate, Steve Fuller; and Don Booz, the son of the founder of the well-known management consulting firm bearing his name. A research assistant worked for one or more professors, wrote case studies, and carried out research and administrative assignments. My work involved a new project on the use of motion pictures and other audiovisual aids for training and marketing purposes in business and as possible vehicles to augment classroom discussion at the school. The professor in charge was Sterling Livingston and my co-researcher was Harry Hague. The three of us had worked together on the Navy Supply Corps manual before returning to Harvard. The Harvard project descended directly from the Navy work. We thought we might start a company some day that specialized in management training, using some of the techniques we were exploring in our research efforts.

In the summer of 1947, Hague and I rented an apartment for several months in the fashionable Back Bay section of Boston. It was located on the third floor over an expensive restaurant called Joseph's. With monthly salaries of $250 each, the two of us subsisted on canned corned beef and tuna and tried to ignore the inviting aromas from the restaurant as we climbed the stairs to our quarters.

One weekend in May, Nan and I had a date on a Friday night and again at noon the following day. She thoughtfully offered to lend me her father's car so I could return to Boston from Wellesley and pick her up the next day. I parked the car in front of my apartment, not knowing that overnight parking was forbidden. A ticket was sent to the car's registered owner, one Richard Mather Weiser, with a notation that his car had been parked from midnight until morning. In those straitlaced days, he had some difficulty comprehending his daughter's explanation about the Friday and Saturday dates and the innocent, though illegal, presence of the car alongside my apartment in the midnight hours.

During the summer, my brother Joe drove from California to pay me a visit. Nan was away with her family for a month at Black Point, a lovely town on the Connecticut shore. I told Joe that Nan and I wanted to get married and that I was anxious for him to meet her. We drove to Black Point and Joe and Nan hit it off from the first moment. They listened to me from the living room when I went out to the kitchen to ask Mr. Weiser's permission to marry his daughter. I heard them giggling as I tried to tell my future father-in-law about the company we hoped to start, unable to say persuasively what the company was going to do because we weren't sure ourselves. As a man who had worked for an established firm for his entire business career, Mr. Weiser wondered how his prospective son-in-law was going to support his daughter. But he gave his permission nevertheless. During a visit to Black Point a couple of weeks later, I gave Nan an engagement ring, and we decided to get married later in the year.

Marriage and Honeymoon

On December 20, 1947, we said our vows at Nan's home in Holyoke. Her sister Jill was the maid of honor and Hague was my best man. Only members of the family and a few good friends witnessed the ceremony, but a large crowd gathered afterward at the Roger Smith Hotel for food, drink, and dancing. We spent our wedding night at the Bond Hotel in Hartford, then drove to New York for several days on the town before returning to Holyoke for Christmas.

It had always seemed to me that a cruise of the Caribbean Islands would be a delightful way to spend a honeymoon. But on my research assistant's salary of $275 per month (Harvard, all heart, gave me a $25 raise when I said I was getting married), there weren't many cruise ships in my price range. I finally found one I could afford, the *Yarmouth*, which sailed out of New York. We took the train to the city and sat leisurely in the bar of the Commodore Hotel sipping drinks before it was time to depart for the ship. It had been snowing on the way down, but we paid little attention to it. I was a lot more interested in my beautiful bride, with her orchid corsage, a new suit, and a pair of high-heeled, open-toed shoes.

When it was time to leave, we went outside to hail a cab. The doorman thought I was joking. Nothing was running: no cabs, no cars, no busses. Our only choice was the subway to Times Square, then a twenty-block walk to the pier on the Hudson River where the *Yarmouth* was waiting.

In all, twenty-seven inches of snow fell, one of the biggest storms since the famous blizzard of '88. A lot of those twenty-seven inches worked their way into Nan's open-toed shoes as we trudged through the snowdrifts to the pier. The poor orchid died on the way, but even in that state it looked better than our fellow passengers shivering under coats and blankets on the snow-filled deck while their rooms were being made ready.

After a wait, we were escorted to what was called our stateroom. It was located in the bowels of the ship and furnished with a double bunk, a narrow upper and lower, and very little else. Not a promising way to begin a marriage. Luckily, I had brought along a flask of brandy, and after the second shot, we began to laugh at our situation and hoped the ship would soon get under way.

We made a brief stop in Miami, then proceeded to Havana for a couple of days ashore. Near the university we heard machine-gun fire and ducked behind a car to avoid a stray bullet. It might have been a preview of the 1959 Cuban Revolution led by Fidel Castro, a minor skirmish that attracted little notice. The rest of the stay was delightful, with swimming at Veradero Beach and a trip to Matanzas on a bus crowded with Cubans.

Our next port of call was Nassau. We went immediately to nearby Hog Island where there was a lovely, crescent-shaped beach. The area was empty except for a small house facing the ocean. It was available for $75 a week including a maid who made coconut drinks. We quickly arranged to get off the double-bunked *Yarmouth* and stay at the beach, returning to New York ten days later when its sister ship, the *Evangeline*, paid a call. After a miserable beginning we had a real honeymoon. Today, Hog Island is called Paradise Island, and there is a large hotel where our little cottage stood.

At Home in Cambridge

Our first home was an apartment building in the midst of the Radcliffe dormitories not far from Harvard Square. It was a short walk to work, across the Cambridge Common and then the Larz Anderson Bridge over the Charles River to the business school. After a few months, Nan got a job as a research assistant for a young Harvard professor, Carvel Collins, who was writing a book called *Sam Ward in the Gold Rush*. Nan helped him to get it done and then went to work on his next project, a book, beautifully illustrated, about famous racehorses of the nineteenth century. She learned about all of them—Ripton, Confidence, Boston, and the others. She could trace their lines of descent from the founding sires imported into England in the seventeenth and eighteenth centuries—the Darley Arabian, the Byerly Turk, and the Godolphin Arabian. For years afterward, she hoped the conversation at dinner parties would turn to the subject of the thrilling horse races of the past. But it never did. The real tragedy was that we couldn't afford the twenty dollars to buy the book when it came out (and Collins was too hard up to give her a copy) and now the book can't be found at any price.

Not being able to afford a twenty-dollar book was typical of the genteel poverty of most of us—young faculty or graduate students—living in the postwar Harvard community. But when money is short, there's no better place to live than a university town with its lectures, art exhibits, concerts, classic movies—all usually at little or no cost—inexpensive restaurants, and informal dinners with friends in the same boat. For those of us from the business school who might have longed for the world of high finance, there were always weekend games of Monopoly where an aspiring tycoon could corner the hotels on Boardwalk and Park Place and get out of jail free with a small paper card.

Nan's parents sometimes joined us for an evening in this world so different from theirs in Holyoke. Her mother, Louise Reynolds Weiser, particularly enjoyed these visits. She had come from a small town in Pennsylvania called Catawissa ("It's near Mauck Chunk," she would explain to people who couldn't immediately place it), became a student leader at Mount Holyoke College, married a man from a prominent Holyoke family, and did more than her share of good works for the city. She loved meeting our young friends and going with us to funky restaurants in Cambridge or East Boston.

On May 26, 1950, our first child, David Reynolds Ignatius, was born. Our apartment was now too small, and we rented a larger place nearby on Arlington Street. It was a Victorian house split down the middle with us on one side and John Morton Blum, a history professor, and his wife and kids on the other. The rent was $75 a month. We had several bedrooms upstairs, a living room, dining room, and kitchen below, and a small garden out back. The water heater in the kitchen had to be lighted every time we washed the dishes or took a bath. The landlord said he would be glad to install an automatic heater in the basement, and raised the rent to $90. I declined an offer to buy the house for $16,000, an absurdly large amount of money for me, and learned thirty years later that it had last been sold for $1.2 million.

Arlington Street had the variety of people that made the areas near Harvard Square such delightful places to live. Across the street was Barrington Moore, an independently wealthy Harvard professor, and his beautiful Japanese wife. Next to them was "Hizzoner" himself, Mayor Deguglielmo of Cambridge. On the other side of the Moores was a quiet family named Vincent that had a lovely farm in Vermont for weekends and the summer months. Their next-door neighbor was a barber. Next to us were an ancient man called "Father," who had once been a Catholic priest, and a woman who looked after him. Up the street near the corner was another Harvard professor who later became a high official in the Central Intelligence Agency.

So many neighborhoods are homogenized, like the Amherst Street area where Nan's parents lived—all upper-middle-class, Protestant, Anglo-Saxon owners and managers of the city's industrial base. Down the hill from them were the people who worked at the mills and factories, typically Irish or Polish, and devout Catholics. In Washington, D.C., where I have lived for more than forty years, many of the neighborhoods are closer to the Amherst than the Arlington model. If you want to see at one time and place people who are rich or poor, black or white, old or young, you only need to buy some shrimp and crabs at the fish market on Maine Avenue or some fruit and vegetables at Magruder's on Connecticut.

Our visits from the Weisers became more frequent now that there was a grandchild to enjoy. David was kind of funny looking at first, but Grampsie, as Mr. Weiser was now called, still found something to admire. "That boy has the most beautiful ears I ever saw," he told Nan when he first looked at David in the crib. Like most young brides, my wife was anxious to show off her growing domestic skills. On one visit, she spent two days buying the finest ingredients and preparing a rich chicken dish with a cream sauce. She left it on the stove while we went to a cocktail party with her parents. When we returned for dinner, the babysitter, a young Harvard student, thanked Nan for having food ready for him. He said it was the best creamed tuna he had ever tasted and apologized for not being able to eat the whole thing.

Motion Pictures

My work as a research assistant continued to occupy me, and in 1949 I was promoted to instructor in business administration. With Sterling Livingston, I coauthored a report on our work that was published in the *Harvard Business Review* and wrote several articles for other business journals. The school's Division of Research published a study I had done on using audiovisual instruction to reduce the incidence of industrial accidents. The problem was a serious one, highlighted by a presidential conference in 1948 that reported no improvement in the overall accident rate since 1932, with injuries running close to two million a year. My study, based on research at a number of companies, examined innovative uses of the motion picture medium in training programs to reduce the frightful human and economic cost.

Livingston and I hoped that money might be available in order to film case studies for use at Harvard and other business schools. The written case study would always be the backbone of the curriculum, but a filmed case in some circumstances could provide important additional detail. Unfortunately, the substantial sum needed for such a project couldn't be found.

An exciting new possibility presented itself at about this time when we met Louis de Rochemont at a conference on documentary films in Boston. Louis was the founder of the popular *March of Time* series shown in movie theaters. He went on to Hollywood and made feature pictures with documentary overtones, "dramas from real life," as he called them, like *Walk East on Beacon* and other thrillers based on FBI source material. His most recent effort had been a movie on race relations in the United States, *Lost Boundaries*, that became a commercial success despite warnings from old Hollywood hands that a subject like that would be poison at the box office. Confident of his judgment, Louis next wanted to tackle another unlikely subject, a motion picture about business in realistic terms rather than in the artificial way that business issues were handled in the typical Hollywood product. He was interested in our Harvard film project and told Sterling Livingston that we should try to work together.

Livingston responded favorably and, with me as his assistant, went to work with his customary energy and zeal. He was happiest when he had a number of things going at once—"keeping three balls in the air without losing his own," as a friend had once described him. He had come from a poor family in Glendale and showed his entrepreneurial talents at an early age. When his paper route had been firmly established, the young Livingston hired another boy to deliver the papers and started a second route for himself.

Louis de Rochemont lived on a large farm in Newington, New Hampshire, outside of Portsmouth. With case studies supplied by Livingston, I worked at the house with Louis, his wife, and several screenwriters attempting to develop an entertaining and dramatic story from the raw business details. The movie was going to be called "The Whistle at Eaton Falls." It would explore technological change at a long-established manufacturing company in a small New England town whose factory whistle, blown at noon every day, was something the townspeople knew they could always count on. The story's intensity was heightened when the head of the union, which had bitterly opposed the introduction of new labor-saving machinery, became president of the company when the previous president died. His widow thought the union head had leadership qualities like those of her late husband.

Early Navy Projects

Although the de Rochemont work began to occupy more of my days, I continued to spend some time with my coworker, Harry Hague, on the Harvard project. After completing a study of his own, Hague resigned from the school to work full time on an educational program, Industries that Supply the Navy, for Supply Corps reserve officers that the Navy had asked Livingston to undertake. The teaching material consisted of illustrated pamphlets on major industry groups prepared by faculty members from Harvard in their spare time, all coordinated by Hague. I wrote a couple of the studies myself, on the paint industry and the railroads. Usually the studies were accompanied by industrial motion pictures that described the products or processes.

The Navy was pleased by the favorable response to the industry series from its reserve officer training groups and asked Livingston to undertake another assignment. The follow-on effort, Functions of the Naval Administrator, was developed in conversations among Livingston, Hague, and me, and it zeroed in on managerial problems that naval officers faced: planning for change, building an organization, delegating work, and coordinating an executive team. Each of the subject areas was presented through a recorded case study. Accompanying the recorded material was a detailed instructor's guide. It was an innovative adaptation of the famed case study method and a way to attain effective results when the instructor was not a professional teacher.

Hague oversaw the industry series, and both he and I were busy helping Livingston get the naval administrator program off the ground. The volume of work was also becoming more than was appropriate for Livingston to handle from his position as a Harvard professor. He asked me whether I would consider leaving the school, joining Hague, and starting a company to produce teaching materials. For the time being, I would continue working with de Rochemont on the movie project and help Hague to produce the naval administrator series.

The idea of forming a company was something we had discussed for months. The three of us were longtime friends. We came from the same town, went to the same high school, college, and graduate school, and had worked together in the Navy and at Harvard. So it seemed only natural for us to want to continue our collaborative efforts. We believed the techniques we were developing in the naval administrator case studies had promise for executive training programs at U.S. corporations at a time when such programs were in their infancy. Moreover, the idea of starting a new venture, though uncertain and not fully developed, appealed to me. My wife was an adventurous person and thought that creating a new business would be more fun than going to work for an established company like the one where her father had toiled for forty years.

I had very much enjoyed the academic life at Harvard, as I had also enjoyed my service in the Navy. But I was quite certain that neither career was something I would be happy doing for the rest of my life. With one child already and others likely to follow, I had some hesitation about giving up an assured income, but decided, nevertheless, to resign my position in the summer of 1950 to join Hague in this new endeavor. It turned out to be a decision I never regretted, and it led eventually to a period of government service that was the high point of my working career.

Three

What's in a Name?

It was a perfect New England morning, bright and sunny, as one occasionally sees in Maine and more often in Boston and Cape Cod, with the clear blue skies reminiscent of Southern California before the smog settled in after the war.

The phone in Professor J. Sterling Livingston's office rang on that lovely June morning and the voice at the other end said, "You guys have given me all I need to draw up the papers except the name. What do you want to call this outfit? Get right back to me because I'm leaving for the Cape in twenty minutes."

It was John Woolsey, the lawyer drafting the legal documents to establish our new corporation. "You got any ideas?" Livingston asked me.

Neither Sterling nor I nor our third partner, Harry Hague, had attended to this important detail. One reason was our reluctance to name the company in an explicit way, which might limit the range of activities we pursued. And Hague and I thought Sterling would want to name the company after himself, and, as the ones who would do most of the work, we preferred an impersonal title.

Our office was going to be located in Cambridge. We were all from Harvard. "How about Harbridge?" I asked, not sure whether the contraction made any sense.

"Harbridge what?" Livingston asked. Then he said "Harbridge Associates." "Not too bad." Then he had another idea. "Why not 'Harbridge *House*'? It sounds like 'Random House.' We're going to be publishing some case studies and other things so why not be a 'house'? I like it."

"So do I," I said. "It doesn't tie us down to any one thing. Let's go with it."

John Woolsey got to the Cape on schedule and our new venture had a name. The three of us would own all the stock, with Livingston at 60 percent, and Hague and me at 20 percent each. The two of us would work full time at salaries of $300 per month, about what we had been earning as Harvard Business School staff members. Livingston would contribute time as necessary and take the lead in securing new business. Temporarily, until we were more firmly established, he would live on his income from the school, where he was rapidly becoming one of the most popular professors.

Financing the Company

We needed money to get started in business and got it by selling stock to ourselves. Hague and I had to put up $5,000 for our 20 percent shares, and Livingston $15,000 for his controlling interest.

The $5,000 investment seemed fair and reasonable except for one thing: I didn't have the money. Living on $275 a month with a wife and a young child had kept me nearly broke. I had picked up a little extra from several articles I had written, but that money had been spent months ago. In fact, I had pawned an old overcoat for $20 one Saturday morning to get enough money for a dinner party that night for some of our friends.

Mr. Bradlee, the loan officer at the Cambridge Trust Company, said the bank was willing to lend me what I needed if I could put up some collateral—a house, some shares of stock—that sort of thing. I didn't have what he wanted. The only thing I and Nan had of value was wedding silver—a flatware service from her parents, a coffee and tea service from my parents, goblets, trays, serving spoons, specialty items such as pickle forks, and enough silver nut dishes to handle a week's output of the Planters Peanut Company. Mr. Bradlee said I was "piling on," mentioning all these items, and that the flatware and the coffee and tea service would be sufficient to secure the loan.

We began to think next about where in Cambridge to locate our offices. Hague had been working out of his apartment. Nan and I and baby David were house-sitting in Weston at Professor Myles Mace's comfortable house until he returned from vacation in a month. Until we found office space, I worked from a desk in Mace's study.

The Korean War Sets Our Course

Along with the desk and bookcases in Mace's study was a large television set, a luxury we didn't have at our own house. I avoided the temptation to turn it on during working hours until a major event commanded our attention. On June 25, 1950, North Korea began an attack across the 38th parallel into South Korea. The United Nations Security Council met in an emergency session and the dramatic proceedings were televised. A resolution was passed without encountering a Soviet veto because the Soviet representative was temporarily absent. It called upon UN members to assist in meeting the aggression. On June 27, President Truman, without asking Congress to declare war, ordered U.S. forces to come to the aid of South Korea in what was called a "police action."

The Korean War gave a direction to our fledgling company that we had not intended. While we were continuing to produce the remaining industry studies and the new naval administrator series, the Navy came to us once again. To carry out the greatly expanded weapons procurement program required for the war, the Navy needed to reacquaint its regular officers and reservists called to duty with the lessons learned from the large-scale production programs in World War II. It urgently wanted a "negotiator's handbook" for their use. Because

Sterling Livingston had taught industrial procurement at Harvard and had written his doctoral dissertation on naval purchasing, the Navy hired him and Harbridge House to prepare the handbook. Getting office space quickly and hiring additional staff members became a high priority.

We soon located suitable space in Harvard Square above the Harvard Co-op, a cooperative store that sold school supplies and clothing. A faculty wife who knew how to type was hired as a secretary. Two recent graduates of Harvard Law School came aboard to work on the handbook. Livingston and Hague supervised that job, and I looked after the naval administrator series along with my work on Louis de Rochemont's motion picture.

The de Rochemont Movie

The Korean War was going badly and so was Louis's movie. We went through several rewrites, dismissing the writer and hiring two more. Even Louis's wife helped write it as we struggled to fashion a script that was both realistic and entertaining. The final shooting script for *The Whistle at Eaton Falls* was completed in September 1950.

For director, Louis chose the well-known Robert Siodmak. The cast members included Lloyd Bridges as the union leader turned company president, Dorothy Gish as the widow of the president Bridges replaced, and Ernest Borgnine as a good-hearted union man. The film was shot on location in New Hampshire and Maine.

Trouble soon developed between de Rochemont and Siodmak, so bad they refused to talk to each other. I was working on the picture virtually full time as a "production associate." Louis asked me to mediate the situation and I did what I could to bring the two talented and temperamental men closer together. The underlying problem was the story itself. The further along we got in its development, the more we deviated from the original purpose of making a realistic motion picture about business. It had become superficial, offering improbable approaches in demanding situations.

Neither Livingston nor I were paid for our work. Instead, we were given part ownership of the movie, in my case 2 percent. If it had been a commercial success, my small interest would have amounted to real money. Unfortunately, it did not succeed because its inherent contradictions were never satisfactorily resolved. De Rochemont asked me to stay with his production organization on a permanent basis. I thanked him and declined.

Two New Staff Members

Two of our early hires were unusual choices. The first was Robert Angus Brooks, Rab to everyone. He was a tall, handsome, rather private man, the son of a Scottish mother and an American father. Born in India, where his father managed a jute mill, Rab was sent at age four to live with his grandmother in Scotland. He attended a strict and demanding boarding school where a boy's knuckles were rapped and his bottom caned if he failed to do his lessons properly. When his father was transferred to Boston, Rab was enrolled in Roxbury Latin School. His brilliance and fine classical education left little for Roxbury Latin to impart, so his teachers packed him off to Harvard at fifteen. He graduated summa cum laude, the top man in his class, four years later. Thereafter, he was appointed a Junior Fellow, one of a select group of unusually able people in the program started in 1933 by President A. Lawrence Lowell of Harvard. The fellows were encouraged to pursue whatever intellectual task interested them, without any supervision by senior faculty. Arthur Schlesinger Jr., for example, wrote *The Age of Jackson* when he was a member of the elite group. Brooks studied the playwrights of ancient Greece and Rome, and later earned a PhD in the classics.

My friend David Ulrich, who was second to Brooks in academic standing in their Harvard graduating class, had introduced me to Rab, then teaching in Harvard's distinguished but very small Greek and Latin Department. Anxious to earn some extra money, he worked part time on our Navy training programs. The classics department was so small, he told me, that a tenured faculty appointment was years away. I asked him whether he would consider joining us at Harbridge House and he said he would. I was elated by his answer, but Livingston's reaction took the wind out of my sails. "Why should we hire some guy who teaches Greek and Latin?" he asked. "How many times in your life will you have a chance to hire the top man at Harvard at the age of nineteen?" I responded. "If he fails, he fails, but my guess is that a guy that smart will probably be running the joint someday."

Brooks began full-time work as the editor of the *Negotiator's Handbook*. Among his responsibilities was preparing a complex and detailed index on a very tight schedule. An editor at Harvard University Press told him it was impossible to do that big a job in the time allowed. Undaunted, Brooks took all the strips of typeset copy home, spread them out on two card tables in his living room, worked through the night and early morning, and completed the massive effort on time. When Livingston asked him what he had used as a model for the index, Brooks said *A Study of History*, Arnold Toynbee's great work. You get that kind of added value when you hire a scholarly guy.

Brooks quickly became a leading member of the firm. He acquired a solid grounding in computer technology and led a Harbridge House team in Europe that converted NATO's supply and weapons inventory from manual to computer records. He left the firm for government service in the mid-1960s, and when he returned to Harbridge House he was elected the company president. Washington called again in the 1970s and he became deputy to the legendary head of the Smithsonian Institution, Dillon Ripley. Several years later, an aggressive cancer ended his life.

The second of the two unusual early hires was in some ways a more unlikely candidate than Brooks. He was Peter Temple, a theatrical producer, director, actor, and founding member of the celebrated Brattle Theatre in Harvard Square. Owlish behind tortoise-shell glasses and with a deep baritone voice that gave a sense of importance to every word he uttered, Temple, as a lad in Minnesota, had played "Jack Armstrong, the All-American Boy" in the popular radio program at the time it was first conceived.

The Brattle Theatre was one of Cambridge's cultural landmarks. There I saw Paul Robeson, Jose Ferrer, and Uta Hagen in Shakespeare's *Othello*, and Peter Temple as Captain Vere in *Billy Budd*. Unfortunately, the Brattle Theatre's income did not match its artistic achievements, and Temple told me one day at lunch that he thought it might go under. He had earned an MBA at Harvard Business School after the war, before starting the Brattle with several others. He said he was interested in our company. I thought he would be a good addition because of his business school education and his demonstrated leadership in starting the theater. In time, he led many of our projects and became a vice president before leaving to form his own highly successful management consulting firm, Temple, Barker, and Sloane.

From this experience and others, I believe that hiring the smartest people you can find is better than employing someone who simply meets the technical requirements of the position. This is especially true in a management consulting firm, where identification of problem areas and consideration of possible solutions requires a disciplined and penetrating mind. An individual can learn technical know-how on the job; the brains come from God.

Whatever latent interest there was in pursuing film projects was entrusted to Temple, and the rest of us, finally including Temple, were drawn into Korean War supply and procurement problems. My first venture of this sort was the aircraft industry purchasing course in 1952. More than fifty cents of each contract dollar awarded to Lockheed, Boeing, and the other prime contractors for aircraft and missile programs was spent by the companies' purchasing departments with subcontractors and vendors. How good a job were they doing, the air force wondered? Were their people equal to the task of managing major subcontracts and integrating the work of each of them into fighter and bomber aircraft? If not, any failings would reflect adversely on the Air Force.

A committee from the defense companies in Southern California contacted Harbridge House and asked if we could begin at once and teach the first session in the fall of 1952. I led a team to Los Angeles to prepare case studies for the course.

The first session got underway at the UCLA Business School. Livingston and I taught the first classes and worked with the UCLA instructors who would handle the follow-on sessions. Eventually, the course was presented by the University of Washington for Boeing and other defense contractors in the Pacific Northwest, and by Fordham University for East Coast contractors. More than nine hundred buyers and supervisors attended the course at its several locations. Harvard professor Howard T. Lewis included ten of our cases in a revised version of his landmark textbook, *Procurement: Principles and Cases.*

Command Management

The Army learned about Harbridge House from the work we had done for the Navy and the air force. The Army told us about a new emphasis on good management and said their officers needed specialized training in putting business concepts into practice.

Legislation had been recently enacted that required the armed services to establish systems of financial inventory control to replace the item controls traditionally employed. The Army could tell you, for example, how many 3 x 5 cards it had, but it was unable to say how much money was tied up in its office supplies inventory. In a further effort to encourage efficiency, the military departments established stock funds and industrial funds that permitted a kind of "buyer-seller" arrangement. Their purpose was to introduce the element of cost when ordering supplies or requesting industrial services. If the commander had to "pay" for the supplies and services rather than having them issued to him, he would presumably be more cost-conscious, spending the money as though it came out of his own pocket.

An early question was what to call the school. If the new venture were called a management school, officers would object because the Army's function was command; if it were called a command school, its emphasis on management would be degraded. We decided to call it the Command Management Conference. The Army accepted our detailed planning report and established the new school on management principles and techniques in 1953 at Fort Belvoir south of Washington, D.C. Harbridge House wrote the case studies for the curriculum, taught the first session, and helped the military faculty to carry on.

The Army Logistics Management Center

Williston B. Palmer was "old Army." The Army was his whole life. He lived at Army posts in this country and abroad, worked tirelessly on each of his assignments as he rose in rank, rode horses in the daytime, and studied military history at night. Because he was in love with the Army, he never thought it necessary to marry. Indeed, when his younger brother Charley, who, like Willy, achieved four-star rank, decided in his early fifties to get married, Willy told him that if the Army had intended him to get married, it would have issued him a wife.

Williston B. Palmer scared younger officers. He liked to sweat their palms and give them a hard time. It was not unusual for Palmer, seated at his Pentagon desk deep in study of an official paper, to disregard an officer he had summoned, keeping him standing for five minutes or more, wondering whether to open his mouth. Finally, Willy would swivel around in his desk chair and stare at the poor man with a look on his face that seemed to say, "Do I awe you?"

In 1953 Palmer, accompanied by his assistant division commander, William C. Westmoreland, came to Harvard Business School to meet with Professor Georges Doriot, a revered faculty member who had been appointed as a general in the Quartermaster Corps during World War II. General Palmer wanted General Doriot to advise him about setting up an Army supply management course, along the lines of Harvard's Advanced Management Program, using case studies as the main educational element. Westmoreland, the handsome, soldierly officer who later commanded U.S. troops in Vietnam, had attended the management course and was keen on the HBS approach to business education. Doriot said he was too tied up with other commitments but suggested that Palmer see Professor Livingston, whose firm, Harbridge House, might be available.

Livingston and I met with Palmer and Westmoreland and learned what they had in mind. Palmer had been selected to be the Army's assistant chief of staff for logistics (G-4), a key player in the General Staff who oversaw the Army's Technical Services, such as Ordnance and Quartermaster. He believed that the Army school system did a first-rate job for the combat arms but fell short in providing advanced training for officers responsible for managing the chain of supply. Would Harbridge House be interested, he asked, in working with him in developing a new course and then preparing the needed instructional materials?

It was obvious at once that Palmer's project was the biggest thing that had come our way. We would be working at a high level in the Army for a period of many months. If we did a good job, our growing reputation for turning out quality work would take on added luster. We told Palmer that we were fully capable of handling the assignment. We did not know then that Palmer expected that more would come from his course than the training of Army supply managers.

Livingston thought I should handle the work. I said I wanted Rab Brooks as my principal assistant and Livingston agreed. A week later, Brooks and I went to Washington to meet with the officers Palmer had designated to get things started. Brig. Gen. Andy McNamara from the Quartermaster Corps and Col. John Lane from the Transportation Corps were the chief liaison officers. We discussed the scope of the project, what it might cost, how our staff would work with Army representatives, and what the key milestones should be. Palmer was anxious to get the course under way as soon as possible, and Colonel Lane said his principal function was to "keep a blowtorch to our ass" to make sure we finished on time. Brooks and I returned to Cambridge to prepare a comprehensive proposal. It would be by far the largest contract ever awarded to us. We returned to Washington for further consultation, reviewed the proposal with the Army, and agreed to get started at once. We shook hands, then repaired to our hotel to celebrate our good fortune with Cuban cigars and a couple shots of Scotch.

In a planning report that Harbridge House subsequently wrote for the Army, we explained the need for supply management education:

In an earlier day logistics support was fully decentralized and refreshingly simple; each soldier brought along his own bow, and food for the troops and hay for the horses were easy to find in the surrounding countryside. In many ways, it was a happier day. Kingdoms could change hands on a field in an afternoon. There was glamour in cavalry charges. The civilian population was usually able to avoid involvement in the carnage of warfare; there was no fallout problem with the crossbow.

The industrial revolution brought power to industry and firepower and mobility to warfare. The arts of war were modified to take advantage of the new weapons made possible by an expanding technology. Although the principles of strategy remained constant, the means by which strategic principles were carried out changed dramatically. Now the means are enormously complex weapons systems. The problem of devising tactics to employ these means is perhaps overshadowed by the effort necessary to place them at the disposal of the tactical commander.

Providing the means of warfare constitutes the support activity. An essential difference between an Army today and in the past is the importance today of supplier-related support: the activities necessary to develop, procure, produce, supply, and maintain the means of warfare. To do the job properly requires specialized skills, an array of management tools, and a high order of management competence. These skills have typically been found in the best-run American corporations; they have not always been present in the Army. With good reason, the Army has concentrated on the development of troop leaders and has done so with magnificent results. Now, there is a growing realization that an individual officer cannot be an equally capable tactician and logician, and that experience acquired in duty with troops might not wholly fit an officer to deal with the problems associated with procurement, production, and supply.

To get the job done we assigned a team of eight staffers under the overall direction of Brooks and me. The Army decided to locate the school at Fort Lee, near Petersburg, Virginia, and began assembling the permanent staff and faculty. We worked long hours to meet the tight deadlines, sometimes arriving at Fort Lee with a case study just in time for its scheduled use in class.

General Palmer wanted the chiefs of the Technical Services to become familiar with the supply management course and asked us to conduct a special two-day seminar for them prior to the first session of the three-month course in September 1954. The tech services, each commanded by a general of at least two-star rank, were powerful, proud, and largely independent organizations that included Quartermaster, Ordnance, Signal, Engineer, Chemical, Transportation, and Medical. With Palmer and his principal assistants, the tech service chiefs and some of their key deputies assembled at Fort Lee to discuss case studies from the course as though they were enrolled students. It was a challenging experience for me and the two others who taught the class, Livingston and Brooks. Some of the participants were formidable figures—Maj. Gen. Bruce Medaris, for example, the spit-and-polish chief of Army missile development; Lt. Gen. J. H. Hinrichs, the imperious chief of Ordnance; and the wise old fox, Andy McNamara, who became the quartermaster general. Palmer said very little except to encourage the chiefs to send their best people. They did, and the first class graduated on December 22, 1954.

During the period when we were preparing and teaching the supply management course, I had several opportunities to meet privately with General Palmer and we became good friends. He told me that his primary purpose in starting the course was to fulfill a neglected area in the Army's educational system. He also wanted to use the course to establish greater control over the tech services. He believed they operated largely independent of General Staff direction. A student of military history, he explained to me how the Army as a whole was an uncoordinated force until Secretary of War Elihu Root between 1901 and 1903 instituted fundamental reforms that established a general staff. The changes Root made did not go down easily, and more than one general officer resigned in protest. Palmer wanted to enhance the power of his position as logistics chief over the tech services, but he knew that if he took any direct action, he would cause an explosion. "I have in mind the eventual organizational chart," he said, "but it would be a terrible mistake to publish it. I want everyone to begin to act as the organization chart anticipates. When that happens, it won't be necessary to issue an organization chart. And even if we did, nobody would take any notice because the chart would simply confirm what was already going on."

In later years a major reorganization placed the tech services within a newly created Army Materiel Command, where their separate technical jurisdictions, blurred by advances in electronics and the missile, required strong, overall direction.

The supply management course continues to this day, serving not only the Army but the other services as well.

Go West, Young Man

One evening in the fall of 1955, I came home from work and asked my wife if she wanted to move to California or Germany. She looked at me, dumbfounded. "What are you talking about?" Nan asked. "Why are we moving?" I replied that we didn't have to move but that there were two major projects being offered to Harbridge House, one in Germany concerning the NATO supply system, and the other in Los Angeles for an Air Force pricing school. "I can have either one of them," I said, "but we have to decide right away."

My wife was a New Englander who had grown up in Holyoke, Massachusetts. She disliked the cold and snow of the Northeast and the long winter months. "April is the cruelest month," she often said. "You think it's time for spring, but it's still cold and unpleasant." One story famous in family lore is that the real reason Nan married me was that, as a Californian, I would take her there to spend our lives together. Instead, we settled down in Cambridge, Massachusetts, and braved the winter snow. Two lovely girls followed David: Sarah Brooks Ignatius, born November 20, 1951, and Amy Louise Ignatius, born April 17, 1954. A lot of Nan's time each day was spent zipping the three kids into and out of the heavy snowsuits that were the uniform of children in the Northeast. As for me, a return to the place of my boyhood was an attractive proposition. It didn't take long to decide to travel west rather than east. Rab Brooks took over the German assignment, and the Advanced Air Force Pricing School was mine.

The pricing school was a major project of the Air Materiel Command (AMC) in Dayton, the huge headquarters that bought air force weapons and supplies. The AMC decided to establish a professional educational program, the most thorough offered by the armed services, to enable procurement personnel to do an aggressive, informed job of negotiating fair and reasonable prices for the air force's costly weapons systems. The command wanted the school to be located in the center of the aircraft and electronics industry—Southern California—so that the participants could meet with company executives and spend time at their manufacturing facilities.

My parents let us stay with them until we found a place to live. I spent my first few days house hunting, and came upon some beautiful land in Chatsworth, at the far end of the San Fernando Valley. "How much are they asking for it?" my father inquired. "Five thousand an acre," I replied. "My God," my father said, "that's chicken-farming country not worth more than a hundred dollars an acre." "When was the last time you were out that way?" I asked. He paused for a moment and then said, "Before the war." "Which war?" I asked.

As it turned out, buying land and building a house was not in the cards because of the scope and urgency of the new project. A day or two later, Nan and I came upon another Valley property, in Encino. A Spanish-style house on what had been an orange ranch, it came with a couple of acres of oranges and lemons, avocados, artichokes, and exotic fruits like loquats. The rooms were grouped around a patio, with a huge sycamore tree in the center. In back were a guesthouse with a stone fireplace and a forty-foot swimming pool. The price for the whole spread was $38,500.

There was office space available on Ventura Boulevard in Encino, a mile and a half from our house. We planted our Harbridge House flag there. The quarters had enough room for the full-time and part-time people we would need to write the case studies for the pricing school. The Air Materiel Command wanted the first session to get under way within a year, and there wasn't a moment to lose.

Two bright young men were hired to help with the research and the teaching: Peter Laubach, who had been Professor Robert Anthony's assistant in the accounting course at Harvard, and Stephen Falk, a cocky but capable person with an HBS degree. Sterling Livingston played a major role, and he and Professor Howard Lewis came out from time to time to assist us, along with Assistant Professor Stanley Miller from Harvard. Several UCLA assistant professors rounded out our staff.

The air force intended to send its top people to the twelve-week course, beginning with the first session in February 1957. Our research was conducted at Lockheed, Douglas, Hughes, and other leading companies familiar to us from our earlier work on the aircraft industry course. I sent Laubach east to the Ford Motor Company where Phillip Caldwell, later the company chairman, agreed to let us develop a case study on how automotive parts were priced. It enabled us to contrast commercial practices with the more constrained procedures of government procurement, with its laws, regulations, and congressional oversight.

Most of our time was spent at the aircraft companies that were producing new fighter planes in large quantities for the Korean War. For example, at one company we developed a case on "sustaining engineering." In contrast to engineers who designed aircraft, sustaining engineers concentrated on production problems. Among the many questions about this generally unfamiliar work were how much sustaining engineering was needed and how the department's costs should be allocated to a particular aircraft program. After teaching the case in the morning, we followed up with a plant visit in the afternoon to meet with sustaining engineers. Through discussions with them and observation of their work, our air force participants acquired a better understanding of the production process and a better feel for what it should cost.

Company executives often came to class, commented on the case studies, and discussed them with their air force counterparts. One case involved a company that promised to deliver an electronics component with a "tunable magnetron" that enabled it to operate on various frequencies in combat. When delivered, it contained a far less desirable fixed magnetron. Company representatives and the air force students had a lively argument on what should be done. Should the company be penalized for failure to deliver what it had promised? Should it return some of the money it received on the contract? If it were not penalized, would that be fair to the competitors who lost the contract because they could only deliver a fixed magnetron?

When I took accounting at Harvard, Professor Clarence Nickerson said on the opening day that the course would be simple: "All you need to know is that debits are toward the window, credits are the other way, and only God knows what cost is." But our air force participants had to rely on themselves. In intensive sessions with Dr. Laubach, they looked at endless categories of cost, discussing which ones were *relevant* to the contract and how they should be *allocated*. Under Laubach's tutelage, they became experts on fixed, semifixed, and variable costs, able to deal confidently with contractor representatives.

The course also devoted time to negotiating techniques. Mock negotiations were held with two air force officers role-playing the contractor and the buyer. At the conclusion, each one was asked to state the agreed-upon terms. There was usually a wide variation in the two summaries, emphasizing how contract disputes can later take place. The sessions underscored the importance of writing down the conclusions and ensuring that each party agreed, rather than relying on oral understandings and memory. As the old-time movie producer Sam Goldwyn said, "An oral agreement isn't worth the paper it's written on."

Several classes followed the initial one, with our Harbridge-UCLA faculty leading the discussions. In time, the Canadian government asked us to prepare a shorter version of the course for their Department of Defence Production, which Laubach, Falk, and I conducted at McDonald College in Montreal.

After work, I would swim with our kids in our pool, and on weekends we would entertain friends with barbecue and swimming parties. Every morning, we drank tall glasses of orange juice from the summer and winter varieties that grew on our property. "We threw away better oranges in California," we used to say, "than we bought in Cambridge." Nan learned to play tennis and took evening classes at UCLA, the beginning of a life-long habit of continuing her education in her free time. Eventually, our fourth child, Alan Paul, was born at a hospital in Burbank on September 10, the same day as Nan's birthday. Alan, called "Adi" by his brother and sisters, was a truly ecumenical baby, born of a Protestant mother and father at a Catholic hospital and delivered by a Jewish doctor.

With the air force pricing school firmly established, we hoped to find other work as a basis for operating a West Coast branch of the company. We got one or two small jobs but not enough to justify our presence, other than the air force course. Most important, I was getting bored with my work. It was repetitive and I wasn't learning anything new.

Our West Coast office was really an appendage, and the main body continued to be Cambridge and later Boston where the firm relocated. I began to handle projects initiated at the main office. One was a personal request from Thomas D. Morris, a deputy assistant secretary of defense, for a comprehensive book on the differing supply systems of the Army, Navy, air force, and marines. Morris saw many opportunities for saving money by reducing the duplication inherent in the separate systems and viewed the book as an important piece of documentation. His deadline was unusually tight; the book had to be written in a three-week period toward the end of the year, 1958. Because most of the technical information was at our Boston office, we gathered our family together and moved in with Nan's parents in Holyoke for the Christmas recess. I set up a desk and telephone in a third-floor bedroom. With voluminous material supplied to me from Boston, I completed Morris's book on time. I enjoyed working under pressure and expected that there would be other urgent projects coming to the attention of our main office. I decided, with Nan's concurrence, to return to the east.

We sold our house for $42,500 to a UCLA professor. On a trip to Los Angeles in the 1980s, Nan and I stopped by the house. It had been totally redone. The owner, a record producer, came to the door in his bathrobe when I rang the doorbell at ten in the morning. He told me he had paid $2.5 million for the place. I couldn't bring myself to tell him what Nan and I had paid.

Go East, Young Man

Because we had no place to live in the Boston area, we rented a house for the summer in Cape Cod. I worked in Boston, stayed at the Harvard Club, looked for a house, and flew to the Cape on weekends.

After looking at houses in Boston, I found one in Weston, a country town west of the city that was still governed by town meetings. There was a spacious, grassy public common and an excellent school system. Businesses were limited to one of each kind: a drugstore, hardware store, market, and plumber. Houses had to be on at least two acres of land. An HBS classmate, Ward Carter, was the town manager.

The house was what Bostonians called a "postwar" house, that is, after the Revolutionary War. It had been built in 1785 by Artemas Ward for his sons. Ward had been the senior commander at the Battle of Bunker Hill on June 17, 1775; two weeks later, George Washington took command from him of all the American troops. The Ward house was faced with narrow clapboards and had large windows, seven fireplaces, and wood paneling throughout. There was a small hill in back where the kids learned to ski and an ice-skating pond at our neighbors, the Wilkinsons. Without a moment's hesitation, we bought the house for $52,000 and moved in at the end of the summer.

My father had often told me that I would get better value if I bought an older house. "New houses have fancier kitchens and more bathrooms, but they aren't built solid like the old ones," he said. When I told him I had bought a house built in 1785, he answered that he was awfully glad I had finally followed his advice on something, but in this case I had carried a good thing too far.

By this time the Harbridge House staff had grown to more than a hundred talented men and women. While most of our work continued to be performed for the government, an increasing number of commercial projects came our way. With several others, I prepared an executive development program for General Electric. Another team took on a major assignment for Volkswagen. Day-to-day administration and responsibility for financial matters were capably handled by Harry Hague. Sterling Livingston continued to play a central role, particularly in the development of new business opportunities.

Two projects gave me a chance to mix work with pleasure at overseas locations. The first was for the Economic Development Administration (Fomento) of the Commonwealth of Puerto Rico in the summer of 1960. Its purpose was to investigate problems of locally owned and managed manufacturing enterprises, and led to the establishment of a management education and research center in San Juan.

I spent a month in San Juan with Nan and our four children. Our apartment was across the street from one of the fancy tourist hotels, and Nan and the kids used its swimming pool during the day. Puerto Rico was an exciting place to be. Its governor, Luis Muñoz Marin, was an uncommonly able politician. He offered tax advantages to U.S. corporations interested in locating plants there, and persuaded his people to take a long view of their economic well-being. The lower wages prevailing in the commonwealth were a primary reason why companies wanted to locate there. Once the process of development got underway, wages would rise, as in fact they did.

The other project was a special program for the State Department. It dealt with the problems arising from a decision to permit civil servants with special talents to enter the elite foreign service without taking the rigorous examinations required of foreign service officers. A weeklong seminar, for which we prepared case studies, was held in Nice, France, for officers in the European and African areas to examine some of the controversial aspects of the initiative.

By far our most significant work at this time was for the U.S. Navy's Special Projects Office, under the direction of Adm. William Raborn and his brilliant technical leader, Capt. Levering Smith. Raborn was given unprecedented authority to develop the Polaris missile and get it quickly to sea. The times were dangerous with both the Soviet Union and the United States armed with nuclear weapons and the means for delivering them. An urgent need during the Cold War was an invulnerable U.S. weapons system to deter nuclear war. The Polaris missile, to be launched from a submarine deep in the ocean, was the nation's chosen weapon. Developing a missile that could be fired from underwater and reach its target with great accuracy was a challenge like no other.

Our connection with Polaris stemmed from testimony Sterling Livingston had given, as a recognized expert on military procurement, before the Senate Preparedness Committee. Admiral Raborn was in the audience and asked him to take a look at the Polaris contracting arrangements. Livingston discussed incentive contracting with Raborn, a subject included in the Advanced Air Force Pricing School. Incentive contracts rewarded success and penalized failure through adjustments in the profit rate. Raborn said he wanted Harbridge House to work with the Polaris contractors to see whether incentive contracts were applicable for the urgent development program.

Livingston worked on the problem with officials in Washington, and I spent time in California with Lockheed and Aerojet. When the time came to brief Raborn and his staff, Livingston made an overall, introductory presentation and I followed with data from the contractors. I mentioned in passing that I had come across a problem at Aerojet that might cause difficulty. Raborn was "all ears"—anything that might cause a problem or slow the schedule for Polaris always got his immediate attention.

The problem involved Aerojet's responsibility for developing the solid fuel missile. The missile body had to be strong enough to withstand the enormous pressures when the fuel ignited yet light enough to be launched from the submarine. Aerojet placed subcontracts with a number of companies that offered both traditional and nontraditional solutions. The winner expected to be rewarded with a lucrative production contract for all the missiles needed for the program. A problem arose when Aerojet failed to clarify whether the winning subcontractor or Aerojet itself would handle production of the successful design. Raborn stopped the briefing, called Dan Kimball, Aerojet's CEO, from the briefing room and said that he wanted the matter to be clarified at once in order to avoid continuing argument that might slow the work.

The briefing resumed with the focus once again on specific incentive arrangements. Ultimately, contracts were awarded that employed concepts from our study.

The Special Project Office's remarkable technical achievements were accompanied by some important managerial innovations. The best known was PERT, the Program Evaluation and Review Technique. PERT tracked each of the many components and subsystems that had to come together in conformity with the overall schedule, and alerted Raborn when and where problems might occur. It was a sophisticated advance over prior schedule planning and control methods. PERT used inputs from Lockheed, Aerojet, General Electric, and the many other companies working to make Polaris a reality. With this information, a computer would calculate the "critical path" toward the key milestones and the final completion date.

Two Important Telephone Calls

Sometime before Christmas 1960, Livingston received a call from Adam Yarmolinsky, a recruiter for the incoming administration of President John F. Kennedy. He wanted names to consider for the important position of assistant secretary of defense (installations and logistics). The job involved responsibility for procurement, supply, transportation, maintenance of weapons and equipment, and the array of depots, arsenals, shipyards, bases, and other installations in the vast defense establishment.

Livingston asked if I had any suggestions. I mentioned Tom Morris, the former deputy assistant secretary for whom we had prepared the book on the supply systems of the armed services. Morris had been a management consultant and was a keen analyst of complex issues. In a few weeks, he was selected for the position by the newly appointed secretary of defense, Robert S. McNamara.

Early in March, while I was in Chicago on an assignment, I received a call from Elvis Stahr, Kennedy's new secretary of the Army. He asked if I wanted to be considered for the position of assistant secretary of the Army (I&L), the Army counterpart to Morris at the Defense Department. I said I was hard at work with Harbridge House, and that after years of toil the firm was becoming profitable. I told him I wanted to serve in the government someday when my financial circumstances had improved. Stahr responded, "Okay, I understand what you're saying, but why don't you stop by the Pentagon anyway on your trip back to Boston?" It was difficult to say no to his cordial invitation. I changed my airline reservation for a stop in Washington, and it led to the end of my eleven-year career with Harbridge House.

Harbridge House continued to grow in influence, size, and stature. Hague and Livingston were the presiding members, one managing the business and the other attracting new business. A consulting firm specializing in transportation issues, headed by Professor Paul Cherington of the Harvard Business School, was merged into Harbridge House and added talented people like Charles Baker, a future undersecretary of transportation. Several leading members of the firm—Rab Brooks, Ron Fox, and Baker—departed for service in Washington. The company relocated its offices to Arlington Street, looking out on the Boston Public Garden, across from Commonwealth Avenue and the elegant Ritz Carlton Hotel.

In the 1960s, the company was bought by Sears Allstate, then reacquired by the Harbridge principals. Later, when the major auditing firms began to develop their consulting arms, Harbridge House was acquired by PricewaterhouseCoopers in 1993 and absorbed within that distinguished company. For a venture that started life with no clear idea of exactly what it wanted to do, Harbridge House had a forty-five-year run of increasingly important work and provided a rewarding life for hundreds of men and women. It was a pioneer in the field of case-method-based executive training, and helped the armed services of the United States and other branches of the government to carry out their responsibilities in a more efficient manner.

Four

You're in the Army Now

THE SECRETARY OF THE ARMY'S OFFICE WAS ONE OF THE LARGEST on E-ring, the prestigious outer corridor of the five-sided, five-storied Pentagon, which had been built hurriedly for use in World War II. Plans to convert it into a military hospital when the war ended did not occur because the Defense Department's large postwar establishment required numerous buildings including the Pentagon.

Secretary of the Army Elvis Stahr sat behind an enormous desk, which was flanked by Army and secretarial flags. He had served briefly in a midlevel position in a prior administration and was dean of the University of West Virginia law school when asked to become the secretary. He was a dark-haired, slender, good-looking man, cordial and courteous. During the two months he had been in office, he had managed to fill all the secretarial positions except for the one responsible for procurement, supply, and the Army's base structure. From what he had heard, he thought I was a highly qualified candidate. "I want you to meet Steve Ailes and Powell Pierpoint," he said, "and let them tell you more about what we're doing."

The office of Undersecretary Steve Ailes, a floor below, was almost as big as Stahr's. Ailes, who was responsible for manpower and external matters, was from a prominent West Virginia family, and his grandfather had once been the governor. Color-blind, he had served in World War II as an attorney in the Office of Price Administration. He left a thriving antitrust practice to accept the Army position.

Ailes had a ready supply of funny stories, a quick mind, and a perpetually smiling face. I liked him at once. Like Stahr, he said he had heard good things about me, and asked me to tell him about some of my Harbridge House work for the Army. He said I would enjoy being part of the secretariat. "The problems are tough and the hours are long," he said, "more demanding than in civilian life. Not everyone is good enough to handle the pressure." I thought he was trying to discourage me but then realized he was offering a tempting challenge.

Ailes said I would be working closely with the general counsel. "When you hear the name Powell Pierpoint," he said, "you get a mental picture of a stuffy Wall Street lawyer. But when you actually see him, you find out that's exactly the way he looks." Pierpoint joined us, and though he talked in ponderous tones, he was anything but stuffy. He had come to know Ailes during an interminable antitrust trial. He said I'd be joining a good crowd and doing important work. I told them what I had earlier told Stahr—that I wanted to serve in the government some day but at a time when I was better off financially. "Talk it over with your wife," Ailes said, "and then get back in touch with us."

Nan listened attentively while I recounted my Pentagon conversations. Ailes had gotten to me with his "not everyone is up to it" gambit, I said. I liked Stahr and Pierpoint and Ailes, and figured I would enjoy being part of the team. But then I repeated my mantra about wanting to serve in the government some day, but now was not the time.

Nan often had shown an ability to get right to the heart of the matter. She looked at me and said, "Maybe when you're ready to go into the government, nobody will want you to come." That did it! I phoned Ailes and said if he and Stahr wanted me, I was ready to come to Washington.

Nan was reluctant, as was I, to give up our house in Weston but thought that government service would be rewarding for the entire family and me. Since it was March, with several months to go before

the school term ended, she would stay in Weston and join me with the
children in June. We decided to sell the house, mainly because we
needed the money to buy another one but also because we wanted to
avoid the worries and distractions of renting a 175-year-old house during a four-year absence in Washington. It was snapped up for $57,500.

I met with Harry Hague to handle the details of my resignation from
Harbridge House. My salary was $35,000 a year, and the assistant secre-
tary job would pay $20,000. My Harbridge House stock, along with the
equity in our house, were my main assets. There was no market for the
stock so a formula had to be devised to establish its value. My 20 percent
share of what was now a successful company was worth $45,000, Hague
calculated—not very much for eleven years of hard and often pioneering
work. I thought a large amount should be added for the residual value of
projects I had handled, but nothing of this sort was seriously considered.
The Harbridge House money, together with a $10,000 gain from buying
some stock in the Paddington Corporation, a distributor of Scotch whisky,
was going to have to see us through as we undertook new obligations at
a salary substantially below what I had been earning.

Getting Started

With business and family affairs settled, I traveled alone to Washington and took up temporary residence at the bachelor officers' quarters
at Fort Myer, near the Pentagon. I saw Ailes when I reported for work,
and after a friendly greeting he said he was sorry to hear about my
grandmother. I didn't have a grandmother any more and thought he
must be referring to Nammie, Nan's ninety-eight-year-old grandmother. "My God," I said, "has Nammie died?" Ailes burst out laugh-
ing. "You don't understand," he said. "It's opening day of the baseball
season and you need an ironclad excuse for getting out of here, like
your grandmother just died." So the demanding work of the Pentagon
began at Griffith Stadium where the Washington Senators took on the
visiting team after the ceremonial first pitch. Some tough problems!
Some long hours! Not everyone's good enough to handle the pressure!

Work began in earnest the following day. I was installed in the assistant secretary's office but worked as a consultant for six weeks until my FBI clearance had been completed and I had been officially nominated by President Kennedy and confirmed with the advice and consent of the Senate. A member of the Defense Department's General Counsel's office, Jack Stempler, helped me to get ready for my senatorial appearance and saw to it that I conformed to the expected ethical standards. This required primarily the divestiture of any stock I owned in companies that did business with the Department of Defense. All I had left was fifty shares of Ginn and Company, a Boston school textbook publisher. Along with Lockheed and Boeing, Ginn was a "defense contractor" because it had sold more than $10,000 worth of textbooks to overseas schools. When I got rid of the shares, Stempler said I was ready to face the Senate.

The Senate confirmation hearing was the biggest thing that had ever happened to me. The chairman asked me to tell the committee about my qualifications, and I began to describe what I had done. None of the members seemed to be paying much attention as I rambled on with what I thought were fascinating details of my life. One member talked to his staff assistant. Another spoke with the senator seated next to him. The chairman left the hearing room to take a telephone call. Mainly they wanted to make sure I didn't own any defense stocks and that I would give full and candid testimony when I appeared before Congress. Though I was crestfallen at their seeming lack of interest in me, Stempler said I had "done good," and I was subsequently confirmed without controversy. My official certificate of appointment bears the signatures of John F. Kennedy and Robert S. McNamara and is dated May 19, 1961.

The Army's Turn

There can't have been many times in our nation's history when it was more exciting to be part of the civilian leadership of the United States Army. First, there was a sense of high expectation in Washington

because of the popularity of the dashing new president and his sophisticated, beautiful wife. Old-timers in the city, the so-called cliff dwellers,
likened it to Franklin Roosevelt's era, when a swarm of Harvard and
Yale intellectuals sought an opportunity to serve under a magnetic
leader. "Ask not what your country can do for you," Kennedy had said,
"ask what you can do for your country." And so many responded! The
Pentagon gathered many of the "best and brightest." McNamara had
left the Ford Motor Company only a month after he had become its
president. His deputy, Roswell Gilpatric, was a leading New York
lawyer who had served as an assistant secretary of the air force in the
Truman administration. The new Navy secretary was John Connally,
who later became governor of Texas. Heading the air force was Eugene
Zuckert, another former assistant secretary, who had been an assistant
dean at the Harvard Business School when I was there as a student.
Cyrus Vance was the general counsel, and a young lawyer named Joe
Califano was one of his underlings. The redoubtable Paul Nitze handled the Pentagon's international relationships, and Harold Brown,
one of two people McNamara once said were even smarter than he
was, directed the research and engineering effort. The list went on and
on: Charles Hitch, a future head of the University of California, was
the comptroller, and under him were the famous (some military officers would say "infamous") whiz kids, the systems analysts led by the
brilliant Alain Enthoven. And, of course, there was the self-effacing
but resourceful and effective Tom Morris. You could put an administration together around people like this, and that's just what Jimmy
Carter did, with Cyrus Vance as secretary of state, Harold Brown as
secretary of defense, and Joe Califano as secretary of health, education, and welfare.

There was another reason why service in the Army was attractive
at this time: the Army's day had finally come. It had been neglected
and poorly funded during the previous decade because of the doctrine
of massive retaliation, officially adopted as our governing strategy in
1953. Under this doctrine, the United States would respond overwhelmingly to any Soviet aggression with its arsenal of nuclear
weapons. The doctrine's purpose was to deter aggression, but if deter-

rence failed and nuclear weapons were employed in a general war, there would be little need for sustained combat on land, the Army's historic mission.

A former Army chief of staff, Gen. Maxwell D. Taylor, wrote a book in 1959 after his retirement called *The Uncertain Trumpet* that argued for a larger Army and more powerful conventional forces, in addition to the nuclear deterrent. Taylor agreed that top priority should be assigned to atomic deterrent forces, "clearly capable of surviving a surprise attack and inflicting unacceptable losses on the USSR." What he objected to was reliance on massive retaliation to cope with all military challenges. "Massive Retaliation," he wrote, "could offer our leaders only two choices, the initiation of general nuclear war or compromise and re-treat." What was needed was usable combat power.

Taylor's arguments influenced the new administration, and he was recalled to duty as a presidential advisor. McNamara promoted his ideas and came to believe that the doctrine of massive retaliation could have the unintended effect of deterring ourselves from applying mili-tary power to back up the foreign policy objectives of the United States. Dean Acheson, secretary of state under President Truman, told President Kennedy that reliance on nuclear weapons for the defense of Europe was a dangerous course. He favored using conventional forces for as long as possible before resorting to nuclear weapons, a strategy General Taylor had called "flexible response."

Taylor's and Acheson's arguments carried great weight with Presi-dent Kennedy, but it was the Berlin crisis of 1961 that led to the expan-sion of the Army that Taylor had urged. Access to Berlin was a basic principle of U.S. foreign policy. When Berlin was threatened by the Soviets in 1948, the United States responded with a remarkable airlift that continued until the Soviets backed down. Berlin was the central topic again when the new president met with Premier Nikita Khru-shchev in Vienna on June 3, 1961. Khrushchev said Moscow would sign a treaty with East Germany before the year was out, and then the West-ern powers would have no rights there. If they were asserted, it would be a cause of war, Khrushchev said. Kennedy returned to Washington in a somber but determined mood. The need to reply to Soviet pressure with less than the full weight of a nuclear response was clear, as Acheson had urged.

The president recognized that larger, better-equipped conventional forces were needed. He ordered McNamara to expand the Army from eleven divisions to sixteen fully combat-ready ones, for a total troop level of one million. Kennedy went on television on July 25 to announce a request for an additional $3 billion in the defense budget and the authority to call up 150,000 reservists.

On August 13, while Kennedy was vacationing at Hyannis Port on Cape Cod, a wall of various materials (later reinforced with concrete) was constructed overnight, dividing Berlin. Intelligence reports indicated that East German and Soviet troops were moving to encircle the city. Kennedy sent Vice President Johnson to Berlin as his personal representative, and several days later he ordered a battalion of Army troops in armored vehicles to move down the autobahn to Berlin. The call for an expansion of the Army and an increase in the defense budget emphasized our resolve. And always undergirding everything in U.S. defense policy was the availability of nuclear weapons and the willingness to use them if vital interests were threatened.

I was not involved in the strategic decisions; nevertheless I had my own views. A stable, invulnerable deterrent was the single most important national security requirement. The Polaris submarine and missile system best met this fundamental need, and whatever funds and resources it required should be provided. I also believed that the air force manned bombers were an essential part of the deterrent force because they could be recalled if necessary. Their relative vulnerability was mitigated by the stringent procedures and oversight of the Strategic Air Command, headed by one of the great military commanders, Gen. Curtis LeMay. I was less certain about the air force missiles because they seemed to be more vulnerable than the bombers.

The concept of "usable combat power" was appropriate for the circumstances. Our strategic nuclear deterrent was not "usable." Its purpose, almost by definition, was not to be used. It was intended rather to deter the USSR from use of its strategic weapons so that there would be no need to use ours. We were in a condition of mutual deter-rence. Within this context, however, the Soviets were on the move in Europe and Asia, and when vital U.S. interests were threatened, we needed military power to reinforce our diplomatic initiatives, usable power that could be brought to bear without the two of us blowing up the world. Flexible response seemed to me to be the right strategy, provided it was accompanied by an invulnerable nuclear deterrent.

Buying the Weapons

My job as the civilian official responsible for procurement was to buy the new weapons and equipment for the Army. I knew what I was doing because of direct involvement with military procurement during the Harbridge House years. More important, the military officers and career civilians recognized the value of this previous experience and worked productively with me. Indeed, shortly after my coming on board, the deputy chief of staff for logistics, Lt. Gen. Robert Colglazier, proposed that the Army staff get out of the procurement business. "I'm interested in what we buy and when we buy, but not how we buy," he said. The transfer of his people to my office enabled a worthwhile consolidation of military and civilian personnel and eliminated a layer of review.

The items on the Army's long shopping list included the traditional Jeeps and trucks of all sizes along with such new or improved weapons as the M-14 rifle, the M-113 armored personnel carrier, the M-50 machine gun, and the M-79 grenade launcher. Although I was familiar with contracting procedures, I had no experience with Congress or investigating committees. My first problem in this area arose with production of the new rifle.

The M-14 was lighter than the M-1, the standard rifle used in World War II. It was reasonably accurate and capable of automatic fire but difficult to control in the fully automatic mode. It had been developed by Army Ordnance at Springfield Armory, a historic part of the Army arsenal system. Harrington & Richardson (H & R), a New England gun manufacturer, had won the contract for the gun.

Harrington & Richardson had difficulty producing the M-14, and the Army became increasingly concerned as deliveries lagged. The Army decided to establish a second source to catch up with deliveries and as a hedge if H & R could not overcome its problems. A number of companies indicated interest in becoming the second source including, surprisingly, H & R itself, who proposed to establish a new facility in West Virginia to produce the gun. West Virginia, as everyone knew, had been especially important in John F. Kennedy's campaign for the presidency; when he won the primary there, he overcame a belief in the minds of many that a Catholic could never become president.

As the procurement secretary, I believed I should do the best job I could to meet the Army's needs competitively and at fair and reasonable prices. In this, McNamara and his deputy, Ros Gilpatric, always supported me. If the purpose of the second source was insurance against the possibility that H & R might fail, then it made little sense to rely on that same company as a "second source" no matter where its plant was located. Army procurement personnel had said as much to H & R representatives, but the company sought a meeting with me. I was a bit nervous when the large delegation arrived. It included the state's two senators, Jennings Randolph and Robert Byrd, Representative Harley Staggers, some local officials, the H & R top brass, and the company's aggressive lawyer, Charles Colson, later a key figure in President Nixon's Watergate scandal. They made their case at length and I listened respectfully. But we went ahead with our plans, and the second source contract was awarded to Olin Mathieson.

The M-14 matter had hardly been settled before I learned that I was going to be investigated by Congress—not over the gun, but for the award of a contract for the M-113 armored personnel carrier to the Food Machinery Corporation (FMC). The Investigations Subcommittee of the House Armed Services Committee, chaired by Edward Hébert of New Orleans, summoned me to appear. The hearing had been instigated by the well-known and highly regarded Paul Porter, the attorney for a company that failed to win the lucrative contract.

Chairman Hébert opened the hearing by saying that it was a bit unusual because it was about the award of a contract to the low bidder. "What this committee wants to know," he continued, "is why this

company is always the low bidder." I said the contract was for additional quantities following the initial contract, also won by FMC.
Therefore, the company had an inherent advantage over its competitors because of the experience gained in the prior contract. The company had always done a good job for the Army, I said, and was regarded
as an efficient low-cost producer.

The hearing dragged on for a while but never seemed to be going
anywhere. No report was issued, but a newspaper columnist, Drew
Pearson, wrote a piece critical of the Army. Because a senior Army
Ordnance officer had gone to work for FMC on his retirement, the
committee felt that something might have been amiss. Today it is so
commonplace for officers of all the military services to begin second
careers with defense contractors that nobody gives much thought to it.
In those far-off days, it was regarded with suspicion.

As time went on, I testified on many more occasions. Although I
can't say I welcomed an invitation to appear, I soon overcame any initial fears and approached them without undue concern. It helped that I
respected the Congress as an institution and that I attempted to reflect
that in my demeanor. Additionally, I found that the Congress respected
a witness if he took personal responsibility for his decisions and
explained fully what he had done and why. Though some members
might have favored a different course of action, they seemed satisfied if
the witness defended his position and gave responsive answers. Hearings were tiring no matter how many times I appeared. It was necessary to concentrate hard on each question and to consider why it was
being asked and where the line of questioning was leading. It also
helped to realize that sometimes an individual senator or representative was less interested in what the witness said than he was in his own
remarks for the record or the folks back home.

Family Reunion

For the first year and a half in Washington, we rented a house near Ward
Circle on Massachusetts Avenue where a statue of Artemas Ward, the
original owner of our Weston house, stood proudly in the center while

automobiles rushed around him. Nearby was the excellent Horace
Mann grammar school, which all four of our children attended, fol-
lowed by private school: David and Adi went to St. Albans School,
Sarah to Holton-Arms, and Amy to the National Cathedral School.

After the owners of our house returned from an overseas assignment, we bought a house two blocks away on Fordham Road. It was
something of a struggle to keep afloat on my government salary. The
equity in our Weston house was applied to the down payment on the
Fordham Road house. The money I had brought from Massachusetts
was deposited in savings accounts, and the interest helped to pay the
bills. It was a declining amount each month as we drew out money for
our expenses, violating the Boston rule of never touching capital. By
the time I left government service, our savings were gone.

There were some expenses I was able to avoid. A government car
took me to work and brought me home, so we got by with only one car.
Most of our entertainment was at official functions—receptions for visiting dignitaries, retirement parties, and fancy dinners at private
houses or government quarters—so we saved something there. King
Faisal of Saudi Arabia hosted the most elaborate party. Guests were
offered whole roasted lambs on ornate tables served by waiters in
native dress. It reminded me of my sister's comment years ago when
Faisal's father, Ibn Sa'ud, entertained President Roosevelt with a feast
of roasted camels. My sister imagined the waiters asking the guests
whether they preferred one hump or two.

Like many New Englanders, Nan was not very good at small talk
and had to learn the technique of saying a little and circulating a lot,
always remembering to "punch the right tickets" so that the honored
guests were properly recognized. We both learned to abandon our
casual ways of arriving stylishly late. At a general's fancy quarters at
Fort Myer, we arrived at 7:25 for a 7:30 dinner. Nan told the driver to
go around the block because arriving early was worse than arriving late.
We got back at 7:34 and found that we were the last of the sixteen
guests to arrive.

Although many weeknights were devoted to official functions, we
reserved Sunday for our family. During my entire period of govern-

ment service, we never accepted an invitation for Sunday. With long hours of work, often beginning before the children arose and sometimes ending after they had gone to bed, I saw little of them, but I made up for my absences on Sunday. The neighborhood kids, in and out of our house during the week, learned to stay away on Sunday because that was our family day.

For several years, our vacations consisted of a week's stay at Fort Story on the Virginia shore where the Army had a few simple houses available at modest rents.

Finally a word about our cats. In Massachusetts we had a playful pet called Cookiehead, and her two kittens, Swimmie and Johnie. In Washington there was the regal Chrissie who lived to an astonishing age for a cat. She had a remarkable sense of smell and would rush from the third floor to the kitchen the moment a can of tuna was opened. Her black and white kitten, Elvis, named for the teenage idol, met an unfortunate end from a neighborhood basset hound. Chrissie's other kittens were the odd couple, Charlie and Rusty. Charlie was fluffy, weightless, beautiful, and voiceless. Rusty was chunky, heavy, loud, and rather confused, especially when she saw her reflection in a mirror, causing her to become temporarily disoriented. I had dogs when I was a boy, not cats, but my kids and Nan loved our kittens and I grew to tolerate them and came to like Chrissie very much.

Tom Morris and the Materiel Secretaries

Each of the three military departments was organized in a mirror image of the office of the Secretary of Defense. The comptroller at Defense, for example, could work conveniently with his counterparts in the Army, Navy, and air force, as could the head of research and development and the other principals. The similar organizations facilitated communications and enabled the Department of Defense as a whole to function more effectively.

No one was better at getting people to work toward a common goal than my friend Tom Morris. As the assistant secretary of defense (installations and logistics), he had a broad span of responsibility, covering the spectrum of logistics (procurement, supply, transportation, construction, storage and distribution, maintenance, and communications) as well as the base structure worldwide, which consisted of posts, terminals, shipyards, depots, overhaul facilities, arsenals, airfields, and thousands of units of family housing. Although supported by an experienced and able staff, even a person who worked as hard as Tom Morris could not get the job done without working with and through the military departments. His points of contact were the service-level I&L secretaries like me in the Army and my Navy and air force counterparts. With Tom, the four of us were the materiel secretaries; under his leadership we pursued identified goals, testified before the Congress as a group, and shared ideas on the best way to solve problems.

Morris had a background in both government and management consulting. During World War II he was a management engineer in the Navy working with talented people like Mark Cresap and Dick Paget. When the war ended these two, along with Bill McCormick, founded the firm of Cresap, McCormick and Paget (CMP), with Tom next in line to the named partners. The firm became a recognized leader in the management consulting field along with Booz, Allen, and Hamilton; McKinsey & Company; and one or two others.

Tom's life was his work and he was unhappy only when he was idle. Once, he was flying with Dick Paget to Washington, and just as the airliner was about to land at National Airport, a military plane from a nearby airfield collided with it. The airliner went down in the Potomac River below. Tom and Dick struggled to the surface, Dick with a broken leg and Tom with a broken heart. He spit out a mouthful of river water and shouted, so the story goes, "Where's my briefcase?"

On another occasion, a couple of junior members of the firm conspired to get Tom out of the office at a decent hour and go to a movie to relax. They sat down in their seats in the darkened theater with Tom on the aisle. When one of the younger men looked to see if Tom was enjoying the movie, he saw him working on an organizational chart with only the illumination of the tiny aisle lights to guide his hand.

Tom had left CMP for the government in the 1950s as a deputy assistant secretary of defense. He returned to CMP after a couple of years only to be called back in 1961 by Robert McNamara to run the I&L area. McNamara placed a high priority on I&L–type problems, and in Tom he had the perfect person to lead the effort.

One of the first needs Tom identified was for a small, independent group of experts—a management consulting group—to augment the efforts of the civil service and military personnel. These outside experts, he believed, could provide a refreshing point of view, approaching old problems with new insights. Because I also had a management consulting background, Tom sought my ideas and assistance. He put together a proposal that McNamara bought at once and took to President Kennedy for approval: the establishment of the Logistics Management Institute (LMI) as a nonprofit organization. Sterling Livingston, my former partner at Harbridge House, was asked to help recruit staff members and a governing board. McNamara flew to Chicago and persuaded Charles Kellstadt, former head of Sears Roebuck, to be LMI's first chairman. The initial board members included such notables as Stanley Teele, dean of Harvard Business School, and Peter Drucker, the well-known author, educator, and management consultant. LMI more than fulfilled its expectations and tackled difficult questions such as appropriate profit rates for government contracts and ways to reduce waste in the enormous spare parts inventories carried by all of the services. Over time, LMI grew substantially in size and influence and today, some forty years after its founding, employs more than five hundred people working on problems for Defense and other departments of the government.

The most comprehensive undertaking Morris set in motion was the Cost Reduction Program, a Defense-wide effort to identify areas in the logistics system where significant savings could be achieved through better management. An important aspect of the program was the closure of unneeded bases.

One of the pleasures of working with Morris was the flexible use of his people and mine. I "loaned" experts to Tom so that their knowledge would benefit the department as a whole. Tom detailed one of

his most senior civilians to my office for two months to work on an
international logistics problem. Shifting people around so they can
make a difference is commonplace in industry; it is far less common in
the government, where strict personnel rules and practices apply.

I often worked out of Tom's office and sometimes he worked out
of mine. Morris had a weekly meeting with Secretary McNamara, and
on several occasions, where Army matters were involved, he took me
with him. In this way, I got to know McNamara personally, and we
found that we had several things in common: we were both Californi-
ans, both graduates of Harvard Business School, and both members of
the faculty there for a brief period.

On one memorable occasion, I spent the night in Morris's office
getting some material ready for McNamara to take early in the morning to a meeting with President Kennedy, who was vacationing on
Cape Cod. The materials included a list of equipment for the Army as
an add-on to the defense budget occasioned by the Berlin crisis. With
data provided by the Army staff, I arranged the items in several
columns on a yellow pad, with high, low, and "best buy" quantities for
each of them. The list totaled several hundred million dollars. At six in
the morning, unshaven and a bit weary, I handed my pad to McNamara and started to explain what I had done. He paid no attention to
what I was saying and instead quickly examined the method I had
employed. While I continued to talk, he picked up his pen and scrib-
bled at the top of my paper "OK RSM."

In a later conversation with McNamara he said he was often skeptical of papers brought to him with the initials of several people who
had presumably gone over the material. "I'd rather have one person
really run the problem through his brain," he said, "than all these initials that may not mean anything." Apparently, he thought I had done
just that when he gave the list his approval.

Secretary Stahr congratulated me on the quick acceptance of the
Army's list, and we awaited the official approval from the defense
budget office. Quite some time went by with no word from on high.
The budget officer, Joe Hoover, was a career employee with a reputa-

tion for being a tough guy to convince. People said the first word Joe spoke when he awoke in the morning was "No!" I showed him my paper with "OK RSM" on it and he said, "You may have McNamara's okay but you don't have mine." I learned at that moment where real power resided in a bureaucracy. After several days of consultation, the authority was granted.

One Thanksgiving Day I was working in Tom's office. Nan was expecting to serve turkey dinner around six in the evening, but I kept phoning her to say we were still at work and she continued to delay the dinner. By nine she gave the kids something to eat and put them to bed. At around ten, Tom's secretary Sally Moser sent out for some pizza. It came back with double cheese and pepperoni. At around midnight we finished what we were doing and took a look at our Thanksgiving dinner. The cheese had congealed and the pepperoni had drowned in melted fat.

Tom worked so hard that I worried about his health. But as time went by with more long sessions in his office, I began to think that I should worry more about my own health. I needn't have. Hard work, when done for a purpose and with people you admire, isn't hard at all. Not everyone has a chance to work with people with such high standards as Morris and McNamara, and I'm glad I did.

Trips Abroad and at Home

Visits to Army posts in the United States and abroad or to contractors' plants were a necessary part of the job. Sometimes they were impromptu and quick. One morning, for example, I mentioned to Gen. Bill Rosson that I was tired of seeing the Army only through the papers that crossed my desk and was anxious to view it in real life. By three that afternoon, we were on a Pentagon helicopter heading for Fort Bragg, North Carolina, home of the famous 82nd Airborne Division and the soon-to-be famous Green Berets, the Army special forces championed by the president and his brother, Robert Kennedy. Before sundown, we had seen some combat exercises using the weapons and equipment I had been ordering, which were becoming available in large quantities. We got up before dawn the following morning for a parachute jump from the Army's new Caribou airplane. The jumpers were my hosts—generals and senior colonels—including Rosson himself. I watched them with admiration and envy. Sometime earlier, a civilian official visiting the base as I was had jumped out of a plane on a similar morning exercise. Although he landed without injury, the officers were deeply offended that a civilian had acted impulsively without the proper safety instructions.

Sometimes the trips were carefully planned and of long duration. My first trip of this kind, in late 1961, was the obligatory tour of Army logistics installations and troop units in Europe. With me on a military aircraft were members of my staff, several senior logistics officers, and Nancy, with a schedule of her own to meet with wives' groups at the places we visited. The itinerary included a long weekend in Garmisch for relaxation and sightseeing.

One of the first people I saw on the trip was an old friend, Gen. Fred Campbell, whom I had met in the mid-1950s on Gen. Willy Palmer's project. I showed Fred the schedule and asked if he could find a way for me to spend more time with Army combat units. He said the 3rd Armored Division was at Grafenwohr, the Army's major training area in West Germany. It was commanded by Maj. Gen. Creighton Abrams, one of the Army's greatest leaders. He called Abrams's aide who said I could come to Grafenwohr instead of Garmisch.

I had heard of Abrams but never met him. He was a daring soldier who had won two Distinguished Service Crosses in World War II and led the tank column that broke through the Nazi encirclement of the 101st Airborne Division in the Battle of the Bulge. His picture had appeared on the cover of *Time*.

Abe was about medium height, squarely built, gruff, and taciturn. He provided me with Army boots and warm clothing ("You never want to be cold in the field," he said). We boarded a helicopter, and before landing at each stop where his units were deployed, he would say something like "Now you're going to see Lieutenant Smith and Sergeant Jones, and they're going to want to tell you about what they do." After we landed, Smith and Jones would take me in hand, and Abrams would wander off to talk to someone else. I asked questions about the new rifles and tanks and other equipment and got a firsthand report on their effectiveness. General Abrams wanted me to hear directly from his men. Most senior officers I had encountered wanted to hear what the visiting official was being told so they could correct anything that seemed amiss. Not Abe! I was impressed by his confidence in his men and grateful for his willingness to let me explore questions that were on my mind. When they had been answered, I signaled to him and we boarded the helicopter for the next stop.

Abe didn't say much during the day, but he came alive at night. He was a great talker, colorful and incisive, with a voice that rose to a crescendo when he wanted to make a point. He liked to drink Scotch, smoke cigars, and listen to classical music. So did I. We began during those several days in the field a friendship that lasted until his untimely death on September 4, 1974. I believe, and many others agree, that he was the finest officer of his generation.

A visit to Vietnam was almost as necessary as the European trip in order to understand the Army's logistical needs and problems. At a later point, I will discuss Vietnam at length because it was the major preoccupation of my Pentagon years. The Vietnam trip began shortly after my return from Europe and acquainted me for the first time with the terrain and circumstances we faced.

A feature of the visit was a meeting with President Ngo Dinh Diem. Gen. Paul Harkins, our commander in Vietnam, accompanied me to the palace and sat next to me during what turned out to be a long meeting. Diem was dressed immaculately in a white suit and smoked one cigarette after another, consuming almost the entire pack. He never stopped talking. I never interrupted. Neither did Harkins. Diem never asked me a question. He just talked on and on, saying he needed more troops, more supplies, and more U.S. support if he was going to win the war. He talked about the French and where they made their mistakes and how he could defeat the Communists if we gave him enough help.

I can't remember another foreign leader so caught up in his own words or so self-important. With his fate depending on the willingness of the U.S. public to support the effort in Vietnam, I had imagined that he might want to hear from a visitor, if only briefly, about what the mood was in our country and whether we would give him all he said he needed.

Short trips to the plants of Army contractors, particularly when a program was in trouble, were another necessary part of the job. The first contractor trip I made was arranged by my military assistant and included a dinner with the heads of several leading companies at Perino's, one of the best and most expensive restaurants in Los Angeles. I learned later that the companies had paid for the entire evening. It was the first and last time that anything like that happened. There was simply no place for this sort of thing where government procurement was involved. Luckily, there were very few instances where problems of this type arose, and the ones that did were minor. For example, one company sent me a box of fruit at Christmas. I wrote a letter of thanks and explained that I had contributed the fruit to Army welfare. I thanked another company for sending me a book and said it had been donated to the Army library. Rather than trying to decide whether one gesture was all right but another one wasn't, it was easier to reject them all.

Sometimes trips were required for ceremonial reasons. When the thirty-five-thousandth tank rolled out of the Chrysler tank plant in 1963, I was invited to the celebration. I asked if anyone was still around who had worked on the first one and several old-timers were rounded up to join in the festivities. Army commanders always wanted the Pentagon brass to appear at their posts because it gave them an opportunity to involve local leaders at the reception in honor of the visitor. I learned on trips like this never to sit down on a parade ground bench. You could always be sure it had just been painted and would ruin a nice pair of pants.

GAO and Readiness

The General Accounting Office (GAO), an arm of Congress, is headed by the comptroller general of the United States who is appointed for a fifteen-year term of office by the president, with the advice and consent of the Senate. A large and influential organization, GAO audits the financial records of the government and, at the request of Congress or on its own initiative, conducts investigations of governmental programs or individual actions, such as the award of contracts. (In 2004 its name was changed to the Government Accountability Office.)

Sometime after I joined the Army secretariat, the GAO issued a report that criticized the state of readiness of Army combat vehicles and equipment. This report was followed by several others that reported the same type of problem in differing Army units. The Army staff had "answered" the reports with general comments on corrective measures, but the tone of the responses was defensive, more negative than positive.

I had been taught that the auditor was a source of help who alerted management to situations needing correction. The GAO reports seemed to be factual and based on careful observation. They said that shortages of spare parts and failures of maintenance were impairing the Army's ability to carry out its combat mission. That there was not one report but a series of them, all highlighting the same problem, was an additional cause of worry.

The reports clearly identified the trucks and other vehicles down for one reason or another but assigned equal weight to each deficiency. For example, one truck might have a cracked rearview mirror and another might have a cracked engine block. Each one counted as a single deficiency in the GAO total. But the deficiencies were quite different in terms of mission fulfillment. You could go to war with one but not with the other.

The GAO was right, up to a point, in claiming that readiness was impaired, but it had no competence to raise broader and more fundamental questions: Readiness for what? Should there be a single standard of readiness for all Army units, regardless of location or mission? What standards should be used to measure readiness? The Army, not the General Accounting Office, should address questions of this kind.

After studying the reports and thinking about the problem, I told Secretary Stahr that the reports raised legitimate questions but neither they nor the Army responses offered much in the way of a solution. The subject of readiness was important, politically sensitive, and needed more attention than it was getting. One approach we might consider, I said, was a weekend conference away from the day-to-day pressures of the Pentagon, attended by both the civilian and uniformed leaders of the Army.

Stahr discussed my suggestions with the chief of staff. He reacted favorably but said he wanted his operations deputy, Gen. Harold K. Johnson, to look into the matter and advise him. I had come to know General Johnson quite well from early morning breakfasts with him in the Army dining room when I was a "bachelor" at Fort Myer. He was one of the most principled individuals I had ever met, deeply religious, dedicated to the Army, and grateful to be alive after suffering the horrors of imprisonment in a Japanese camp after the fall of Bataan in the Philippines.

Johnson decided that the readiness questions deserved the kind of attention a weekend conference would provide. He recommended that it be held at Fort Monroe, a hundred miles or so from the Pentagon, and supervised the preparation of the agenda and the briefings that addressed the problems and offered solutions. The approach was positive and thorough. The Army leaders listened to the briefings, discussed the problems they raised, and evaluated the proposed solutions. The conference concluded that a whole new approach to readiness was needed.

Perhaps the most telling indication of the Army's commitment to a new approach was the assignment of General Abrams to oversee the development of a new readiness reporting system. Abrams had only recently returned from his combat command in Europe to a position in General Johnson's operations directorate. Under Abe's informed leadership, standards were produced for materiel, personnel, and unit readiness. A reporting system was installed that presented accurate and timely information on Army combat units. Overall, it was a good example of how professional the Army staff can be when it goes to work to solve a problem. I was glad to have started the ball rolling.

Interservice Rivalry

Anyone who has ever watched an Army-Navy football game needn't be told how intense the competition can be among the armed services. The Army can lose every other game it plays, but if it beats Navy in that final contest, it will have had a successful season.

Interservice rivalry isn't confined to the gridiron. It goes on regularly in the Pentagon. Sometimes it arises in the fight for a larger share of the defense budget. No matter how many times the politicians tell the chiefs that there is no ceiling on the dollars available, they believe otherwise and scramble for each one. Many times the competition is fueled by a new technology that affects the services in differing and uncertain ways. Often it arises from a sincere belief by one service that its concepts for war fighting are superior to competing ones. And in many cases the rivalry stems from arguments between proponents of offensive or defensive weapons.

There are also occasions in which the rivalry is confined to a single service. In the Navy, for example, aviators are sure they can sink enemy submarines with aerial torpedoes. Navy submariners, on the other hand, are confident that their stealth tactics preclude easy kills from the air. In the Army, a similar argument goes on between antitank weaponeers and tank commanders.

Critics of the military believe that interservice rivalry produces damaging controversy that causes the public to lose confidence in its armed forces. They point to such episodes as the acrimonious battle in 1949 between the air force, which wanted many new B-36 bombers, and the Navy, which wanted a new aircraft carrier. An admiral called the B-36 a "billion dollar blunder," and the chairman of the Joint Chiefs of Staff, Omar Bradley, called the admirals a "bunch of fancy Dans." Clearly things had gotten out of hand.

My own view is that the rivalry serves a useful purpose if it is contained within reasonable bounds. I like the idea that each service puts its best foot forward and claims that its weapons or tactics are the preferred way to defeat an emerging threat. I would not want to see a situation in which a service reacted passively to a challenge, withdrawing from the contest so another service could carry the day. It wouldn't breed the aggressiveness one wants to see in the commander who says "I can take that hill" or another who says "Damn the torpedoes, full speed ahead!"

Some of the most profound and unsettling rivalries have resulted from attempts to control a new technology and the weapons it makes possible. In World War I, the airplane made its first combat appearance, and it was evident that it had important implications for the future of warfare. Billy Mitchell, an Army Signal Corps officer, was a pioneer in air combat. His specialty was bombing enemy targets. After the war, he argued strongly for a separate air force, a position opposed by the Army and the Navy. His criticisms became so vitriolic that in 1925 an Army court-martial convicted him of insubordination. He resigned from the Army the next year. In time his prophecies about strategic bombing and the eclipse of the battleship by the airplane were fulfilled.

Another example of how a bold new technology can stimulate intense rivalry among the services arose from the V-1 and V-2 missiles that emerged from secret Nazi efforts during World War II. Hundreds of V-2 missiles were fired on London beginning in 1944. Military leaders saw the great potential of the new technology and struggled to control its development. The Army said it should be in charge because missiles operated under the laws of ballistics and the Army Ordnance Corps was the "pope" of that field. The air force disagreed, arguing that the laws of aerodynamics applied and that it had the last word on that subject. The Navy had both an ordnance branch and an aeronautical branch, each of which laid claim to the missile. In an effort to placate its own claimants, the Navy decided that if the missile had a wing on it, as some of the earlier ones did, the Bureau of Aeronautics should develop it. If no wing was attached, it belonged to the Bureau of Ordnance. The impracticalities of the arrangement were soon evident and the two bureaus were merged into the Bureau of Naval Weapons.

While the Navy was able to settle its jurisdictional claims, the controversy between the Army and the air force continued. The Army had an extensive and long-established arsenal system. Before the emergence of the "defense industry" at the end of World War II, the arsenals were the repositories of knowledge about military science and the places where the arts of weaponry had been kept alive. The Army assigned missile development to Redstone Arsenal under the command of an aggressive and capable ordnance officer, Maj. Gen. Bruce Medaris. Redstone's resources were greatly strengthened with the arrival in the United States in 1945 of some of the leading German rocket pioneers, including the most famous one of all, Wernher von Braun. Von Braun and more than five hundred specialists had fled south from Peenemunde, where the V-2 had been developed, and surrendered to U.S. forces. (More than one hundred were later admitted into the United States.) The Soviets captured Peenemunde and took many German technicians to the USSR.

The air force did not become an independent service until 1948. Lacking arsenals, it turned to industry for its missile development. The Ramo-Wooldridge Corporation played a major role. Simon Ramo, a brilliant electronics engineer, left Hughes Aircraft in 1953 with a fellow engineer, Dean Wooldridge, to form the new company. It later became Thompson Ramo Wooldridge (TRW). A quasi-public organization, the Aerospace Corporation, was later formed under Air Force direction for systems engineering purposes. Another aggressive and capable officer, Gen. Bernard Schriever, exercised overall responsibility for missile development.

The bitterness of the rivalry between the Army and the air force became apparent to the public when General Schriever paid a visit to Redstone Arsenal. General Medaris refused to let him in! I had met Medaris at Willy Palmer's logistics seminar and remembered him as a flamboyant person, given to the dramatic gesture. The lockout of one U.S. general by another must have been unprecedented.

My personal encounters with interservice rivalry lacked the drama of a court-martial or the lockout of a competing general, but they were vivid, nevertheless. Under urging from Secretary McNamara and civilian systems analysts on his staff, the Army in the early 1960s was moving rapidly toward the formation of units up to division strength that employed large numbers of helicopters. Smaller ones were used for observation, and the larger ones like the UH-1 Huey and the twin-rotor Chinook carried troops to battle. The Army wanted to equip the Hueys with a machine gun, but the air force objected. Fearful that the Army ultimately wanted to develop its own air arm, the chief of the air staff, Gen. Curtis LeMay, thought that arming the Hueys was a step in that direction and expressed his strong opposition directly to McNamara. It was a "roles and missions" issue, the air force argued, using the terms employed to define the scope and boundaries for each service.

As the Army's procurement secretary, I had become involved in the air mobile efforts, buying helicopters and helping the uniformed leaders to free themselves from confining specifications that mandated equipment too heavy for use in aircraft. The Huey question came to my attention, and through Tom Morris I had an opportunity to talk to Secretary McNamara about it. I described the problem in simple, non-technical terms. I said I couldn't understand a logic that permitted a machine gun on an M-113 armored personnel carrier used to carry troops to battle but denied a gun on a helicopter that carried troops. Apparently it was okay to have a gun if the vehicle maintained contact with the ground, but if the vehicle lost contact with terra firma then the gun was verboten. McNamara couldn't see the logic of it either and approved the arming of the Hueys. (Later, Huey gunships were heavily armed with automatic weapons and rocket launchers.)

The air force was unhappy with the decision to approve machine guns for use on the Huey helicopter, but it was even unhappier about another Army foray into the air, a fixed-wing airplane with elaborate infrared and other sensing mechanisms. Though I was expected to be an Army partisan in matters such as this, I thought the air force was right that the airplane, called the Mohawk, overstepped the roles and missions boundaries. Fortunately, I was not asked to express an official opinion and was not unhappy when the expensive airplane was denied to the Army.

The other rivalry problem was a complex entanglement over a new rifle. The Army had only recently adopted the M-14, a product improvement over the M-1 standard rifle of World War II. It had been designed, as were all Army rifles, by the Ordnance Corps at Springfield Armory, a place that traced its history to George Washington's time.

Meanwhile, a gun designer named Eugene Stoner came up with quite a different type of rifle called the AR-15 that was being produced in small quantities by the Armalite Corporation. Its stock was made of plastic, not wood, and its parts could be stamped out inexpensively, not hand-machined as with previous rifles. It fired a smaller bullet than the M-14, which meant a soldier could carry many more rounds of ammunition. The smaller bullet also enabled the soldier to control the weapon in fully automatic fire, unlike the M-14. The Army looked at the rifle but rejected it for a number of reasons. General LeMay, a gun enthusiast, also looked at the AR-15 and asked the air force to test it, after which it was adopted as the standard rifle for airmen on guard duty or other assignments.

The whole story of what followed is set forth in great detail in *National Defense*, a book by James Fallows. Army ordnance continued to object to the gun. In 1963 Secretary McNamara designated the Army as the central procurement agency for all the services, and I began to oversee the contracting of initial quantities for the air force, Army special forces, and the Vietnamese. But when Army ordnance got hold of the gun, it declared that it had been inadequately developed and undertook to "militarize" it into what became the M-16 rifle.

The sordid tale is too long to relate in full here. It included an Army inspector general's report that said the Army's tests of the AR-15 had been blatantly rigged, and a congressional investigation that concluded the gun had been sabotaged by Army ordnance. Over a period of time, the problems that arose from "militarizing" the highly successful AR-15 were overcome, and the M-16 version of it became the Army's standard rifle.

How does one make sense of all of this? Many of the reasons are subjective. The AR-15 simply didn't look like a rifle should look, Army purists thought. It had been designed by an outsider, not by Springfield Armory. It had been championed by the air force, hardly a mark in its favor for the Army. Its early proponents were civilian analysts who pushed the Army to adopt it. Although these reasons may explain why the Army resisted the gun, they do not justify the actions taken to prevent its adoption. It was not the Army's finest hour.

When interservice rivalry becomes too intense or gets out of control, the public loses confidence in its military leaders. Although the rivalry serves a useful purpose, it needs to be managed. The best way to do this is to have strong civilian and military leaders at Army, Navy, and air force levels, pushing aggressively to exploit the inherent characteristics of each service. But there must also be highly capable people at the Department of Defense level to analyze and finally decide among the proposals coming from the services. Otherwise, there may be too many solutions offered to meet a particular threat and not enough to deal with another. And clearly, one service's proposal, in a comparative analysis, may be far superior to a competing one. This is the way the Pentagon operated during the McNamara years. Operations were decentralized, for the most part, to the military departments, but final decisions on force levels, weapons, and budget amounts were made by the secretary after review by his staff and the Joint Chiefs.

Reorganizing the Tech Services

Gen. Williston B. Palmer had it about right back in 1953 when he noted that the Army technical services needed direction and control. Less than a decade later, a major reorganization bundled them together into the Army Materiel Command. In the process, the chief of Army ordnance and the secretary of the Army resigned. Change does not come easily in the Pentagon, as Secretary of Defense Donald Rumsfeld has found in his attempts in the George W. Bush administration to transform the military services. The establishment of the Army Materiel Command was no exception.

The seven technical services had a long and proud record of accomplishment, not only for the Army but also for the United States. In many important ways they helped the country to become a modern industrial society. The Corps of Engineers surveyed the land and constructed the dams and waterways, and one of its officers, George W. Goethals, built the Panama Canal. The Ordnance Corps perfected techniques for serial manufacture of guns that became the basis for mass production of civilian goods. The early aviation efforts of the Signal Corps, including the first contract with Wilbur and Orville Wright, helped to establish the modern air transportation system. Walter Reed of the Army Medical Corps conquered yellow fever. The Transportation Corps hastened the advent of container ships. Like developing countries in recent world history in which military forces have built national infrastructures, the United States in its formative years looked to its Army and Navy for nation-building efforts.

Each of the technical services was a fiefdom unto itself. Each one obtained and managed its own financial resources, controlled the education and advancement of corps personnel, and developed weapons and equipment within its own technical boundaries.

What had worked reasonably well throughout history no longer seemed adequate for Army needs after World War II. First, the rapid advances in technology, particularly the near-universal application of electronics, made it difficult to maintain the technical boundaries that defined the services. The advent of the missile further complicated the problem. The rise of the defense industry, driven by competitive pressures, produced new ideas, new products, and rapid development schedules that the arsenals could not match. Army leaders like Gen. James Gavin and Gen. Arthur Trudeau were dissatisfied with the Army's research effort and looked for ways to improve it. Long lead times for getting new equipment into the hands of troops were often blamed on technical service bickering as, for example, in the opposition of the Ordnance Corps to the amphibious vehicles of the Transportation Corps.

The movement toward integration of the tech services was accelerated by the arrival of Robert S. McNamara as secretary of defense. Almost immediately he announced an array of proposals and studies to combine functions of the individual services into Department of Defense (DOD) agencies and to bring about organizational change within individual services, particularly the Army. The first joint agency in the McNamara period was the Defense Intelligence Agency (DIA), set up in August 1961 to organize and manage the department's intelligence resources. A second change, with more sweeping implications, was the establishment of the Defense Supply Agency (DSA) in November of the same year with responsibility for items common to all the services. DSA's first commander was Andrew McNamara (no relation to the defense secretary), the quartermaster general of the Army and the first project officer for the Harbridge House effort to get Gen. Willy Palmer's supply management course under way.

One of Secretary McNamara's many studies raised the question of integrating the tech services into a single command. Despite General Palmer's earlier efforts to bring them under control, they continued to function largely as autonomous organizations with three hundred thousand military and civilian personnel at some four hundred installations.

When the study was completed, a briefing was scheduled for the tech service chiefs to comment. Secretary McNamara made an unannounced appearance. I remember the surprise, if not astonishment, of the Army officers as he entered the room. Many military people viewed McNamara as a remote and hostile figure. He tended to work closely with his own staff and seldom found the time to chat leisurely with members of the armed services. What they didn't know was that he could be a warm and engaging person when he wanted to be, and that's just what he wanted to be in the Army meeting. He disarmed the officers first by telling them that his organization at Ford, as indeed at General Motors and other large corporations, was based on the fundamental line and staff concepts pioneered by the Army. I saw some of the rigid backs relax when he paid this compliment. Then he described what he was attempting to accomplish, how important a strong Army was for the nation's defense, and how a new functional logistics command was long overdue and urgently needed. He told the tech service chiefs that he welcomed their views, but that after a decision had been reached they should support it and not engage in public controversy.

It was time now for the tech service chiefs to respond. Surprisingly, several of them—the surgeon general, the chief signal officer, and the chief of transportation—endorsed the change. The others objected for one reason or another. When McNamara left, Lt. Gen. John Hinrichs, chief of Ordnance, accused the Army staff of letting the secretary of defense take over the direction of the study effort.

A month later Secretary McNamara issued an executive order on Army reorganization that abolished the technical services as independent entities.

The new Army Materiel Command was scheduled by the Army to be fully operational by the spring of 1963. McNamara told Secretary Stahr to accelerate the reorganization so that it would be in business nine months earlier than the Army desired. Stahr protested. He considered McNamara's directive to be yet another intrusion into Army affairs and announced his resignation. Cyrus Vance replaced him in July.

Stahr had always fought hard for Army positions, and that was both his strength and, in the McNamara Pentagon, his weakness. McNamara expected strong advocacy from the service secretaries, but he also thought of them as senior members of a defense team headed by him. I often thought that he might have preferred not to have Army, Navy, and air force secretaries, but he was wise enough to know that any attempt to abolish the positions would be mired in controversy for months or years. So the service secretary remained the man in the middle, subject to pressures from above and below.

I was sorry to see Stahr go. Though McNamara sometimes put me in an awkward position by dealing directly with me, I was always careful to keep Stahr informed. He treated me with the utmost consideration and fully supported my efforts to strengthen Army logistics. Shortly before he departed, he unexpectedly presented me with the

Army's Distinguished Civilian Service Medal. Medals like this are normally given at the end of one's period of service—indeed I got a second one when I left the Army—so Stahr's award had special meaning. My wife and children attended the ceremony and our young son David told me he saw a six-star general—three stars on one shoulder and three on the other. That topped even General of the Army George Catlett Marshall, who had only five.

Cy Vance took over the reins quickly, stamping his imprint on the department. In his first few days at work he sent back to the staff a paper that had been prepared for his signature, saying it failed to make its points clearly and persuasively. The system got the word that there was a new man on the block who expected first-rate staff work.

As the paperwork was being prepared to establish the Army Materiel Command on the demanding McNamara schedule, I got a telephone call at my house early one morning while I was getting ready to go to work. It was Bob McNamara. There was a brief pause while I got over my shock at being home while he was at work. McNamara said: "Now that we have this command in place, who should be in charge of it?" I responded immediately: "Frank Besson."

Besson, a two-star general, was chief of the Transportation Corps. The senior tech officer, at three stars, was John Hinrichs. Hinrichs had opposed the new organization while Besson had favored it. Besson was also younger and more vigorous. He had been a Corps of Engineers officer before transferring to Transportation, and in World War II he had been one of the youngest officers raised to general officer rank. Besson was duly appointed as head of the Army Materiel Command and elevated to four-star rank. Hinrichs resigned from the Army.

Defining and Acquiring the Army "Requirement"

Cyrus Vance brought impressive credentials to the position of secretary of the Army. He was from a distinguished family from Clarksburg,

West Virginia, one of whose members, John W. Davis, was the Democratic Party's candidate for president in 1924. He attended college and law school at Yale, served as a gunnery officer in the Navy in World War II, and joined a leading Wall Street law firm. Senator Lyndon Johnson tapped him for service as special counsel for the Senate Armed Services Committee, followed by a second assignment as counsel to the Senate Special Committee on Space and Aeronautics. McNamara made him his general counsel and a close advisor. Vance was reserved but friendly, decisive but anxious to hear opposing views, and respected for his sense of fairness. Most important from the Army's standpoint was McNamara's complete trust in Vance: McNamara had made him the Army secretary, and we were confident that he would fully support him.

Vance developed an easygoing relationship with the chief of staff, Gen. Earle G. Wheeler. Wheeler, a tall, handsome man like Vance, had distinguished himself as a skillful staff officer rather than as a brilliant combat leader. There was a private door between his office and Vance's, and he would sometimes "come through the woodwork" to confer with Vance informally about a matter before the machinery of the staff cranked out a hard, official position.

Vance made an important organizational change after taking office. He placed force planning and programs under a new assistant chief of staff for force development. The Army needed to have someone with primary responsibility for force planning. The large number of Army units—divisions, regiments, battalions, companies, platoons—including those in the active force, the reserve components, and the National Guard, sometimes defied a simple accurate tally. Lt. Gen. Robert Colglazier, the logistics chief, told me one day that he was never able to get an accurate count of the force structure and had to come up with a tally of his own in order to prepare procurement schedules.

The problem became more complex when one considered the "requirement," that is, the force that should be the basis for current support and mobilization planning. As the procurement and logistics secretary, this was a matter of importance to me. The national strategy was shifting from primary reliance on the nuclear deterrent to an emphasis on usable combat power. To be "usable," a force had to be ready with the equipment and supplies it needed for sustained combat. When I asked the Army's senior military logistics planner what the "requirement" was, he said, rather matter-of-factly, "I suppose the answer is one hundred divisions. That's what we had in World War II."

I was astonished by his comment. Could anyone seriously think that one hundred divisions would ever be mobilized in the age of nuclear weapons? If that was the "requirement," the Army would never be ready, and there would be no realistic standard against which to measure readiness for combat. The Army was authorized for sixteen divisions, and it seemed to me that they should constitute the "requirement" for which equipment and supplies were procured.

It is one thing to develop a requirement for a static situation—that is, sixteen divisions consuming ammunition and other supplies at peacetime rates. It is quite another calculation when expenditures at wartime rates are considered. In war, tanks and trucks are destroyed by enemy fire and ammunition is expended in amounts far exceeding those needed for routine peacetime training.

I learned from my inquiries that Army logisticians had developed a technique for determining the "requirement" that took wartime expenditure rates into account. It was called "D to P." "D" was the assumed date on which combat began. "P" was the date on which industrial production matched combat needs. The time from D to P varied substantially across the spectrum of Army items. For example, it would take far longer for tank production to reach a rate that matched combat losses than for a simpler item, like a truck battery, similar to those in commercial usage. The time to reach P for tanks and artillery and other items where there was no civilian counterpart also depended on whether the production base was "cold" or "hot." If it were cold, that is, if no tanks were in current production, it would take many more months to reach wartime levels than if the base were hot, that is, with tanks in production at minimal levels that could be quickly stepped up if needed.

In short, the D to P concept appeared to be a useful method for assuring that the Army's sixteen divisions would be fully equipped and supplied in peace or war. The "requirement" was defined as the amount needed in peacetime plus the additional quantity needed to cover the gap until production reached wartime demands.

McNamara liked the concept and quickly approved it as the "requirement" to be funded and acquired. He had always opposed the notion of arbitrary budget levels, believing that the nation could afford whatever was needed to enable the armed forces to help carry out U.S. foreign policy objectives. He subsequently issued formal logistics guidance to the Army but insisted that we sign a certificate attesting that the dollars included in the budget request were sufficient to meet the guidance.

No one had ever requested a certificate like this before. It had to be signed by the chief of staff and the secretary of the Army, and there was some hesitancy among the military leaders to go along with the idea. On the other hand, the logistics guidance with its accompanying certificate assured adequate funding for defined Army needs, in contrast to earlier periods when budget levels were inadequate.

The task of preparing the back-up material for the certificate fell to me and to the no-nonsense vice chief of staff, a New Englander with the marvelous name of Barksdale Hamlett. "Ham," as he was called, left his quarters at 4 AM on several mornings to go over the major items with me, one by one, to arrive at the proper numbers. In some instances he would accept a shortage as a reasonable risk. One example was bayonets. "I never saw too many guys put out of action with a bayonet," he said. When I mentioned this to an infantry officer, he laughed and said jokingly that Hamlett was an artilleryman, a long way from the soldier with his rifle and bayonet.

In the midst of all this logistical planning effort, I had a surprise visit from Gen. Maxwell Taylor, the former Army chief of staff, then serving as President Kennedy's special military representative. Taylor said he had heard what we were doing and wanted to say how pleased he was. His words meant more to me than a raise in pay.

Cuba, Kennedy, and Vietnam

Three events of surpassing importance marked the eighteen-month period when Cyrus Vance was secretary of the Army. In October 1962, only three months after Vance took office, the Cuban Missile Crisis plunged the United States into the most dangerous confrontation of the Cold War. A year later, on November 22, 1963, President John F. Kennedy, who had appointed McNamara, Vance, and the rest of us to the positions we held, was assassinated in Dallas. Finally, the situation in Vietnam was becoming more complex each day, particularly after another assassination, that of Vietnam's leader, Ngo Dinh Diem, on November 2, just twenty days before President Kennedy was killed.

The Cuban Missile Crisis, the first of the three events, might have ended in a nuclear war with millions of people killed in Cuba and beyond, including in the United States and the USSR. That the crisis was resolved without a nuclear catastrophe was directly the result of the patience, wisdom, and courage of the man who sat in the presidential chair, John Kennedy. With many of his military and civilian advisors recommending an invasion of Cuba, the president stood firm, exploring diplomatic opportunities that led eventually to Premier Khrushchev's agreement to remove the missiles from Cuba.

The president's advisors were the Executive Committee, a small group of senior officials that included McNamara, Secretary of State Dean Rusk, Gen. Maxwell Taylor, Russian experts like Llewellyn Thompson, Attorney General Robert Kennedy, and a few others. McNamara consulted with Vance and kept him informed of the tense deliberations over the thirteen-day period of the crisis. Vance told me at the outset that an invasion by Army troops was under serious consideration and that I should work with the uniformed leaders to make sure needed supplies and equipment were available and that the movement of invasion forces to points of embarkation was expedited. Those of us occupied with the details knew how dangerous the confrontation was. We learned years later that it was even more perilous than we had realized. Discussions with Soviet officials disclosed that 90 of the 160 nuclear warheads in Cuba were tactical weapons available to the Soviet commanders for use against U.S. forces if they had invaded the island.

On Saturday night, October 27, 1962, at the height of the crisis when it appeared that we might attack the island, I came home from work and did something I hadn't done before. Normally, I would say good-night to our kids if they were still awake and then have a cocktail with my wife before dinner. This evening I told Nan that I wanted to take a walk around the neighborhood. She knew I was preoccupied and wanted to be alone with my thoughts but didn't realize that it was the prospect of a nuclear confrontation that haunted me.

President Kennedy's performance during the Cuban Missile Crisis was his finest hour. The shock of his assassination, some forty years after it happened, is impossible for me to put aside. A youthful president had been killed, the nation had been wounded, and those of us privileged to have served with him felt a personal wound. I couldn't believe he was gone. The only comparable experience in my life was when I learned, as a naval officer at sea in the war against Japan, that President Roosevelt had died. He had been my president since I was a boy of twelve. I couldn't imagine the United States without Roosevelt any more than I could imagine it without Kennedy.

Nan and I were invited to the White House where President Kennedy's body lay in state in the East Room. For the remainder of that long weekend of mourning, we stayed home with our children, watching the unfolding events on television. We grieved as a family, as countless other families did across the nation.

Vietnam was the third surpassing event during Vance's tenure as secretary. Of course, it continued long after he left the Army position, and he played a major role in the drama. But in looking back on Kennedy and Vietnam, many people wondered whether we would have become so involved with the war in Vietnam had Kennedy lived. No one can be sure, but Bob McNamara, for one, thinks not. In his book *In Retrospect* he bases his judgment on Kennedy's handling of the Cuban Missile Crisis. Kennedy wanted to keep us out of war over Cuba, and he found a way to do it. "So I conclude that John Kennedy would have eventually gotten out of Vietnam rather than more deeply in," he wrote. Bob may have been right, but his reasoning is quite speculative. My guess is that Kennedy would have been affected by the same military and political imperatives that drove Johnson.

Procurement

Military procurement is an enormous enterprise where thousands of people at hundreds of buying centers spend billions of dollars for everything from mayonnaise to missiles. Each of the three military departments operates its own purchasing system. Items common to all the services are bought by the Defense Supply Agency (now called the Defense Logistics Agency).

During the McNamara years there was a great deal of interest in making procurement more cost-effective. One aspect of this involved changes in organization, such as the formation of the Army Material Command and the Defense Supply Agency. A second was a department-wide effort to shift from cost-reimbursement contracts to fixed-price types where the contractor bore more of the risk and stood to make a larger profit. A third emphasis was on finding innovative ways to solve old problems.

Multiyear Buys

Congress appropriates money annually and contracts are typically placed for annual requirements. This produces higher prices than a single contract for a multiyear amount.

I became concerned about the waste associated with annual buys and asked my staff to figure out a way to solve the problem. They came up with a fairly simple solution. If the annual requirement for a five-ton truck, for example, was five thousand, we could place a contract for fifteen thousand trucks to be delivered over a three-year period. The truck manufacturers, bidding on fifteen thousand trucks rather than five thousand, would be able to offer a better price because of the greater quantity and the ability to spread their start-up and fixed costs over a larger base.

The prerogatives of Congress were preserved by stating in the contract that if, for any reason, Congress failed to appropriate the necessary money for the second or third year's quantities, the government would owe the contractor the unamortized portion of the start-up and fixed costs that had been developed on the basis of the full fifteen thousand requirement.

I explained our concept to Representative George Mahon, chair of the House Appropriations Committee, and he gave us his approval. The Army placed multiyear contracts for trucks, Jeeps, and other items with predictable requirements. A great deal of money was saved—some estimates run as high as 25 percent—and national security was enhanced by the assurance of stable sources of supply.

Two-Step Advertising

The preferred procurement method is through formal advertising, with the submission of sealed bids and the award of the contract to the lowest bidder. On occasion, a buying agency has doubts about the ability of the low bidder to produce a satisfactory item, but it is very difficult to deny an award and then place it with a company that bid more.

This problem gave rise to an approach we developed called two-step advertising. In step one, companies would indicate whether they were interested in bidding on the contract. Government procurement officials would then look into the companies' qualifications and eliminate any that were clearly unqualified for one reason or another. In step two, the qualified companies would submit their bids and the low bidder would win. The technique was extended beyond the Army to the other military departments as well.

Two-step advertising didn't solve all the problems of dealing with unqualified suppliers. Because taxpayers' money is being spent, any company believes that it has a right to compete for government contracts. In the 1960s the Army faced a serious problem because most of its contracts for generators ended up in the hands of companies that couldn't compete favorably in the commercial generator market and were unable to produce an acceptable Army generator. A generator is vitally important to an Army in the field; a soldier can't stick a plug into a wall socket but must rely on portable generators for the supply of power.

Major surgery was needed to correct the problem. The obvious solution was to default the failing suppliers and place new contracts with recognized manufacturers. When I explained the seriousness of the problem to the representatives in whose districts the failing companies were located, they agreed that corrective action was needed and accepted our approach without protest.

Buying In

Sometimes a contractor submits a low price with the clear intent of finding ways after the contract is awarded to raise the price. Because the government must issue change orders from time to time, the contractor has an opportunity to "get well" by pricing the changes at an unwarranted price. To the extent that this occurs, it penalizes companies that bid honestly only to lose to the one that bid deliberately low.

In a large contract for Army Jeeps, the company that won the award was accused of "buying in" by the losing contractor, who alleged that the Army would end up paying more through the change order process. It occurred to me that a simple remedy might help to discipline the situation. I sent a memo to General Besson, chief of the Army Materiel Command, asking him to submit for my personal approval any change order that raised the price of the Jeep. This was not the sort of thing that a procurement secretary normally did, since he was supposed to be concerned with policy, not details of a particular contract. But it worked in this instance. The only change that was requested and issued lowered the price by the substitution of steel wheels for magnesium ones. In several subsequent procurements, General Besson followed the same approach, telling his buyers down the line to submit for his approval any changes where a buy-in was suspected.

Congressional Environment

Members of Congress have a legitimate and often intense interest in the awarding of contracts that affect their districts. Contracts bring jobs and money to the community, and members of Congress are expected to champion the local contender. When it is necessary to explain to a member of Congress why a favorite son lost to a competitor, he or she will usually go along if the facts are persuasive.

Many people believe that members of Congress determine who receives a contract or at least influence the award by one means or another. I saw very little of this during my Pentagon years. Nevertheless, the practice of having a representative or senator announce the winning contractor fueled the suspicion of influence. In our naivete, Cy Vance and I visited several congressional leaders to explore whether the Pentagon, not the member of Congress, should be the sole announcer of contract awards, but we got nowhere. We decided that the practice created the wrong impression but did little in the way of actual harm.

The only instance I can recall where politics influenced a procurement decision originated in the White House, not the Congress. It was for a machine gun contract for which a reputable company in an economically distressed area of Maine was an interested bidder. I received a telephone call from Roswell Gilpatric, the deputy secretary of defense, telling me that he would handle the matter. He did and the Maine company got the contract. So far as I could tell, it was simply an innocent effort to help a town with an unemployment problem. Nevertheless, I was grateful for Gilpatric's intervention because it protected me, and the Army procurement people, from any charge of political influence.

Musical Chairs

After three years of distinguished service as deputy secretary of defense, Roswell Gilpatric returned to his law practice in New York.

McNamara called on Cy Vance to replace Gilpatric, and Steve Ailes was elevated from the number-two spot in the Army to become the secretary. I was made the undersecretary, beginning officially on February 28, 1964.

Vance had been an illustrious secretary, providing leadership for the Army and also serving as a trusted advisor to McNamara. It surprised no one when he was tapped to succeed Gilpatric. Ailes's promotion was also expected. He had been intensely loyal to the Army, got along easily with the uniformed leaders, and handled his responsibilities with enthusiasm and good results. His principal areas of concentration were manpower issues, a subject of special importance to the Army, and external matters including the Panama Canal and our relationship with Okinawa.

The Panama Canal occupied an important place in the Army's history. As noted earlier, an Army engineer, George W. Goethals, supervised its construction. The Canal Zone was administered by a general of the Corps of Engineers with the title of "governor." The secretary of the Army was the "stockholder" of the canal, and the undersecretary was the chairman of the board of the Panama Canal Company.

I had thoroughly enjoyed my work as the assistant secretary and felt that my experience prior to joining the secretariat equipped me to lead the logistics area with confidence. Ailes hoped that I would dig into Army manpower problems with the same degree of enthusiasm. Though I tried, I never found the manpower area as interesting and comprehensive as the broad field of installations and logistics. The Panama responsibility was different entirely. I became fascinated with the history of the canal and with the emerging and controversial issue of turning it over to the government of Panama.

In December 1964, Tom Morris left the government to return to his management consulting practice at the Cresap firm. McNamara said he wanted me to replace Morris. I was officially appointed as the assistant secretary of defense (I&L) on December 23, 1964. My period of almost four years of Army service had come to an end. I hated leaving Ailes and my many other Army friends, in and out of uniform, but looked forward eagerly to working directly with McNamara and my previous boss, Cy Vance. Vance, meanwhile, recruited his long-time friend and Yale classmate Stanley Resor to succeed me as undersecretary.

I walked up E-ring of the Pentagon, from the Mall entrance where I worked to the River entrance where my new office was located, down the hall from McNamara and Vance, prepared to begin a new assignment that turned out to be the most demanding one of my career.

Me at three with my parents, Hovsep and Elisa Ignatius, Glendale, California, 1923. *Author photo*

Ensign Paul R. Ignatius, U.S. Navy, July 1943. *Author photo*

Our TBF following a wheels-up crash landing at Salton Sea, California, in April 1944. The engine conked out during a steep dive. The plane was a mess but the pilot, radioman, and I were not injured. *U.S. Navy photograph*

The escort carrier USS *Manila Bay* (CVE-61), 1944: ten thousand tons of sheet metal and baling wire that we called the "Manila Maru." It fought the Japanese for two years from the Marshall Islands through the end of the war. *U.S. Navy photograph*

Captain Fitzhugh Lee, twice awarded the Navy Cross while skipper of the *Manila Bay*. *U.S. Navy photograph*

That's me in a flight jacket rushing across the crowded flight deck of the *Manila Bay*. *Author photo*

Wedding day, December 20, 1947, Holyoke, Massachusetts. *Author photo*

In the Rose Garden at the White House in 1961, with President Kennedy more interested in my wife than in me. *Official White House photograph*

Deputy Secretary of Defense Cyrus Vance, center, and I talk with Lt. Col. Melvin Garten of the army's 101st Airborne Division, near Tuy Hoa, Vietnam, in 1966. *U.S. Army photograph*

Defense Secretary Robert S. McNamara with his principal assistants making final DOD budget decisions in the secretary's office, January 5, 1967. *Left to right*: Robert N. Anthony, comptroller; Deputy Secretary of Defense Cyrus R. Vance; McNamara; John S. Foster Jr., director, defense research and engineering; and me, the assistant secretary of defense for installations and logistics. *Official Department of Defense photo*

Reception following the swearing in of the new secretary of the navy, August 18, 1967, the same date that, twenty-five years earlier, I was commissioned as a naval officer. With me are Nancy and our children—*left to right*: David, Amy, Sarah, and Adi—and my boss, Bob McNamara. *Official Department of Defense photograph*

Nan launches the nuclear attack submarine USS *Seahorse* (SSN-669) in Groton, Connecticut, on June 15, 1968. With her is our daughter Amy, the maid of honor. The civilian in the back is Roger Lewis, CEO of General Dynamics. *General Dynamics photo*

On an October 1968 visit to units of the Seventh Fleet off Vietnam, I am escorted on the battleship USS *New Jersey* (BB-62) by Vice Adm. William Bringle, commander, Seventh Fleet, right, and the ship's commanding officer, Capt. J. Edward Snyder. *Official U.S. Navy photograph*

In early December 1968, I joined Adm. Elmo R. Zumwalt Jr. as he inspected a SEAL team at Binh Thuy, headquarters for the Navy's Operation Game Warden forces. *Official U.S. Navy photograph*

A visit with Gen. Creighton Abrams, commander, MACV (Military Assistance Command Vietnam), on my final trip to Vietnam. *Ministry of Defense*

To the surprise of us all, Adm. Hyman G. Rickover, who never went out, showed up at my retirement party in late 1968. *U.S. Navy photograph*

Awarding the Distinguished Service Medal to the chief of naval operations with whom I served, Adm. Thomas H. Moorer, in January 1969. *U.S. Navy photograph*

With Nancy (right) and Katharine Graham, 1970. *Bill Mitchell Photography*

In the *Washington Post* composing room talking newspaper economics to *Post* printers, 1971. *Author photo*

My mother, seated at the Bechstein that moved with her from England to California in 1911. *Author photo*

Five

In McNamara's Band

Robert S. McNamara was at the height of his power when I joined his staff in December 1964. He ruled the Pentagon as no one had before. For years many members of Congress and the public had called for strong civilian leadership to bring greater order and efficiency to the Department of Defense. One influential panel, headed by Senator Stuart Symington and including Roswell Gilpatric, the man later selected by McNamara to be his deputy, had urged new legislation that would strengthen the office of the secretary and diminish the influence of the individual military departments.

With the zeal and energy that were his hallmarks, McNamara came to Washington a month before Kennedy's inauguration in January 1961 and immersed himself in the details of the department, learning about critical issues and the authority of the secretary to deal with them. He telephoned people across the country for their views on defense matters and for their suggestions on individuals he might invite to be his key assistants. By the time he took office in January, he had most of his principal aides on board. He had also prepared a formidable list of study projects to focus the military departments on the problems he wanted to address. From his intensive review, he concluded that he had sufficient authority to accomplish his objectives and those of Senator Symington. In this way he could concentrate on the job at hand

and avoid the protracted controversy that certainly would arise if the proposed legislation were debated in Congress.

With the help of his comptroller, Charles Hitch, McNamara launched a major reordering of planning, programming, and budgeting, the processes by which weapons systems and funding levels were determined. Instead of dealing simply with Army, Navy, and air force requests, he was able through the new procedures to look at basic missions and objectives, irrespective of service identity. The strategic program, the most important of all, grouped Navy Polaris submarines and air force nuclear bombers and missiles into a single package, with all their costs for research, production, manpower, basing, and support set forth over a five-year period. The same approach was taken with the other major packages, such as general purpose forces, airlift and sealift forces, reserve forces, and the like. By highlighting basic missions, the system showed the purposes for which money was being spent, where new investment might be needed, and where too much had been committed.

Coming from a business background, McNamara was particularly interested in the business side of defense, that is, the broad area of logistics and the vast real estate holdings of the department in the United States and abroad. Working with Tom Morris, he undertook steps to improve the management of these business-type activities. For example, he was surprised to learn about duplicate items that served the same purpose in the inventories of the military departments and stressed the need for standardization. Too many purchases were made on a sole-source basis, so he pushed for more competition to get better prices. Suspecting that the department kept open for political reasons many more installations than it needed, he launched a comprehensive review of the entire base structure. Morris put these several efforts into a department-wide cost reduction program that would identify the savings and recognize the individuals and groups that achieved them. McNamara reviewed the results on a regular basis and brought them to the attention of the president.

Robert McNamara took the Pentagon by storm. His dominant manner and the analytical techniques he employed were resented by some of the uniformed leaders. Others simply decided that "if you can't beat 'em, join 'em," and set up systems analysis offices of their own, or sent some of their brightest young officers, like Bob Pursley from the air force and Stan Turner from the Navy, to work with Alain Enthoven's whiz kids.

Much of what McNamara accomplished remains an integral part of the management structure in Defense and other departments of the government. McNamara is a controversial figure today largely because of the Vietnam War. But in 1964 people listened in admiration when he spoke, the Congress was mesmerized by his command of the facts, and in the cabinet he was regarded as the first among equals, with influence far beyond his duties as defense secretary.

The I&L Staff

Sally Moser, Morris's secretary, knew the routines of the office and was extremely helpful in getting me started with my new duties. She had come to Washington along with thousands of other women to help the United States win World War II. Sally's desk was next to the door to my office. Nobody got in to see me without checking with Sally first.

Each functional area had a deputy in charge—experienced individuals respected by the military departments for their knowledge and good judgment. Glenn Gibson, the senior deputy, oversaw international logistics. Paul Riley, a supply management expert, handled storage and supply. Procurement was handled by Jim Bannerman, a legendary civil servant who was later promoted to be an assistant secretary of the Navy. Military construction and installations were Ed Sheridan's responsibility. Sheridan was the office politician. He spent much of each day on "the Hill" talking to senators and representatives about construction projects in their states and districts. Under Sheridan was a live-wire activist, Bill Point, who was in charge of the sensitive subject of base closures. Bob Moot, another legendary civil servant, looked after several areas, including transportation. Moot, in time, became comptroller of the Defense Department.

The deputies were supported by outstanding technical experts. Carl Rolle, for example, knew more about the stockpiles of strategic materials than anyone else in the government. Ed Bennewitz had a genius for organizing data into meaningful reports. Later, when the Vietnam War intensified, I added one of the Army's brightest officers, Maj. Gen. Allen T. Stanwix-Hay, to my staff to oversee, with Bennewitz, the critical area of ammunition production and supply.

The I&L people weren't flashy or shining intellects like most of Enthoven's whiz kids. I&L guys weren't kids and you couldn't find a whiz among them no matter how hard you tried. Instead of advanced degrees from Harvard or MIT, they held undergraduate diplomas from less-known colleges, and in some instances, like the exceptionally capable Bob Moot, had no college education at all.

There was no I&L staff when the Department of Defense was established in 1948 after the end of World War II. The office of the first secretary, James Forrestal, consisted of only a few individuals. Forrestal soon found that he could not properly discharge his responsibilities with such limited resources. As a result, his office grew in size and influence over the years, and under McNamara reached a pinnacle of power. The military departments—Army, Navy, and Air Force—were separately staffed with both civilians and military leaders, but the secretary of defense and his key assistants had overriding authority in most matters.

Meetings with McNamara

When I was a research assistant at the Harvard Business School, I used to look at the intercoms on the desks of executives to see who among them were connected to the chief executive. It was a quick way of determining the individuals and functions that were important to the boss. The intercom on my desk was piped in to McNamara's, an indication of the significance he attached to I&L matters. He could get me by pushing a button, and frequently did, but I almost never called him directly unless there was a matter of exceptional urgency.

Although I saw McNamara often in departmental meetings or on special I&L issues, my formal contact was a weekly half-hour session in his office at 8:30 on Friday mornings, attended also by Cyrus Vance, his deputy. At these meetings, I summarized highlights of what was going on in my area, provided data, and sought his advice or approval when needed on issues.

Each week, like Morris before me, I prepared a tightly written, eight-to-ten-page agenda to guide our discussion. McNamara read and digested each item quickly, then commented on both the details and the larger context. For example, when I showed him a table of profit rates on defense contracts, he questioned why the rates were so high on risk-free cost-reimbursement contracts. Then he launched into a discussion of the importance of profits when companies take risks and how essential it was for them to earn a satisfactory return in order to keep them interested in defense work. "We should think how what we do today will affect the situation twenty years from now," he said.

In meeting with McNamara, it was customary to sit on the chair alongside his enormous desk, which had been used earlier by Gen. John J. Pershing and James Forrestal. I would look directly at McNamara and he would look up from time to time at the clock on the wall in front of him. To McNamara, time was everything. Like caviar or white truffles, it was a gift of inestimable value, not to be wasted. More than once I suggested that he spend some time at the war colleges to let the future generals and admirals know what he was attempting to accomplish, and thereby gain their support. He always said there wasn't enough time for that sort of thing. He told Gene Zuckert something similar when Gene said he should spend more time on the Hill with influential members of Congress.

When the weekly meeting was over, I returned to my office and immediately dictated a confidential memorandum to Sally Moser on the points we had discussed. Then I would meet with my deputies to give them guidance stemming from the McNamara meeting. Before long, it was time to begin thinking about what to include in next week's agenda in the never-ending process of identifying problems and seeking solutions.

It was sometimes intimidating to meet with McNamara, especially when he looked up at that clock on the wall. Occasionally, he would bear down too hard on a point that was more complex than he seemed to realize. I thought it was important when this happened not to be overwhelmed by the vigor of his argument. With one so dominant and quick to make decisions, a subordinate should stand his ground if he thinks it will help to keep his boss out of trouble. Vance understood this intuitively and would often come to my support.

I never saw McNamara shame anyone in the seven years he was my boss. If a person's performance was less than expected, it would be evident without McNamara saying so. Though he examined you closely on some issues, he was prepared to grant wide latitude when he thought you knew what you were doing. It was as though his questions were test borings to discover what was there, to find out if it was the true ore or simply the dross.

McNamara had been a highly regarded teacher at the Harvard Business School. He continued to be a superb teacher at the Department of Defense, instructing me, and Tom Morris, and all the rest of "McNamara's Band" how to analyze a problem and get things done. One way he did this was to insist that we meet with him one-on-one. For example, if it was a maritime policy problem—having to do with shipbuilding, subsidies, the merchant marine, and so forth—I had to discuss it with him without the benefit of my maritime expert at my side. This way, I was compelled to familiarize myself with all aspects of the problem so I could respond to his inevitable probing. He always wanted an informed and reasoned defense of what was being proposed, not simply a loose judgment based on personal experience. With McNamara, there was no such thing as an opinion that was not cross-examined. His approach didn't sit well with some of the senior officers, unaccustomed as they were to having their views challenged.

McNamara's managerial revolution—what he did and how he did it—deserves careful study at schools of business and public administration. He believed that an executive accomplished things when he became directly involved in the issue, helping to shape its parameters, rather than waiting for a solution to be served up to him. Cy Vance, as able a person as anyone is likely to meet, told me once that he never could have accomplished all that McNamara did.

McNamara's legacy, as I said earlier, is tarnished because of the Vietnam War. Qualities he so effectively brought to bear in his managerial innovations were inadequate in dealing with the challenges of Vietnam. Today, he works tirelessly on behalf of world peace and on the need to get rid of nuclear weapons. He has written several books on this issue and on the Vietnam War. My time with McNamara was well spent and he continues to be a valued friend.

The Cost Reduction Program

Early in the Kennedy administration, Tom Morris presented McNamara with a recommendation to establish a DoD cost reduction program. It would have goals for each of the military services and for the general areas where savings would be sought. The auditor would validate the results, and the individuals and groups that produced the savings would be identified and honored in ceremonies conducted by the secretary and the president. Uniformed and civilian leaders would work together to achieve the goals, with Morris and the I&L assistant secretaries in the military departments overseeing the effort. Innovations by one service would be made known to the others via frequent newsletters and publicity of various sorts.

The Cost Reduction Program that resulted was organized around three broad areas: buying only what we need; buying at the lowest sound price; and reducing operating costs. Savings ranged across the entire defense establishment and included everything from phone calls to missiles. For example, a shift from paying for individual calls to a flat monthly rate saved $385,000 in fiscal year 1965. In that same year, a $39-million air force contract for 1,200 Sparrow missiles was cancelled when excess Sparrows were found in Navy inventories. The overall goals amounted to real money. In FY 1966 the department reported savings of $4.5 billion, with a long-range goal of $6.1 billion in FY 1969.

President Johnson was so impressed with the DoD Cost Reduction Program that he wanted the other cabinet departments to initiate
similar efforts. To this end, he scheduled a briefing at the White House
in July 1965 so that McNamara could explain how the program operated. At the last moment, McNamara was unable to appear and Vance
had another engagement. The job was given to me. I got some charts
together, rushed to the White House, and somewhat nervously began
my briefing. Each time I opened my mouth, the president spoke up in
the booming and enthusiastic manner for which he was famous and
exhorted his cabinet to look hard, *hard* for ways to save money. I never
got much beyond the first few charts, but the president seemed to
think he had accomplished his purpose and sent a nice letter to me
with a copy to McNamara.

Base Closures

Barely a year after he became secretary, McNamara announced a comprehensive list of some seventy-five military bases for closure or consolidation. It was a bold move and caught everyone by surprise. Since
so many members of Congress had called for reducing defense expenditures, it was difficult for them to complain about actions that saved
millions of dollars. The typical response was that seventy-four were
good choices, but one of them was clearly wrong. The one that was
wrong, of course, was different for each representative who spoke up.
McNamara said he was willing to reverse a decision if the facts on
which it was made turned out to be incorrect. The decisions stood up
to challenge and analysis and none of them was changed.

Assembling a list of bases to be closed involved painstaking work
over a period of many months. Each of the military departments was
asked to designate installations no longer needed and to develop plans
for how the closure would be carried out, the number of people
affected, the impact on the community, the expected savings, and any
costs incurred in shutting down the base. The work was cloaked in

secrecy and presented to McNamara for his review in closely guarded papers marked "Eyes Only."

McNamara recognized at the outset that a program of this kind needed safeguards to cushion the impact on the community and on the employees no longer needed. He said no individual should bear the full brunt of the change, no matter how worthwhile it was. Accordingly, he directed that every person losing a job would be guaranteed one somewhere else in the defense establishment. He also directed that an economic adjustment program be inaugurated within I&L to work directly with the communities to find other uses for the base. Often the results were quite favorable, with the land and structures put to new, productive uses.

Occasionally, we informed a senator or representative of an action before its announcement the following day. We got mixed reactions. For example, when I told Leverett Saltonstall, the "proper Bostonian" senator from Massachusetts, that we intended to close the Watertown Arsenal, there was a silence for a moment before he spoke. "Mr. Ignatius," he said, "I take this harder than most. My family went up from Boston to found the town of Watertown. But if you tell me the arsenal isn't needed any more, I'll go along with the decision."

The response from Senator Edmund Muskie of Maine was quite a different matter. When he learned that we were going to close the Portsmouth Naval Shipyard, he reacted angrily. He chewed me out over the phone, almost burning up the wires with the heat of his emotions, telling me I was bullheaded and inflexible and that McNamara would hear from him immediately. I got Bob on the intercom to warn him.

One of our most contentious closures was the Springfield Armory, also in Massachusetts. It had been the place where generations of Army rifles had been designed and produced, and the local member of Congress and the Springfield community put up an epic battle. We no longer needed Springfield because better rifles were being designed by industry. We believed the armory property would interest private manufacturers and that the city would benefit from getting the federal property back on the local tax rolls. With the ups and downs of defense contracting, we also thought that jobs would be more secure if private companies took over.

We couldn't persuade our opponents to accept our arguments. They demanded that we produce further documentation and initiated a widespread newspaper and letter-writing campaign. McNamara agreed to meet with the Massachusetts delegation in January 1965, and subsequently he and I visited the armory for further discussions with angry community leaders.

On the day of our visit, the local newspaper carried a dramatic two-page display. On one page was a picture of Gen. George Washington with the caption "He Opened It!" On the facing page was a picture of Secretary Robert McNamara with the caption "He Closed It!" The opposition continued and an outside study was conducted, but eventually the local people began to work affirmatively with our Economic Adjustment Office. A new tenant was found that offered steady employment.

Between 1961 and the mid-1970s, the Defense Department closed or consolidated hundreds of bases. Congressional opposition intensified after McNamara left office, with members of Congress more and more reluctant to give up the economic benefits of military installations in their districts. For an eleven-year period, from 1977 to 1988, not one base was closed, even though there were many that military leaders no longer wanted.

In 1988, Representative Dick Armey offered legislation to break the logjam. He said his proposal would protect individual members of Congress from political punishment at home and from intimidation by the administration. Under the Armey plan, the secretary of defense would appoint a commission to work with the military departments to identify unneeded installations. Their list would then be submitted for the approval of the secretary. After his approval, the list would be sent to the Congress for approval or disapproval in its *entirety:* no individual base on the list could be changed. Hearings on the proposed legislation, at which both McNamara and I testified, were followed by enactment, and the base closure program resumed under the new procedures.

After a couple of cycles, it came to a stop because the Congress refused to authorize a further base closure commission.

Standardization

Standardization in the Department of Defense can take many forms. Usually, it means the adoption by all of the services of a single item rather than having several similar items for the same purpose. Because the Army, Navy, and air force need trashcans, for example, it is wasteful for them to purchase and carry in inventory three different versions of the same thing. There were many cases where one service bought an item under its own stock number while another had an excess of essentially the same thing cataloged under a different number.

The I&L staff presented McNamara with many examples of this type that for one reason or another had not been standardized. One was the smock worn by military butchers: each service had its own, differing in inconsequential details. McNamara said there was no threat to national security if he chose one of them, no matter which one. He made quick decisions on several other articles of this sort, saying there was no penalty for error if he picked the "wrong" one: the important thing was to make a decision and not let the matter languish. In one instance, he tried but failed to get a belt buckle for all the services. The Army and the Navy agreed on a black metal buckle but the Marine Corps wanted to keep its own distinctive buckle. I told McNamara that we should abandon the effort. The savings didn't amount to much and there was no point in aggravating the marines over something they cared about. He agreed with some reluctance.

Standardization can take other forms. The Army had a different chassis for a gun, a howitzer, and a vehicle when one of them could have served the three applications. Separate chassis meant separate research programs, separate production runs, separate testing, separate spare parts inventories, all far more costly than having a single item. When I brought this to McNamara's attention, he quickly agreed and directed the Army to select one of them as the standard chassis.

Sometimes, attempts to standardize with a single weapons system met with intense opposition. The most celebrated example of this in the 1960s was the F-111, a fighter airplane McNamara wanted for both the air force and the Navy. The Navy fought the joint program and eventually went its own way with another aircraft. During this same period, somewhat better results were achieved with the F-4, used primarily by the air force but also by the Navy.

Another aspect of standardization is reliance on commercial standards and commercial items rather than military specifications and specially designed military items. When it is possible to use the commercial product, the price is usually lower and the spare parts support less costly. Even here, though, the services sometimes can't seem to avoid making alterations. For example, the familiar yellow school bus was purchased for the children of military families overseas. Someone got it into his head to raise the step an inch higher on the buses for the military schools. It took a lot of time and money to correct the silly mistake. Another example, mentioned earlier, was when the Army insisted on militarizing the AR-15 rifle, with unfortunate results. Though it had long resisted the purchase of commercial trucks, the Army, under Gen. Frank Besson's prodding, bought three-quarter-ton commercial trucks, with good results.

A Changing Workload

The nature of my work began to change after a conversation with Deputy Secretary Vance in February 1965. Vance told me that he expected the conflict in Vietnam to intensify and that I should analyze the logistics feasibility of Operation Plans 32-64 and 39-65, the Southeast Asia contingency plans. Vietnam had been in the background of everything we did, but we were far more concerned about Europe and the Soviet threat to Berlin. Under President Kennedy, our Vietnam policy was to help the South Vietnamese to defend themselves, and toward this end he authorized a force of sixteen thousand U.S. military advisors to provide training and assistance.

Despite our help, the situation in Vietnam worsened when Buddhist leaders, in addition to the Viet Cong guerrillas, opposed President Ngo Dinh Diem. In November 1963, South Vietnamese officers assassinated Diem in a coup, and a military junta took over the government. Increasingly, U.S. officials began to doubt whether the government could survive. In August 1964, U.S. destroyers in the Tonkin Gulf reported attacks by North Vietnamese naval vessels. Soon thereafter, the Senate passed the Tonkin Gulf resolution with only two dissenting votes. The resolution gave President Johnson advance authority to take whatever action he deemed necessary to defend South Vietnam. Though not a formal declaration of war, it amounted to about the same thing. Later on, the resolution became highly controversial when investigation showed that one of the attacks may never have taken place. Additionally, the North Vietnamese may have been understandably confused because there were U.S.-sponsored covert operations taking place in the area near the destroyers. On February 19, after further deterioration of the situation and more provocative attacks, President Johnson authorized regular strikes by U.S. warplanes against targets in North Vietnam. It was a major escalation of the war.

During Tom Morris's tenure, the I&L staff had concentrated on the supply management improvements and the range of activities embraced by the Cost Reduction Program. McNamara wanted no letup in this effort, saying good management practices were entirely compatible with efforts to support the war. He made it clear to me that he wanted both an aggressive base closure program and further progress in competitive procurement. When I said our Vietnam workload might delay the comprehensive white papers he wanted on our worldwide base structure, he said I could hire outside consultants if I needed help.

What McNamara had accomplished was an important part of his legacy, and he didn't want the war to divert him or me from his ongoing goal of managing the vast department with the greatest possible effectiveness. His situation was not unlike that of his boss, President Johnson. The president did everything he reasonably could to prevent the Vietnam War from interfering with his own legacy, the Great Society program.

With the help of a wonderfully capable staff that I augmented to meet wartime demands, I was able to keep the cost reduction effort on track and even to make further improvements. It is also fair to say that from the time of my conversation with Vance about the Operations Plans in early 1965 until September 1967, when I left the I&L job, my principal and at times exclusive focus was on the war.

The review of the war plans indicated that the most severe logistics constraint was insufficient capacity to receive and support the troops. My office began to develop a list of what we called "prudent actions" to deal with the problems uncovered in the review. With events moving rapidly, McNamara told me to form a steering group to meet daily to expedite needed actions. The group included Gen. Richard Meyer, the JCS logistics head; Joe Hoover, the budget officer; and Jack Stempler from the legal office. It was clear to all of us that a large-scale construction program was an immediate priority. Though some improvements in airfields and port facilities had been made in prior years, they were only the beginning of the logistics infrastructure that would be needed.

The Military Construction Program

In the introduction to *Southeast Asia: Building the Bases*, the official history of construction for the Vietnam War, the program was called "the largest single effort in military construction history." It was also described as "the first time that civilian contractor employees were guarded by and worked with military construction troops." Before it was completed, more than $2 billion had been spent on a workforce of fifty thousand and for construction equipment valued at $150 million and materials worth $200 million. The contractor was a giant consortium of Raymond International, Morrison-Knudson International, Brown & Root, and J. A. Jones—called RMK-BRJ. Among the projects completed were

- Six ports with twenty-nine berths for oceangoing ships
- Six naval bases

- Eight jet airfields with ten-thousand-foot runways
- Hospitals with sixty-two hundred beds
- Fourteen million square feet of covered storage
- Housing for 450,000 Vietnamese servicemen and their dependents
- Sixteen hundred miles of paved roads

In Thailand, $500 million was spent through another huge consortium to build six jet airfields, paved roads, and improvements in port areas.

Secretary McNamara approved an initial construction goal of $1 billion after a hurried trip to Vietnam. Jack Bonny, head of the construction consortium, told me that he planned to reach a level of $35 million of construction a month by May of 1966 and $40 million by October. The work would be done under a cost-plus-fixed-fee contract.

Bonny expressed his concern about a problem that was also worrying us. The construction goals would require large numbers of ships to bring all the materials and equipment for unloading at overtaxed port facilities. Bonny said he could not wait while ships sat at anchor for days unable to off-load their cargoes. If sufficient port facilities were unavailable, shallow-draft boats would be needed to go to the ships and bring the materials and equipment ashore.

The port congestion that concerned Bonny got worse as time went on, reaching a high of 122 ships waiting to unload in November 1965. It became a matter of presidential concern when McNamara told President Johnson that the concentration of ships anchored off the port of Saigon would be an attractive target for enemy submarine or air attack. Additionally, enemy swimmers might blow up ships loaded with ammunition. I prepared weekly status reports on the port congestion problem until May 1967 when new construction permitted operations to proceed without delays.

Two serious construction problems arose that had to be settled quickly. The first came from an inspection trip that Ed Sheridan made in late 1965. Sheridan said no one had the authority to decide priorities for the services' construction demands, all urgently needed and well justified. Sheridan's solution was a "construction czar" on the staff of the commander, Gen. William Westmoreland. The suggestion met with immediate opposition. Sheridan dropped the word "czar" and titled the position "director of construction." When the proposal was presented to the chairman of the Joint Chiefs of Staff, Gen. Earle G. Wheeler, he turned it down after consultation with CinCPac, the theater commander. Part of the concern was that the construction director could bypass the military chain of command through direct access to the office of the secretary of defense.

I liked Sheridan's proposal because it provided a mechanism for deciding priorities in a situation in which everyone wanted his job to be completed "yesterday." Deputy Secretary Vance also saw its merits and made the decision to go forward, despite the objections. Rather than the individual armed services deciding when construction was needed, General Westmoreland, through his construction director, would do so.

The second problem arose from a discovery in mid-1966 that $200 million in construction had been "underfunded." The services' construction requests had been approved, but when they were priced out by the contractor, they totaled $200 million more than the available funding. The solution we adopted was a common-sense approach: tailor the construction program to the contractor's capability in a concept called "level of effort." The Congress approved our plan and the program moved ahead on the new basis.

There were the inevitable problems along the way, but the overall results were excellent. In its report on construction in Vietnam in the years 1965 and 1966, the General Accounting Office credited the contractor and the Navy's Bureau of Yards and Docks, which had supervised the effort, for a remarkable achievement in mobilizing the forces to get the job done.

Expanding Aircraft Production

Aircraft, both fixed-wing planes and rotary-winged helicopters, played a significant role in the Vietnam War. The helicopters gave U.S. forces a degree of mobility that the French Army never had in Vietnam.

Although helicopters had been used somewhat in the Korean War, it was in Vietnam that they became as fundamental to the Army as a tank or a truck. They were used for reconnaissance, for carrying troops to battle, for supply and medical evacuation, and, when armed with guns and rockets, for deadly attacks on enemy troops.

One of the earliest units to deploy to Vietnam was the 1st Cavalry Division, commanded by former Army Secretary Elvis Stahr's military assistant, Maj. Gen. Harry Kinnard. The Cav had been reshaped around the air mobile concept, and arrived in Vietnam with its hundreds of helicopters.

To meet the Army's widening helicopter needs, we were producing the two basic models—the single-rotor Huey and the twin-rotor Chinook—at fairly high rates, sixty per month for the former and five per month for the latter. With helicopter losses in combat certain to rise at the same time that more helicopters would be needed to equip units headed for Vietnam, production had to be increased. At our regular Friday meeting in July 1965, McNamara told me he wanted a plan for boosting output.

On Monday morning I flew to Ft. Worth with two Army aviation specialists to meet with officials of Bell Aircraft, builder of the Huey. Bell said it could increase production to one hundred Hueys a month by May 1966 through a major expansion in its subcontractor and vendor base. This was a faster and more feasible approach, Bell explained, than expansion at the company itself. We spent the day asking questions and going over details. On the way back to Washington, we prepared the Huey portion of our report for McNamara.

At midweek, the three of us flew to the Philadelphia area to meet with officials of Boeing-Vertol, producer of the Chinook. They presented a plan for a step-up from five to fifteen per month by November 1966. The fifteen-ship rate was high enough for our needs, and the plan to attain it was well conceived. At 8:30 Friday morning, with the Huey and the Chinook work completed, I made my report to McNamara and he approved the new production rates.

Bell did a magnificent job, meeting every milestone in the advance toward the one hundred per month rate for Hueys. I met frequently with the chief executive, Edwin J. Ducayet, to review progress and to make sure that any problems were brought to my immediate attention. I had similar meetings with General Besson, the Army's capable logistics chief, who was often present during the conversations with Ducayet. The three of us were in this thing together and we needed to keep one another fully informed at all times. Bell eventually raised the rate to 150 Hueys a month.

The experience at Boeing-Vertol was less successful, at least in the early stages of the buildup. Vertol had been a pioneer in the helicopter field and was well regarded for its engineering ability, but it had limited production experience. When Boeing acquired Vertol it tended to leave it alone, believing that rotary-winged aircraft required special knowledge that a maker of fixed-wing aircraft, like Boeing, didn't possess.

When the buildup of Chinook production fell behind schedule, I met with Bill Allen, the Boeing chief executive. Allen told me that Boeing's hands-off policy had been a mistake. He said he was sending one of his top production men from Seattle, Bob Tharrington, to take charge at Vertol. Tharrington responded as Allen was sure he would, and Vertol got back on schedule. Allen, one of the great men of aviation, told me privately and in confidence that Boeing was going to lose $200 million on the Chinook work. He never asked for any relief and never made any public outcry.

While the Army was stepping up helicopter production, the air force was buying more F-4 fighters and C-130 and C-141 cargo planes. These programs, together with production of aircraft for the Navy and the commercial airlines, were beginning to tax our capacity in some critical areas, such as aluminum forgings and extrusions. The problem was exacerbated by our huge purchases of aluminum matting for hastily built airfields in Vietnam.

For critical situations like this, Department of Defense needs were given priority treatment through "DO ratings." The DO rating required the manufacturer to set aside a portion of its capacity to meet military demands. Commercial aircraft had also been included in the government's rated-order system. Because of the increasing bottlenecks in forging, extrusion, casting, electronic components, and machine tool capacity, we decided in May 1966 to withdraw our support for commercial airplanes. We immediately got complaints from the aircraft manufacturers and their trade associations. They said they couldn't produce civilian airliners, including the new jet-powered 707, without the benefit of DO orders. Under the program as it stood, if Boeing placed an order for a commercial landing gear a day before McDonnell ordered one for a fighter aircraft, the commercial order would be favored over the one for the fighter. I told McNamara we couldn't live with a situation like this, and that was why we had withdrawn our support. He told me to do what I could to ensure that military needs didn't disrupt the civilian economy, which frankly didn't help me very much.

The aircraft manufacturers furnished us with the specific details we requested on the harm they would suffer if the DO ratings were withdrawn. The secretary of the treasury made a personal appeal to McNamara, saying that many of the new jet aircraft would be sold to foreign airlines, helping our balance of payments. This last argument carried the day, because the president himself was worried about our payments balance, which he always referred to as the "gold flow" problem. The DO ratings were reinstated for commercial airliners, and both sides—the manufacturers and the government—said they would try not to step on one another's toes. Douglas Aircraft missed some deliveries of its new jet airliners but cooperated, along with Boeing, to avoid interference with urgent military schedules.

Ammunition

The manufacture and timely delivery of air munitions for the Vietnam War was the most persistent, complex, and contentious element in our entire procurement and production program. Nothing is more serious in logistics support than a shortage of ammunition. Real or imagined shortages can resonate in the press and the public, agitate the Congress, and alarm the commanders in the field. Accordingly, ammunition received daily top-level attention.

The difficulties in the ammunition supply program arose from the gigantic quantities of bombs, rockets, artillery, and rifle rounds expended in the war. In 1966, we planned usage of 538,000 tons of bombs, almost as much as the yearly usage of 576,000 tons in Africa and Europe during World War II. The 1966 production rates were inadequate and had to be increased significantly.

Artillery ammunition in Vietnam was also expended at exceedingly high rates against enemy targets and in what was called harassment and interdiction fire, which was employed against enemy troops that might be infiltrating U.S. positions, particularly at night.

So far as I knew there was never a time when a shortage of ammunition impeded combat operations, but we had to stay on top of the problem to ensure an adequate supply. One close call required immediate action. It occurred at the end of an inspection trip by Vance and me to Vietnam and Thailand in 1966. U.S. ambassador Henry Cabot Lodge invited us to lunch in Saigon along with some military commanders and embassy officials. As we were leaving, the senior air force commander in Vietnam, Gen. William Momeyer, asked if he could have a word with me. "We're running out of ammunition," he said softly. "I hope you will look into it."

I told Vance about the brief conversation and reported it to McNamara on Saturday morning after our lengthy flight back. McNamara told me to turn around and fly immediately to Honolulu to meet with CinCPac, Adm. Ulysses S. Grant Sharp, who ran the air war in Vietnam, to find out what was going on. I flew there the next day for urgent discussions with Sharp and his staff. We found a number of problems. First, bombs dropped in air operations in March exceeded the planned level by 25 percent. Second, political demonstrations by dissident Buddhist groups near the port of Hue prevented bombs from being unloaded from ammunition ships. Third, air force inventory reports were not prepared on a "complete round" basis, with the bomb, its fuse, and its fins grouped together. In a number of cases, there were too many fins or not enough fuses for the complete bomb assembly. We also learned that ammunition in a ship waiting to unload was reported as "on hand" when in fact it was not in the hands of troops.

We took action at once after returning to Washington. First, I spoke to Navy Secretary Paul Nitze and Chief of Naval Operations David MacDonald and obtained their permission to "lend" bombs to the air force. Second, we drew on reserve bomb stocks in western U.S. depots and sent them to Vietnam. Third, we increased bomb production. Fourth, we encouraged the air force to adopt the complete round method for reporting bomb inventories. Finally, we clarified our reporting so "on hand" meant what it was supposed to mean. I learned many years later that the chairman, General Wheeler, had calmed down the Joint Chiefs by telling them not to worry about any bomb shortage because "Paul was on top of the problem."

Our procurement policy for bombs was "never let production drop below current consumption." It was an easy policy to state but a hard one to achieve. There were many reasons for this. First, the air force quite understandingly had lost interest in "iron bombs," the kind we were dropping in Vietnam. With the availability of nuclear weapons and the prospect of "smart bombs" guided to their targets by high-tech gadgetry, it believed that iron bombs were a relic of the past. Indeed, when we started up the production lines, we found that the government-owned tooling to make the bombs had been sold for scrap. The poor fellow who sold it, undoubtedly at a fraction of what it cost, must have thought he did a good deed for his country by getting money for some worthless metal.

It took a while to get production going. We had three companies making the Mark-81 bomb (250 pounds), and five making the Mk-82 (500 pounds), including such well-known firms as U.S. Steel and American Machine and Foundry. There were work stoppages at some plants, delayed delivery of tooling at others, and so many problems at one company that we came close to defaulting it. My staff and I made frequent visits to assess progress and to let the companies know how vital their work was.

The main problem, however, was the galloping rate of consumption, the increase month by month in the tons dropped. We were continually accelerating production that had already been accelerated. In April 1966, we raised the Mk-81 and Mk-82 levels and settled on an air munitions program of 65,000 tons per month. By March 1967, we realized that 65,000 tons, higher than bomb production in World War II, was not enough, and increased the rate to 80,000 tons.

Two months later, with the tempo in Vietnam rising, McNamara approved a 92,000-ton rate for FY 1967 that included a huge increase of Mk-82s. The 92,000-ton program was premised on 800 B-52 sorties (individual flights) per month, and about 30,000 tactical sorties, that is flights by aircraft smaller than the giant B-52s. I told McNamara that CinCPac had recommended an increase from 800 B-52 sorties to 1,200, and that some preliminary thought was being given by the Joint Chiefs of Staff of raising the rate to 2,000. The tonnages required, together with additional tonnages for tactical sorties, Army air munitions, and training purposes, would total 131,000 tons. With another 100,000 tons per month for ground munitions, we would likely exceed the nation's entire capacity for making explosives.

I was so busy placing contracts and expediting production that I had little time to think about the human aspects of what we were doing. When I did, I was appalled by the amount of ordnance we were expending on a rural country with no well-established industrial base. On more than one occasion, I spoke to Army Secretary Resor about the huge quantities of artillery ammunition for "harassing and interdicting" purposes. He said he was also concerned and would do what he could to reduce it.

Because of the scope and complexity of the ammunition program, I had appointed General Stanwix-Hay of my staff as a special assistant for air and ground munitions, and later promoted him to be a deputy assistant secretary. One of our most pressing needs was accurate and timely information on production, stockage, and expenditure. Stan, with Ed Bennewitz, developed formats for this purpose that were the most sophisticated inventory management tools we had ever had. Some forty items were included in what we called our "controlled munitions" program. Bob McNamara was so pleased with the approach that he hoped it could be extended across the entire Department of Defense inventory. It never happened because there were too many items to manage, and not enough managers like General Stanwix-Hay. However, we got partway toward McNamara's goal by including 286 major items in an intensive inventory management effort. They included aircraft, mines, missiles, torpedoes, sonobuoys, electronics equipment, and so forth. The controlled items list represented a significant portion of what was being used in Southeast Asia. Accordingly, it was helpful for production planning as well as for assessing the materiel readiness of U.S. forces.

Shortages

There were times in the war when we didn't have enough of something to meet all of the demands for it. Sometimes, it was an item of clothing. At other times, it might be concertina wire or canvas tents or bulldozers or aluminum matting. In a few instances, it was having enough components to support equipment in combat and the accelerated production schedules. We had all of these problems, and McNamara hated every one of them. He was acutely sensitive to any criticism of his conduct of the war. When Representative Gerald Ford (later President Ford) charged him with mismanagement because of a suspected ammunition shortage, McNamara went on the attack, mobilizing facts and figures to refute Ford and calling the alleged shortages "baloney."

A shortage that caught the attention of the press, particularly the editorial cartoonists, was the "bare-ass Marines" problem. There was a period early in 1966 when many military clothing items were in short supply, particularly those for the Marine Corps. At one point twenty-five items were on the critical list, but we managed to work them down to only two, the overcoat and the raincoat. The Marine Corps commandant, Gen. Wallace Greene, was still unhappy, however. He complained to me and a lot of others. One newspaper ran a cartoon of a marine with a barrel around his middle to hide his nakedness. The clothing shortages didn't affect forces in Vietnam, but at training centers new recruits were unable to draw their full complement of clothing.

An agonizing problem, as noted earlier, was meeting both combat demands and accelerated production schedules with only a limited supply of component parts. The rapid buildup of the helicopter fleet was our most acute area. We, of course, gave priority to troop needs. To get the most out of our limited assets, we centralized inventory control under General Besson and let him decide when to fly parts to Vietnam or send them, when he could, to the manufacturers.

Flag Poles and Red Balls

Timely information was vital in managing critical supply areas. In the Pentagon, we had both too much information and not enough. There were piles of routine reports on combat consumption, but we only learned about an impending bomb shortage from a quiet remark at a Saigon luncheon.

To give us advance warning of potential shortages, we established a special system called Flagpole Reports. ("Run it up the flagpole so everyone can see it.") The first Flagpole Report arrived from Vietnam in September 1965. It listed emerging problems in the availability of aircraft flares, 40-mm gun ammunition, collapsible petroleum storage tanks, tropical combat boots, and several other items. My staff followed up on each item with the military services. Their corrective actions were reported each week in my SecDef agenda notes. The critical items stayed in the notes until supply returned to normal.

A second measure for dealing with urgent needs was the Red Ball Express. We were concerned about reports that a high number of vehicles—trucks, jeeps, armored personnel carriers, helicopters, airplanes—were inoperable because there were no parts to fix them. Vehicles were simply wearing out faster in Vietnam than in other places. The cause was laterite, an abrasive soil found in Vietnam. Laterite soil and dust would get into wheels and other moving parts and shorten their lives.

Paul Riley of the I&L staff, together with Army officers and General Meyer of the Joint Chiefs of Staff, put together a rapid resupply system to ease the problem. Each day, needed parts were flown on what we called Red Ball Express flights from Travis Air Force Base in

California to Saigon. The planes had large red ball markings for all to see, and space on them was guaranteed. Daily reports were prepared showing what was shipped and the weight and dimensions of the shipment. By September 1967, when I left the I&L job, we had airlifted 23,915 tons of cargo to Saigon.

McNamara immersed himself in the details of the Red Ball reports. Was he a micromanager inserting himself into minutiae best left to people at the operating level? I think not. He wanted to see the details so he could find out how the system was functioning. Then he could hold people's feet to the fire until the progress he sought was attained. In short, his philosophy of management was to decentralize operations and look to his immediate staff for review and analysis of performance.

His approach worked. For example, on October 29, 1965, McNamara, Vance, and I examined some detailed Army shortage reports and then had an extended discussion on what to do. I said the major problem was the tremendous tonnages of supplies that had not been properly segregated, recorded, and brought under supply system control. Needed parts were probably there but nobody could find them. The situation was likely to get worse before it got better because the Army was continuing to push supplies to Vietnam at a rate of almost a million tons per month. Problems of this kind, I said, were not going to be solved by brief visits from high-ranking officials. The only way to untangle the mess was to assemble a team of knowledgeable military and civilian personnel from depots and supply control points and send them to Vietnam for as long as it took to identify the supplies and bring them under control.

McNamara nodded and said, "We're sitting on a volcano." Vance agreed and asked me to join him that same afternoon for a meeting with Secretary Resor and Assistant Secretary Rab Brooks, whom I had recruited from Harbridge House, to discuss the composition of the depot team. McNamara thought it should not exceed fifteen people, but that was too small a number. We might need as many as five hundred, but that was something for the Army to decide. "If the Army can't do the job," McNamara said, "we should send management systems experts out there." He said he was prepared to dispatch Tom Morris, who had returned to the Department of Defense as assistant secretary for manpower, to solve the problem.

It wasn't necessary to send Morris, or Paul Riley, or experts from management consulting firms. The Army went to work on its own. First, it stopped "pushing" enormous quantities of supplies before they had been requisitioned. Second, it provided the supplies requested in metal "Con-ex" containers that protected them from the weather and from damage or pilferage. Each container was carefully marked to indicate its contents and served as a small storage site until the supplies could be properly warehoused.

The Army also organized quick-response teams prepared to fly to Vietnam on forty-eight hours' notice with the parts and the tool kits to get its vehicles rolling again.

McNamara's interest in detail helped all of this to happen.

Strikes and Work Stoppages

Strikes and work stoppages were a constant threat to our ability to meet demanding production goals for ammunition, aircraft, aluminum matting, and our many other critical needs. Our policy was to maintain strict neutrality with respect to the substance of labor-management disputes. Instead, we analyzed the impact of each impending or actual work stoppage and developed contingency plans to deal with the situation as best we could. In a number of instances, I was invited by federal mediators to meet with the parties. My role was simply to impress upon them the criticalness of their work and ask them to resolve their differences quickly. Other defense officials did the same thing.

An example illustrates the problems we faced. Olin Mathieson was a major supplier of rifle ammunition and explosive powder for guns of various sizes. The workers had been on strike for sixteen days, and our situation was becoming untenable. The strike affected not only the ammunition Olin was making but also the production schedules at other companies that depended on Olin for delivery of explosive powder.

Secretary Resor twice telephoned representatives of both management and labor to urge prompt settlement. He also requested the Federal Mediation Service to bring the labor and management negotiators to Washington. Deputy Secretary Vance telephoned the president of Olin to impress upon him the seriousness of the situation. I telephoned the assistant secretary of labor with the same message. Meanwhile, the Army prepared the paperwork for a Taft-Hartley injunction to get people back to work. The strike was finally settled and production resumed.

In another instance, the Brotherhood of Locomotive Firemen and Enginemen struck eight railroads across the nation. The potential impact was severe. Fortunately, the union stated that troop trains, hospital trains, and freight essential to operations in Vietnam would be moved. Under the provisions of the Railway Labor Act, a federal judge ordered the union back to work.

An impending strike in April 1967 at Avco-Lycoming, the company that made the engines for both the Huey and Chinook helicopters, probably caused the most concern. I told McNamara and Vance that we could not afford the loss of a single day's production. Our paperwork for a Taft-Hartley injunction had been prepared. But Secretary of Labor William Wirtz had told me that he opposed using presidential power in this dispute since LBJ had intervened in a labor dispute just the week before. I urged McNamara to help me and he said he would. I got quite emotional about it, saying we had employed every device we could think of to avoid grounding helicopters in Vietnam or stopping production lines in the United States. McNamara followed up and an eighty-day injunction was issued.

In June, toward the end of the eighty-day period, we learned that a ten-day strike might take place in July, after the end of the injunction period. I prepared a memo from McNamara to Joe Califano, President Johnson's assistant for domestic affairs, urging presidential intervention. Meanwhile, Jim Kerr, the Avco president, called me to say that management's last offer was an increase of forty-two cents an hour, but at the appropriate time he would go to fifty-two cents or fifty-four cents. He couldn't go any higher, he said, because the business at Lycoming was producing little if any profit. He said further that he believed the union's demands amounted to ninety cents. The mediator in the case told me that the union was likely to settle at around eighty cents.

I mention all of this detail because it shows how deeply we became involved when labor disputes threatened critical programs. We never expressed an opinion on the merits of a dispute, but in every reasonable way we did what we could to avoid a cessation of work. The Lycoming dispute was settled through the mediation process.

Economic Issues

President Johnson never wanted his support for the war in Vietnam to be at the expense of his dreams for a Great Society. As A. J. Langguth states in his masterful history, *Our Vietnam*:

> Johnson had barely touched on the war in his State of the Union address to Congress (1965). He had spoken instead of funding a new program for national health care for the elderly to be called Medicare. Johnson also pledged to create a Department of Housing and Urban Development that would oversee the rebuilding of America's cities. He would make federal aid available to students in preschool—through a Head Start program—and in college through sixty education bills; their cost would total several billion dollars.

The president's place in history would depend on reaching these lofty goals. He was keenly aware of the increasing costs of our deepening involvement in the war. He knew that as commander in chief, he must support his forces in combat, at the same time assuring the necessary funds for his ambitious domestic program. We would become, in effect, a "guns and butter" economy, with constant pressure from the president and his administration to keep prices from rising and fueling a dangerous inflation.

As the civilian official responsible for the multibillion-dollar defense procurement program, I became an unwitting player on many occasions in the struggle to keep a lid on prices. In these encounters, I also addressed issues of foreign trade and domestic policy.

Imports of Jeweled Watches

In April 1965, President Johnson asked the director of the Office of Emergency Planning to undertake a study of the effects on the national security of imports of watch movements. The subject was controversial and we knew the few remaining domestic makers of jeweled watches would carefully monitor it. These companies, like Bulova and Hamilton, faced stiff competition from foreign companies and from makers of inexpensive pin-lever timepieces. The domestic makers asserted that they were essential to national security because they made fuses for bombs and artillery shells. I was assigned as the DoD representative.

In our study, we looked at a variety of possibilities, including setting up an "in-house" capability if the watchmakers went out of business. We concluded after much thought that the national security would not be impaired if they went under because we could meet our needs with imports of pinions and gears from the Swiss, and from new types of fuses made by electronics companies. McNamara was opposed to protective tariffs and supported the administration's efforts to remove trade restrictions. He strongly endorsed our conclusions.

We came under intense pressure from the domestic industry but didn't budge from our position. Retired Gen. Omar Bradley, a World War II hero who was now the president of Bulova, called on McNamara and then visited me in company with some of Washington's most distinguished lawyers. Their advocacy of protective tariffs went against the grain of administration policy, and we at Defense were unable to substantiate the companies claim that they were essential to the national security.

Food Purchases

The Department of Agriculture did not want our purchases of food to have an adverse impact on consumer prices. After consulting with the military departments, we made many changes in our food purchases, substituting items "in season" for those in short supply.

In March 1966, the deputy secretary of defense told the military departments to stop buying butter and to substitute margarine instead. At the time, butter cost seventy cents per pound and margarine only sixteen cents. Since we were buying about a million pounds a month, the fifty-four-cent differential amounted to a savings in excess of a half million dollars a month. Additionally, medical authorities certified that margarine was nutritionally equal to butter.

It was not long before the press and the public got hold of this one. Newspapers began to write about the "Guns and Oleo" economy. Letters from the public asked whether butter was served in the White House, or why we were denying the "best" to our fighting men. Several people sent in dollar bills, requesting us to apply the money to purchases of butter. We stuck by our guns and bought the margarine.

President Johnson solicited other nations to join our effort in Vietnam. Among those responding favorably were Australia and New Zealand. Their representatives said they hoped we might increase our purchases of lamb, an important export item for both countries. In November 1966, the United States agreed to buy 5.9 million pounds of boneless cuts, in increments of 3.5 million and 2.4 million pounds. When I told the head of the Defense Supply Agency, my old friend Andy McNamara, about this, he winced and said, "My God, Paul, don't you know soldiers won't eat lamb? You can feed them pork or beef, or chicken, but please no more lamb." Like it or not, more lamb showed up on military menus.

When it was time in May 1967 to place contracts for the second increment, we found that Australians had been buying more lamb for their own use because their supply of beef had declined. Accordingly, the price of lamb had risen by up to six cents a pound. Since buying 2.4 million pounds would worsen the situation, the Army decided to delay the purchase until prices were more favorable. It was a plausible explanation. But to my dying day, I will always believe that the wily Andy McNamara somehow managed to manipulate prices so that his beloved soldiers could eat the pork they loved instead of the lamb they hated.

Stockpile Issues

The government maintains stockpiles of various materials needed in time of war. Some of them are rare metals obtainable only from foreign sources. Others, like copper, are available from both the United States and overseas. The enormous quantities of aluminum in the stockpile came from "pay and take" contracts during the Korean War. The government had encouraged a reluctant industry to expand its capacity by agreeing to purchase excess or unsold aluminum for the stockpile. The companies were also obliged to buy back the aluminum under certain circumstances.

Copper. The Department of Defense needed vast amounts of copper for ammunition and other purposes. Artillery rounds, for example, contained a rotating band of the malleable metal. When the round was fired, the spiral grooves in the gun barrel imparted a spin to the projectile that made it more stable and accurate. Our copper requirements in 1966 amounted to 109,000 tons, or roughly double the 1965 quantity. One ammunition supplier told us that it would have to pay sixty-three cents per pound for additional copper, as opposed to the current price of about thirty-six cents, because of a tightening market. To ease the situation, we released 35,000 tons that were surplus to the current stockpile objective of 775,000 tons. We also agreed to reexamine the assumptions on which the objective was computed.

The release of materials from the stockpile was a sensitive matter. The affected industries always feared that the stockpile quantities might be dumped on the market, depressing prices. People in the Defense Department usually wanted to safeguard the stockpiles to ensure that they would be available when needed. There were few subjects of greater interest to the Congress than the stockpiles. With all this in mind, the president seemed prepared to make further releases of copper but wanted his special assistant, Joe Califano, to keep a close eye on the situation. We were able to muddle through without the dramatic confrontation with the industry that occurred with aluminum.

One final note on copper: Kennecott, one of the largest copper companies, announced plans for an open-pit mine in the heart of Glacier Peak Wilderness in the state of Washington, part of the national wilderness protection system. Kennecott's plans were within the law, but conservationists who feared devastation of the pristine landscape vigorously opposed them. The need for copper for the Vietnam War was cited as a reason for the proposal.

In an article in the July 1967 issue of *Harper's*, Paul Brooks reported: "The final, unanswerable opinion came—amazingly, from the Department of Defense. Assistant Secretary Paul R. Ignatius has written Senator Henry M. Jackson that 'Because of the length of time to bring the mine into production and the relatively small amount of additional copper that would result therefrom,' it is doubtful that its contribution would be 'sufficient to outweigh the inevitable damage to the natural beauty of the wilderness area.'"

Aluminum. The confrontation between President Johnson and the aluminum industry was a classic example of how the administration fought to keep the lid on prices during the Vietnam War. In an extensive article in the February 1966 issue of *Fortune*, Gilbert Burch, wrote

> If any episode in recent business history deserves to be talked about for a long time, it is the twelve-day imbroglio that began last October 29, when Olin Mathieson Chemical Corp. raised the price of aluminum by a half cent a pound. The affair reached its climax when Johnson ordered Gardner Ackley, Chairman of the Council of Economic Advisors, to issue a bull against the industry, and when Secretary McNamara, also on orders from L.B.J., beat

the industry to its knees by threatening to dump 300,000 tons of stockpile metal on the market.

Robert McNamara, in his book *In Retrospect,* describes how he first learned of the situation. He had left Washington on a Saturday afternoon to see his son play his last football game in Concord, New Hampshire, and planned to return on Sunday. When he checked in at his hotel, there was a message to call the president at once:

> When I did, he came on the phone and shouted "Where are you?" I patiently explained where I was and why. "I want you back here immediately to get that damn aluminum price down," he snapped. I said I knew nothing about the aluminum price, and, in any event, he had a commerce secretary to handle such matters. "Well, if you want to put your personal pleasure ahead of the welfare of your president and your country"—he paused—"then stay where you are." I said: "I'll make you a deal. Marg [Mrs. McNamara] and I will see the game this afternoon and I'll be back in my office early tomorrow morning." He slammed down the phone.

That's how McNamara learned about it. Here's how I learned. Nan and I had accepted an invitation for a cruise on the Potomac for Saturday night. Shortly before we were to depart, the phone rang and it was McNamara. He said he wanted me to learn everything I could about the aluminum industry and the government's huge aluminum stockpile: "Come to my office at 6 AM Monday morning and make me an expert on the subject."

We told our hosts we couldn't join them, and then I got busy on the phone. I called Paul Riley, my deputy in charge of supply. He then called Carl Rolle, the stockpile expert in my office, and told him to meet with me early Sunday morning and give me a crash course on the aluminum stockpile. Rolle did a good job and I learned what I needed to know. The main point was that we had much more aluminum than necessary. The stockpile objective was 450,000 tons, and our hoard of aluminum contained in excess of 1.4 million tons.

Early Monday morning I met with McNamara for about a half hour before he left for a meeting with Secretary of Commerce John Connor; Lawson Knott, head of the General Services Administration and the custodian of the several stockpiles; Joe Califano; and others. A meeting with the industry—Alcoa, Reynolds, Olin Mathieson, and Kaiser—was set for Wednesday morning with Lawson Knott and me as co-chairs. I told the industry executives about our enormous requirement for aluminum for airfield matting, aircraft, and as a major ingredient in explosive powder. I said the government wanted to dispose of two hundred thousand tons in 1966 and asked them to work with us to develop a plan to do it. Meanwhile, the president's press secretary, Bill Moyers, announced that there was no connection between the stockpile discussions and the price increase. With Lloyd Cutler, the lawyer representing Kaiser Aluminum, I began to work on a plan whereby the industry would buy back not only the two hundred thousand tons in 1966 but also the remaining 1.2 million tons on an orderly basis over the next several years.

While I was busy at the GSA meeting, there was a lot going on backstage that involved the president, Robert McNamara, and the Alcoa president, John Harper. I was not informed of these discussions. Alcoa, on the basis of what it understood (or perhaps misunderstood), thought it was safe to raise its price by a half cent, as Olin had done earlier. It also said that it would raise the price of fabricated products on a selective basis.

The president was upset by Alcoa's action. When our talks at GSA resumed on Friday evening, I took a tougher line, saying we expected the industry to buy back two hundred thousand tons beginning immediately. I suggested several ways this might be done and how the remaining stockpile tonnages could be released. The industry made a counteroffer, which I relayed to McNamara. He told me to say that the government wanted to wait until the following morning to make up its mind. The meeting broke up at 11 PM.

We resumed discussions Saturday morning and there was little that I had to offer. I reiterated our position that the industry had to buy back two hundred thousand tons in 1966, and that we would have to talk about the remaining tonnage some time later. I read them a copy of a press statement that McNamara would make shortly. At his press conference, McNamara said the government had tried to reach an understanding with the industry. Gardner Ackley followed him and said the price increases were unjustified.

Alcoa's executive vice president, Leon Hickman, who had attended the GSA meetings, then held a press conference of his own. He challenged the good faith of McNamara and me, and said that the industry and government representatives had been close to an agreement on Friday night. From my standpoint, I thought that what he said was about right. The president saw things differently. Hickman's remarks provoked him, and on Tuesday the government said it might have to release three hundred thousand tons of the surplus aluminum.

The matter was finally settled when John Harper, the Alcoa president, met with McNamara. Alcoa agreed to roll back the price. The plan on which Cutler and I had been working was developed in further detail and accepted by both parties. Everyone came out a winner, it seemed to me. The government got some money for a surplus it didn't want. The industry got rid of the huge stockpile that, like the sword of Damocles, hung over its head threatening prices if it were ever "dumped." The huge demand for aluminum for the Vietnam War continued unabated, and the stockpile release helped to meet it without distorting the price level.

There was obviously more going on in this confrontation between a powerful president and a powerful industry than negotiations about a stockpile. The president, concerned with larger issues, wanted to discipline the industry, to show his willingness to "jawbone" when prices were raised. If he could succeed with the aluminum companies, which he did, it would be a signal to other companies that might be thinking about raising their prices beyond the general guidelines of the Council of Economic Advisors.

Finally, neither McNamara nor I had any business being a part of these negotiations. As McNamara had told the president, he had a secretary of commerce to handle matters of this kind. He reflected on this in *In Retrospect*, saying that both Presidents Kennedy and Johnson "often asked for my advice and assistance on matters outside the secretary of defense's jurisdiction. This complicated my life." I might add that it also complicated mine.

Musical Chairs II

Cyrus Vance resigned as deputy secretary of defense in the summer of 1967. He had a painful back problem that had recurred after a first surgery several years earlier. Sometimes we had to meet with him while he was lying on an Army cot in a small room across the hall from his spacious office. He was a man of the highest integrity. I respected him above all others for his strength of character and his innate sense of fairness.

It came as a surprise to no one that Vance was succeeded by Navy Secretary Paul Nitze. Nitze was a distinguished presence and had been around since the early days of World War II, when James Forrestal brought him from Wall Street to Washington. He had served in the Kennedy administration as the assistant secretary of defense, responsible for international security affairs and for liaison with the State Department. He succeeded Fred Korth who had replaced John Connally when he resigned to run for governor of Texas.

Who would succeed Nitze? The two people who were considered, I was told, were John T. McNaughton and me. McNaughton had served in the Pentagon as the general counsel, then as the assistant secretary in charge of international security affairs, the position Nitze had held earlier. He was McNamara's trusted and influential advisor on Vietnam strategy and policy. McNamara selected him to be the new Navy secretary.

Shortly after his selection and before he got down to work, McNaughton took a brief vacation trip with his wife and son. All three were killed in a tragic airplane accident. Sometime later, McNamara called me to his office and said he wanted to offer me the opportunity to be the Navy secretary. He said the job carried a lot of prestige but was less important than what I was doing. He hoped I would stay where I was and continue the progress we had made. I told him that after three years in the same job, I was looking forward to a change. I also mentioned my duty on a ship in World War II and said I had a real fondness for the Navy.

McNamara asked Tom Morris, his manpower assistant secretary, to take the I&L job. I had succeeded Morris as I&L secretary three years earlier when he departed for the private sector. Our careers had intertwined in mysterious ways. I had suggested Tom as the person best qualified to be McNamara's first I&L secretary. I learned several years afterward that it was Tom Morris who had suggested my name to Elvis Stahr in 1961 when he was looking for someone to be the Army I&L. McNamara told me to spend as much time as I could to make sure Tom was fully up to speed on all the changes we had made to get the ammunition and equipment to Vietnam.

The last of my regular Friday morning meetings was held on the first of September. The agenda topics began, as usual, with the Red Ball Express Report ("Looks good. Things are up and running."). The next subject was another old favorite, competitive procurement of ocean shipping ("Don't let up the pressure, Paul."). Then there was the report on the controlled munitions ("I wish we had everything under control like this."). After that, copper ("We're going to have to release some more from the stockpile."). Then a short note on a strike at a rifle plant (no comment). After this, some new information on import controls for zinc and lead (no comment). I mentioned that I had recommended that General Stanwix-Hay be awarded the U.S. Army's Distinguished Service Medal ("Great idea."). Finally, I said I wanted to talk about a personal matter. The Navy wanted me to take a five-day trip to Europe in October and speak on maritime affairs at a NATO symposium. McNamara interrupted: "Don't take the trip! We've got too many important things going on here. Send someone else!" Then he said he wanted me to keep working with him on stockpile matters after I became secretary of the Navy. "It won't take much time away from your Navy work," he said.

That's how the biggest job I ever held came to an end. The topics we talked about were the same ones we had wrestled with for the past three years. They were, in fact, more important than the trip to Europe, but the trip did sound rather nice. I was looking forward to my new job but thankful for the experience of the old one. Under McNamara's relentless prodding, I had found sources of energy and initiative in myself that I didn't know were there. They lay dormant until awakened by the man sitting opposite me.

Six

At the Helm

THE ANNOUNCEMENT OF MY SELECTION TO BE THE SECRETARY OF the Navy pleased my wife and me, but it almost killed her parents, Richard and Louise Weiser. The person responsible for their near-fatal mishap was the very one who had appointed me, Lyndon B. Johnson. President Johnson was famous for zealously guarding his appointments until he was ready for them to be made public. When word leaked out about his intent to appoint a prominent Washington lawyer to be the undersecretary of a cabinet department, he pulled back the nomination and picked someone else. I didn't want anything like that to happen to me, so I told Nan not to say a word to anyone, not even her parents. They learned about it from their car radio. "Did you hear that, dearie?" Mr. Weiser exclaimed, distracted momentarily from his driving. "Dick," she shouted, "you're going to hit that tree!"

Luckily, I didn't hit any trees during my confirmation hearing on August 17, 1967. It was uneventful except that I was presented as "Paul R. Ignatius of California," having been from Massachusetts at my previous confirmation hearings. McNamara explained to me that President Johnson had preferred the state of my birth to Massachusetts because it might "do him some good out West." Senator John Stennis, chairing the hearing, wanted to know whether I would always give the Congress all the facts when I testified, and I said I would because "I couldn't conceive of the Navy operating without the understanding and support of the Congress." Senator Stuart Symington said some nice things about me, but Senator Harry Byrd of Virginia wanted to know whether I thought a long war in Vietnam would benefit the Soviet Union. That question looked like trouble to me, so I danced around it rather than with it. The Senate approved me unanimously.

The Navy Department

The Army is the oldest of the military services, with the Navy following closely behind. On November 13, 1797, the Congress authorized the Department of the Navy with a chief officer called the secretary of the Navy, "whose duties shall be to execute such orders as he shall receive from the President of the United States, relative to the procurement of naval stores and materials and the construction, armament, equipment and employment of vessels of war, as well as all other matters connected with the Naval establishment." The secretary was also authorized a principal clerk and other clerks to help him. His salary and that of the clerks was $3,000 a year.

The secretary of the Navy and his counterparts in the Army and the air force had no responsibility for military operations. This responsibility was handled by the secretary of defense through the chairman of the Joint Chiefs of Staff and the service chiefs. The principal responsibilities of the service secretaries were to oversee the acquisition and training of personnel, obtain their necessary equipment and supplies, provide for their support, and turn them over for combat to the regional commanders worldwide.

The Navy Department had many of the characteristics of the Department of Defense as a whole. Like the Army, it had ground forces—the Marine Corps. Like the air force, it had an air arm. And, of course, it had ships—combatant and logistics types that could apply force from the sea, and a fleet of submarines operating stealthily under water. Like the air force, it fired long-range strategic missiles. It even proposed, during my period as secretary, a sea-based antimissile defense system at the same time that the Army was exploring land-based systems to intercept incoming missiles. The arguments today over antimissile defense systems are similar to those that were raised thirty-five years ago when these programs were just getting under way.

The two uniformed leaders, the chief of naval operations and the commandant of the Marine Corps, were accountable to the secretary of the Navy for the performance of their respective services. The CNO, Adm. Thomas D. Moorer, had been appointed to his position only a few weeks before me. He was a strong and proven leader, conservative and traditional in manner and outlook. He later served as the chairman of the Joint Chiefs of Staff. The commandant, Gen. Leonard Chapman, was a tall, serious man with a well-deserved reputation for effective military management.

The members of the civilian secretariat matched the high quality of the uniformed leadership. Charles Baird, the undersecretary, had come from industry and became the chief executive officer of the International Nickel Company when his term ended. The I&L assistant secretary was the venerable Jim Bannerman. When he left to become vice president of the University of California, I asked Barry Shillito, president of the Logistics Management Institute, to replace him. The assistant secretary for research and development was Robert Frosch, a scientist with a supple and inquiring mind, who later became the head of the National Aeronautics and Space Administration. I recruited Charles Bowsher to be the financial management assistant secretary. He later served a fifteen-year term as the comptroller general of the United States. It was a strong, highly qualified, and dedicated group that worked with the uniformed leadership in a spirit of mutual respect.

The Navy made available to the secretariat its most promising officers to serve in several capacities. The most important of these was the naval aide to the secretary, Capt. Worth H. Bagley. It was his delicate responsibility to be faithful to the views of the uniformed Navy but always to be intensely loyal to the secretary. Bagley filled the role to perfection. He came from an illustrious naval family. Worth's father was a vice admiral. His uncle Adm. William D. Leahy had been CNO and later President Franklin Roosevelt's chief of staff. Still another relative was Josephus Daniels, secretary of the Navy for an eight-year period beginning in 1913 and best remembered for abolishing alcohol aboard ship. Worth and his brother David, in due course, became admirals, the only instance in U.S. Navy history where two brothers attained four-star rank. When Bagley was reassigned to sea duty, he was replaced by another outstanding officer, Capt. Stansfield Turner, a graduate of the Naval Academy, a Rhodes Scholar, later an admiral, and finally President Jimmy Carter's director of central intelligence.

As an assistant secretary of defense, I had reviewed budget requests from the Navy and the other military departments and recommended changes, usually reductions in the amounts requested. Now, I would be submitting the Navy budget for the knife wielders in Defense to cut to pieces. My practice had always been to look critically at budget requests because I believed that they tended to be inflated with worst-case assumptions. I told Bob McNamara that I was prepared to continue this approach and submit a lean Navy budget. But if the Defense staff then chopped it up, he would have to find a new Navy secretary. McNamara told me to do the job at the Navy level with the assurance that our submission would be favorably received by Defense. I proposed to the CNO, Admiral Moorer, and the vice chief, Adm. Horacio Rivero, that we trim any fat from our budget submission, based on my assurances from McNamara. Rivero was highly skeptical, but Moorer said he was willing to give it a try. We spent long hours finding ways to make cuts and turned in a solid product. To our great satisfaction (and Rivero's surprise) the Navy budget was approved pretty much as submitted. The experience helped to solidify my relationship with Admiral Moorer. We continued to work productively together and got most of the things we wanted.

We Interrupt This Program for . . .

While I was working twelve-hour days to get on top of my new responsibilities, I was interrupted by a plea to restore an officer to his former command or to order a court of inquiry into the circumstances of his removal. The officer was Lt. Cdr. Marcus Aurelius Arnheiter, skipper for only ninety-nine days of the destroyer escort USS *Vance,* on patrol in the waters off Vietnam. He was removed from command because witnesses said he had violated Navy regulations and the orders of his superiors, submitted false position reports, acted in bizarre ways, and conducted what amounted to a private war to glorify himself. Conservative columnist James J. Kilpatrick had written a lengthy article about Arnheiter entitled "He Might Have Been Another Halsey," referring to the Navy's renowned Fleet Admiral. Joseph Y. Resnick, a member of Congress from New York who planned to run for the Senate against Senator Jacob Javits, had taken up Arnheiter's cause and had held a public hearing on the circumstances of his removal.

Arnheiter was praised in the Resnick hearing by Capt. Richard B. Alexander, who had been selected for the choice assignment of command of the battleship *New Jersey,* now being recalled from mothball status to join the war in Vietnam. Arnheiter appeared before Resnick, and in his testimony accused a Navy vice admiral of lying to Congress about his removal from the *Vance.*

Captain Alexander requested an appointment with me and I agreed to see him. He said Arnheiter had been improperly accused, that there had been a miscarriage of justice, and that his removal was a blot on the good name of the Navy. "Mr. Secretary," he said in the document he prepared for our meeting, "what all your officers will demand to know is just how in hell this could happen in the United States Navy!" Alexander's comment was widely reported in press articles, most of them favorable toward Commander Arnheiter.

The file on the Arnheiter case must have been three feet thick. It was carefully reviewed by my able legal assistant, Capt. Horace Robertson. Robbie said the Navy had acted properly and saw no need for a court of inquiry or the restoration of Arnheiter to his former command. I respected Robbie's judgment but said I wanted to read the file myself to make sure Arnheiter had been treated properly. Worth Bagley said I didn't have the time for this sort of thing and should rely on Robbie's recommendation.

For a week, partly during the working day but mainly at home at night, I went through the whole account, including all of Arnheiter's fitness reports from the time he graduated from the Naval Academy.

There was a common thread running through them over a twenty-year period—Arnheiter might become a great officer if he ever developed better judgment. I couldn't find anything in the file that warranted the need for a court of inquiry. I was particularly troubled by Arnheiter's skirting of the rules of engagement in a situation where the president of the United States had established tight controls on the conduct of combat operations. I went beyond the file and thought about skippers of Polaris submarines armed with nuclear missiles of unimaginable destructive power and the need always to be sure of their fidelity. I thought also that I would not be happy having my own sons serving under Arnheiter's command.

When I issued a statement saying I saw no reason for further inquiry, Resnick called for my resignation. Meanwhile, Admiral Moorer summoned Captain Alexander to his office and dressed him down for intemperate behavior in attempting to influence the secretary of the Navy on a sensitive matter. He was reassigned from the *New Jersey* to a desk job in Boston.

The negative articles continued for several days, and then favorable ones began to appear in *Time, Newsweek*, and other publications. The *Time* article in the December 1967 issue described examples of Arnheiter's highly unusual behavior, and compared him with Captain Queeg in Herman Wouk's classic, *The Caine Mutiny*. Witnesses said he had tried to run a private war, had almost gunned down fleeing refugees, and had written his own commendation for a Silver Star for gallantry. Eventually, James Kilpatrick wrote a generous article suggesting that he may have been wrong about Arnheiter. Neil Sheehan, who had covered the story for the *New York Times*, wrote a lively book called *The Arnheiter Affair.* He signed my copy with a nice note saying good judgment had prevailed. Resnick failed to win a Senate seat and died in 1969. Arnheiter resigned from active service in 1971.

The Pueblo Incident

At 4:30 in the morning on January 23, 1968, I was awakened by a phone call from Admiral Moorer. He wanted me to know that the USS

Pueblo had been captured by the North Koreans and escorted into Wonson Harbor. Moorer said everyone had been informed and that there was nothing I needed to do. "We should issue an ultimatum and get the ship back," he said. I told him I would see him in the Pentagon in an hour or so.

Bob McNamara was on the phone when I reached my office and wanted a complete report from the Navy. Admiral Moorer had an inquiry already under way. The *Pueblo* had been engaged in gathering signals intelligence in Wonson Bay, although the cover story was that it was merely an oceanographic ship engaged in research in international waters. The Soviet Union for some years had conducted signals intelligence like this using fishing trawlers equipped with special electronics gear. A friend and colleague, Eugene Fubini, who had worked with the legendary Enrico Fermi in Italy before coming to the Pentagon, had recommended to McNamara that we do what the Russians were doing. The Navy agreed and fitted out the *Pueblo* and several other small cargo ships for the intelligence mission. Although they had a limited amount of armament under cover on the deck, they were innocent-looking vessels not expected to attract much attention.

The capture of the *Pueblo* and its secret equipment and intelligence information was startling news. As the facts began to emerge, it was learned that North Korean subchasers and torpedo boats had surrounded the ship, opened fire (killing one sailor), and then escorted it into Wonson Harbor. The eighty-three crew members were removed and charged with spying in North Korean territorial waters. The crew had attempted to destroy some of the sensitive equipment and heave the secret papers overboard, but much valuable information remained that would undoubtedly end up in Soviet hands. The *Pueblo*'s captain, Comdr. Lloyd M. Bucher, had radioed for help, but there were no U.S. aircraft or ships near enough to render assistance.

The North Koreans had a field day at the expense of the United States and the *Pueblo*'s crew members. With their usual heavy-handedness, they trumpeted the incident for its worldwide propaganda value. The *Pueblo*'s crew members were tortured. Under the brutal circumstances, they tried or failed to meet the stern demands of the Code of Conduct requiring that "when questioned, should I become a prisoner of war, I am bound to give only name, rank, service number, and date of birth." They acknowledged the ship's intelligence mission and signed statements, prepared by their captors, that admitted guilt and offered apologies.

The United States gained the release of the crew eleven months after their capture by signing an apology—which was then renounced after the crew's release. In December, the Navy convened a court of inquiry. The court members were highly critical of Commander Bucher and pressed him repeatedly about why he had surrendered his ship. He stated that he had received fire from the North Koreans at point-blank range. "I considered that any further efforts . . . would result in severe damage to either the ship or, more importantly, the men on the ship," Bucher said. "I was completely and hopelessly outgunned." In *Bridge of No Return*, a book on the ordeal of the *Pueblo* by its operations officer, F. Carl Schumacher Jr., and George C. Wilson, military correspondent of the *Washington Post*, the authors explain: "The Captain of the *Pueblo*, as he saw his situation, was on his own, with only two options: lose his ship and his men, or lose his ship and save his men. He chose the latter."

The court of inquiry asked crew members why they had been unable to live up to the Code of Conduct, and they described their torture and harsh treatment. They were beaten, denied food, and forced to make false confessions. Schumacher acknowledged that after three days of beatings, he had broken the code: "It becomes a matter of how much you can take before you find a way around the torture." Three of the crew members, according to the record, contemplated or actually attempted suicide.

The court of inquiry completed its work on January 23, 1969, after I had left office. It recommended that Commander Bucher be brought to trial by general court-martial for permitting his ship to be searched while he still had the power to resist, failing to take immediate and aggressive protective measures, and related charges. My successor, John H. Chafee, former governor of Rhode Island and a decorated Marine Corps officer in World War II and the Korean War, had to decide the next step. In May, he announced his decision: "I make no judgment regarding the guilt or innocence of any of the officers of the offenses alleged against them. . . . It is my opinion that . . . even assuming that further proceedings were held, and even going so far as to assume that a judgment of guilt were to be reached . . . they have suffered enough, and further punishment would not be justified."

I wonder how I would have come out had Chafee's decision been mine to make. I think I probably would have ended up about where he did. George Wilson, a journalist I have known and respected for many years, thought Chafee was "inconclusive," that his "political decision did not stop the suffering of the *Pueblo* men . . . who had done their best under extraordinarily brutal circumstances." God knows that men who were so inhumanly treated merit our most profound sympathy. But if Wilson was suggesting that Chafee should have praised them or declared them innocent, he would have collided with the most fundamental traditions of the naval service—"Don't give up the ship"; "Damn the torpedoes, full steam ahead"; and "I have only just begun to fight." Chafee had to weigh this history against the sympathy he felt for the men, and his "they have suffered enough" conclusion was the proper way to end the matter.

It is never easy to handle intelligence-gathering operations that go wrong. The U-2 incident, in which pilot Gary Powers was shot down on an intelligence flight by Soviet missiles, embarrassed President Dwight D. Eisenhower at a time when he had new diplomatic initiatives under way. In April 2001 the Chinese capture of a U.S. plane that had been conducting signals intelligence dominated the news and required months of negotiation before the diplomats found the right combination of words to secure the release of the plane. In the *Pueblo* incident, the crew members were criticized for apologizing to their captors, but the United States government also apologized to the North Koreans in order to obtain the release of the crew.

Finally, in cases like this in which Americans are tortured, the relevance of the Code of Conduct is called into question. I think the Navy was right to continue adherence to the code—"You have to have something," as Chafee said. But no one who has not been tortured by ruthless captors can be entirely sure how he would behave under similar circumstances.

Personnel Matters

The U.S. Navy, it seemed to me, was the most aristocratic of the military services, owing, I suspect, to its antecedents in the British Navy. Partly because of this, it was the slowest of the services to widen opportunities for black Americans. In November 1967, I announced a program to double the number of black Navy and Marine Corps officers, who numbered only 290 in the Navy and 155 in the marines. With a lot of help from Undersecretary Baird, we began to recruit aggressively at predominantly black colleges and, for the first time, established a reserve officers training program at one of them, Prairie State A & M College in Texas. The Navy worked hard on the new program and within a year the number of black officers had tripled.

Throughout my tenure and continuing to the present day, the Navy has had problems retaining officers and skilled enlisted men. There have been many reasons for this, high among them being the long deployments at sea and the separation from families. Naval aviation was particularly hard hit because of lucrative offers from the commercial airlines. Additionally, growing dissatisfaction with the Vietnam War turned people away from the military. I referred to this in a speech I gave, saying "these unjustified attacks on the military image add to the problem of motivating impressionable young men toward a career in the Navy."

The Navy took a number of steps to overcome its personnel retention problems. More postgraduate education was provided for young officers, first tours at sea for nuclear submarine officers were shortened, more shore duty was made available, and plans were developed to reduce crew size through greater automation of Navy ships. Finally, in 1967, Congress enacted legislation to increase pay scales. Although each of these measures helped, the overall problem remained.

Normally, the secretary of the Navy stands clear of officer assignments, but occasionally there are reasons to become involved. An

immensely talented officer, Adm. Elmo Zumwalt, had the makings of
a future chief of naval operations, but I feared that his prolonged duty
in Washington rather than in combat commands would prejudice his
selection. I persuaded Admiral Moorer to assign him to the top naval
job in Vietnam, under the overall command of my Army friend,
Creighton Abrams, who had replaced General Westmoreland in March
1968. The assignment meant jumping Zumwalt over many officers of
higher rank, but Moorer (I believe somewhat reluctantly) agreed to my
wishes. I wrote a personal letter to Abe telling him that one of the
Navy's brightest officers would soon be arriving. My letter, ironically,
almost led to Zumwalt's rejection. Abe was a stickler for proper procedures, and the protocol for assignments like this was for the chairman
of the Joint Chiefs of Staff to inform him before the assignment
became official. He told Zumwalt that he would have turned him
down except for his longstanding friendship with me. He later told me
that Admiral Zumwalt was the best naval officer he had ever known.

In another instance, I learned that things were not always what they
seemed to be. Admiral Moorer had submitted for my approval the nomination of an officer for a particularly demanding job in the Pentagon
who seemed to lack the proper qualifications. I was hesitant about
rejecting Moorer's recommendation but uncomfortable with his choice.
I discussed the officer with my predecessor, Paul Nitze, who told me
forthrightly that the officer was clearly unqualified. Worth Bagley
saved the day. He suggested that perhaps Admiral Moorer was under
pressure from "the system" to nominate this particular officer and
might actually welcome it if he were turned down by the secretary of
the Navy. I did what Bagley suggested. Moorer never complained, and
then he quickly submitted the name of a highly qualified officer to fill
the position.

The F-111

From the beginning to the end of my eight-year period in the Pentagon, controversy raged over the F-111. It began in 1961 when Robert

McNamara said an airplane with "commonality" features would be suitable for the air force and the Navy, thus saving many millions of dollars. Two companies, Boeing in Seattle and General Dynamics in Fort Worth, competed for the lucrative contract. The source selection board narrowly preferred the General Dynamics proposal, while the Navy and air force chiefs favored Boeing. After further review by McNamara and Air Force Secretary Gene Zuckert, the contract was awarded to General Dynamics. There was some talk about political meddling by Vice President Lyndon Johnson to ensure that the Texas company won. In a spirited defense, McNamara said legitimate questions about the Boeing proposal, not politics, guided his decision. A contentious hearing convened by the Government Operations Committee, chaired by powerful Senator John McClellan, raised many troubling questions, but work on the airplane went forward on schedule.

For the first six-and-one-half years of my time in the Pentagon, I had no involvement with the F-111. Things changed abruptly when I became secretary of the Navy. I found myself in the middle of an emotionally charged controversy that had grown in intensity over a period of many months. The Navy didn't like its version of the airplane, the F-111B. They thought it was too heavy. They thought it lacked the agility to defeat the newest Soviet fighter. It was too big for easy handling on the crowded carrier decks. It was regarded as simply a Navy version of an air force airplane, and, consequently, it was not likely to embody those characteristics needed for naval aviation. The climate was so hot that even if the F-111B were an excellent airplane—which it was not—the Navy wouldn't have wanted any part of it.

The admirals in charge of naval aviation—Tom Connolly and Gerry Miller—were tough, single-minded and justly proud of the Navy's aeronautical achievements. For years, the aviators had fought against the battleship admirals and eventually triumphed. The aircraft carrier task force had become the Navy's principal offensive weapon. Although secure within the Navy, the aviation leaders always kept a watchful eye on the air force, suspicious that Navy missions might be taken over by the rival service or that decisions on the budget would favor the air force. With a war going on, everyone agreed that the

North Vietnamese were the enemy. In the battle of the F-111, the Navy was sure that the enemy was McNamara and the air force.

The situation was extremely uncomfortable for me. I was naturally expected to support and defend the Navy point of view. Bob McNamara, on whose staff I had served for so long, expected me to control the admirals and keep the Navy in the F-111 program. An "unsolicited" proposal from Grumman Aircraft brought the matter to a head. Grumman proposed a new Navy fighter instead of the F-111B. A favored Navy contractor, Grumman had been working on the Navy version of the F-111. McNamara and Roger Lewis, the head of General Dynamics, were furious. Lewis told me that Grumman had sabotaged the program for its own selfish interests and that its proposal, far from being unsolicited, had been instigated by Vice Admiral Connolly. Connolly was anxious to move forward with the Grumman airplane.

Though McNamara was displeased, I told him that we had to face reality and recognize that naval aviators had lost all interest in the F-111. I said Admiral Moorer and I had agreed to undertake a study of a new type of Navy fighter along the lines of the one proposed by Grumman. In any event, I would insist on a competitive procurement instead of a sole-source award to Grumman. Meanwhile, the Navy would continue in the F-111 program.

The Senate held another F-111 hearing, this time chaired by Senator John Stennis. I was the principal witness, along with Admiral Moorer and Vice Admiral Connolly. I defended the F-111 program against a decidedly skeptical chairman. When Stennis asked Admiral Connolly for his personal views, Connolly said the plane was a failure and couldn't be fixed. His comment helped to kill a Navy airplane that was already dying. The Congress ended funding for the F-111B but made money available for a new Navy fighter.

Neither Admiral Connolly nor Admiral Miller fully trusted me. They thought I was loyal to McNamara, not them. They also thought that I would retaliate against Connolly for his outspokenness in the Stennis hearing, but that was nonsense. If I had any gripe against Connolly it was that as a senior officer he should have recognized more than he did the delicacy of the situation we were in. Admiral Moorer fully understood the problem, worked productively with me, and played his hand with finesse.

In 1968, Grumman won the new fighter contract over another favored Navy contractor, McDonnell Aircraft, which had recently merged with Douglas Aircraft. The Grumman plane was designated the F-14 "Tomcat" in honor of Tom Connolly, following the naming of earlier Grumman planes such as the "Wildcat" and the "Hellcat." The airplane proposed by McDonnell became the basis for a new air force fighter, the F-15. Admiral Connolly went to work for Grumman after his retirement. He died in 1996, but his namesake, the Tomcat, is still flying.

Admiral Rickover

Adm. Hyman G. Rickover was rightly called the "Father of the Nuclear Navy." He developed the first atomic-powered submarine, the USS *Nautilus,* launched in 1954. He began his nuclear propulsion efforts in 1947, and his tour as the head of the Navy's nuclear program never seemed to come to an end. Normally, an officer serves in a post for several years, then moves on to another assignment. Rickover went on forever, surmounting such formidable barriers as the mandatory retirement age of sixty-two and the efforts of high-ranking officials to get rid of him. He bulled ahead through all these years, initially against a Navy skeptical of nuclear power and finally against naval leaders who preferred having many conventionally powered ships instead of fewer, more expensive nuclear ones. His single-mindedness and abrasive manner offended his fellow officers and the contractors who built his ships.

I spent a lot of time with "Rick," supported him in some of his objectives, and questioned him on others. He held strong, unwavering views on whatever topic he discussed, whether it was his nuclear specialty or subjects of a broader sort, such as people, organizations, managerial philosophy, or education. He had an original mind, was outspoken, and was not afraid to make an outrageous statement.

One needs a lot of adjectives to describe Rickover fully. He was short, wizened, devious, calculating, manipulative, dominant, demanding, focused, unscrupulous, egotistical, and effective. Though I detested the methods he employed to sustain his power and influence, I believed that the nation was in his debt for his dedicated pursuit of nuclear power to propel submarines and surface ships.

Few people in modern U.S. history have been centers of power unto themselves, free from the checks and balances that circumscribe individual ambition. Rickover was certainly one of them. J. Edgar Hoover, the long-time head of the Federal Bureau of Investigation, was another. Hoover's power derived from information in his files that he was prepared to release to embarrass or compromise a member of Congress or even a president who attempted to thwart him. As a result, he was able to stay in office for many years longer than he should have. As President Johnson once said of him, "I'd rather have Edgar inside the tent pissing out than outside the tent pissing in."

Rickover lacked Hoover's raw power and depended on a combination of bureaucratic ingenuity, a masterful sense of public relations, and an unassailable position as the individual responsible for the safety of naval nuclear reactors. His bureaucratic arrangements allowed him to oppose military authority when it suited his purposes. He could do this with impunity because he was "double-hatted." He wore a military hat as the deputy commander of the Navy Ship Systems Command and a civilian hat as the director of the Division of Naval Reactors of the Atomic Energy Commission. When he disagreed with the secretary of the Navy or the chief of naval operations, he would respond on AEC stationery in his civilian capacity outside the military chain of command. As Elmo Zumwalt described it in his book *On Watch*, "Rick doffed his admiral's suit whenever he found himself in conflict with Navy policy, and sniped at the Navy in his civvies."

Rickover's talent for public relations was unsurpassed. He cultivated the image of a hard-working, cost-conscious, and plain-speaking public servant. His office, located in the "temporary" Navy building constructed during the First World War, was the shabbiest one in Washington. Barry Shillito, my assistant secretary for procurement, occupied a truly grand office in the same building. He said, in his privately published memoir, that Rickover "delighted in comparing my rather ostentatious, Forrestal-designed office with his Spartan quarters, which had also been designed for an effect—but a different effect."

His plain-speaking, plain-living image appealed to members of Congress. Rickover cultivated the influential committees and the individual members with an assurance that a high-priced lobbyist could only envy. As Zumwalt wrote, "Congress doesn't really think of Rick as an admiral at all, but kind of as a Senator." I was appalled on one occasion when I was testifying on Navy programs to find Admiral Rickover, in civilian clothes, sitting up there on the dais with the senators!

Rickover flattered senators and representatives, gave them helpful information, and included them in his activities. For example, when he went out on sea trials in a new submarine, he would send out stacks of letters marked "Aboard the Ship on Sea Trials" to members of Congress and the public. He also obtained from the shipbuilder a quantity of gifts and souvenirs that he would send to his friends and constituents. The ethics of what he was doing raised some eyebrows, but no one thought that he benefited personally or was otherwise corrupt.

Congress willingly responded when Rickover needed help. In 1967, as reported by Zumwalt in *On Watch*, Navy Secretary Paul Nitze wanted to get rid of Rickover. He and Bob McNamara convinced President Johnson that Rickover's time had finally come to an end. Some of the admiral's staunch Senate friends got word of what was going on and raised such a storm that the president changed his mind. Rickover stayed on and continued to be a powerful presence when I succeeded Nitze later in the year.

Rickover and I got started on a good footing because I believed submarines were needed in greater numbers and that nuclear power made them far more lethal weapons. The essence of submarine warfare is stealth. With nuclear power, the submarine was a true submersible, able to remain underwater for extended periods, unlike the older diesel-powered boats that had to resurface from time to time. I persuaded the Department of Defense to increase the rate of attack submarine production, a task made easier because the deputy secretary, Paul Nitze, felt as strongly as I did.

Rickover was deeply offended when I called him forward for a review of cost overruns on one of his specialized programs. Cost overruns, according to the myth he cultivated, occurred in other programs, not his. With financial experts like Chuck Bowsher and procurement experts like Barry Shillito at my side, we worked over Rick's figures as though he was just another project manager. Rickover fumed and sputtered and treated our questions with disdain. Talking down to those who opposed him came naturally to Rickover. I remember one incident when Paul Nitze and I questioned him about one of his submarine projects. He treated us like schoolboys, saying that the Germans called submarines "U-boats" and that submarines operated underwater and had to be strong enough to withstand the pressure.

Defense officials in systems analysis and research and development sometimes challenged Rickover's design concepts. For example, John Foster, the DoD chief of research, raised probing questions about a one-of-a-kind electric power propulsion submarine that Rickover wanted to build. Foster explained his concerns to me, and the more I listened the more I was convinced that he was right. I tentatively decided to oppose Rickover but wanted to hear what the vice CNO, Adm. "Chick" Clarey, recommended before making a final decision. Clarey was an unpretentious, sincere, "solid citizen" sort with a distinguished record as a submariner. We spent a lot of time reviewing Rick's proposed ship and Foster's objections. Clarey was critical of Rickover's methods but stressed repeatedly how the new ship could contribute to the quieting of submarines. Silence was the essence of submarine warfare. Our ships were quieter than the Russian ones and we needed to keep our advantage. Though I continued to have some misgivings, I decided that Clarey was right. To Foster's dismay, I argued in favor of the project and won its approval.

The senior naval officers would probably have applauded if I had tried to get rid of Rickover. They respected his accomplishments but resented his methods. Given Rick's entrenched position in Congress, there was no point in trying to dump him. I discussed Rickover on many occasions with Admiral Moorer. He was more offended than I was by his callous disregard of the chain of command. He also understood Rickover's ultimate source of power. It was not simply his high standing with the Congress, it was his responsibility for the safety of the Navy's nuclear reactors. If he chose to play the safety card, it would trump all the others.

Rickover never went to the Navy's many social functions. It wouldn't have fit his carefully cultivated image. But he surprised everyone by showing up, unannounced, at my retirement party. Perhaps he came because he was glad to see me go. Perhaps he came because I never tried to fire him. I like to think he came because he sensed, despite our differences, that I thought the nation owed him a debt of gratitude and that his place in naval history was secure.

The War Goes On

The Vietnam War was the major concern that occupied my waking hours as it had when I was McNamara's procurement and production chief. The Navy was heavily involved in the conflict. Carrier planes struck targets around the clock, and many pilots were killed or captured. Surface ships patrolled offshore, firing their heavy guns at troop concentrations and structures of all kinds. In the Mekong Delta area of the south, the Navy's riverine forces fought the war from small craft, and Navy SEALS carried out daring missions. The marines, who had led the deployments at the beginning of the stepped-up U.S. effort in 1965, fought bloody battles in the northern sectors.

On January 30, 1968, one week after the capture of the *Pueblo*, the Viet Cong and the North Vietnamese attacked almost every city and military installation in South Vietnam, after a brief truce for the Tet holidays. The Tet offensive surprised the U.S. military commanders and further eroded support for the war. Coming after encouraging reports from General Westmoreland, the scope and intensity of the Tet offensive shocked everyone. Casualties were heavy on both sides, with a final estimate of as many as twenty-five thousand enemy troops killed or captured.

Shortly after Tet, with almost half a million troops in Vietnam, General Westmoreland requested 206,000 more by the end of 1968. I spoke privately to McNamara about my concerns about how the war was going. The initial intelligence reports had presented a confusing picture, citing an apparent collapse of the Army of South Vietnam (ARVN). I told McNamara that he should oppose Westmoreland's request until we understood the situation more clearly. If Tet was a U.S. victory, as Westmoreland proclaimed, why did he need 206,000 more troops? If the ARVN had collapsed, the request, huge as it was, would undoubtedly be followed by an even larger one. McNamara seemed preoccupied with his own thoughts and didn't appear interested in hearing mine. He had always looked on me as someone ready and able to carry out the huge logistics tasks rather than as a counselor on war policy.

On February 23, 1968, Bob McNamara submitted his letter of resignation to President Johnson. It did not come as a surprise. The president thought McNamara had gone "soft" on the war, and so did several important Senators who had LBJ's ear. McNamara said in his memoir, *In Retrospect*, that "I do not know to this day whether I quit or was fired. Maybe it was both." His last official act on the Vietnam War was to oppose Westmoreland's troop request.

McNamara was appointed to head the World Bank, a position very much in keeping with his views on helping poor nations to rise from poverty. It was time for him to leave the Pentagon—perhaps past the time when he should have left. He had told the president that "we could not achieve our objective in Vietnam by any reasonable military means, and we should therefore seek a lesser political objective through negotiations." Bob was tired, tense, worried about his wife's health, and torn apart emotionally over a war for which he was responsible but which he thought unwinnable. I was worried about his health when I saw how haggard he looked. Although I would miss him, I thought it was the best thing for him personally to depart.

McNamara's replacement was Clark Clifford, who was sworn in as secretary of defense on the first of March. Clifford had been an advisor to presidents, beginning with Harry Truman. President Johnson had depended on his counsel and advice for years, even though he held no public office. He had been a "hawk" in the early years of the war, but now, at the president's request, he began a top-to-bottom reexamination of our effort. A so-called Clifford Group was assembled that included the secretaries of state and treasury, the chairman of the Joint Chiefs of Staff, the director of the CIA, and other high officials. Their immediate task was to review Westmoreland's troop request and then advise the president. In addition to his meetings with the cabinet officials, Clifford began each day with a discussion of the war with his "8:30" group, which consisted of his deputy, Paul Nitze; George Elsey, his personal assistant; Paul Warnke, the assistant secretary for international affairs; Phil Goulding, his public affairs officer; and Col. Robert Pursley, his military assistant. Clifford wanted to know whether we could ever prosecute the war successfully, even if we provided thousands of troops beyond those in Westmoreland's request.

The broader group of cabinet-level officials could not reach agreement on the question of more troops. Clifford himself came to the same conclusion as McNamara had before him—that the president should deny Westy's request.

While these important meetings were taking place, far from the probing eyes of the press, a leak of major consequences occurred. The *New York Times* learned about the troop request, and on March 10 it published its account. Other papers across the country followed suit. The effect was devastating. Even those members of the public who had long supported the war effort began to doubt its wisdom. We may have "won" the Tet offensive, as measured by enemy casualties, but we "lost" Tet and perhaps the war itself because of Tet's impact on U.S. public opinion.

Clark Clifford stated in his memoir, *Counsel to the President,* "What changed my opinion on the war was, in the end, the failure of the war's supporters, especially the military, to make a convincing case that we could achieve our objectives at an acceptable cost to the nation. The simple truth was that the military failed to sustain a respectable argument for their position."

Events began to unfold quickly. In the New Hampshire presidential primary, an antiwar candidate, Eugene McCarthy, got almost as many votes as Lyndon Johnson. Two days later, on March 14, Bobby Kennedy told Clifford that he might become a candidate for president in the hope of changing the policy on Vietnam. President Johnson still had not made up his mind on how to respond to Westmoreland's request, but he said he would discuss the war in a major speech to the American people. Working with Harry McPherson, a respected member of the White House staff, Clifford attempted to make the speech less warlike. He succeeded. On March 31, in his televised address to the nation, the president said he had ordered a cessation of the bombing attacks except in an area where an enemy buildup threatened our positions. He announced further that he was sending an additional 13,500 troops to Vietnam. His closing words stunned the nation: "I have concluded that I should not permit the presidency to become involved in the partisan divisions that are developing in this political year. . . . Accordingly, I shall not seek, and I will not accept, the nomination of my party [for president in the 1968 election]."

Meanwhile, each of us carried on with our responsibilities in the rapidly changing environment. Clifford left the day-to-day operations of the Pentagon to his able deputy, the veteran Paul Nitze. I met with Clark in regularly scheduled or special meetings, usually with Nitze present. The differences between Clifford and McNamara were immediately apparent. Clark was beautifully tailored in double-breasted suits and starched white shirts. McNamara looked rumpled, with a buttoned-down shirt and a tie that sagged below the collar. McNamara's huge desk, which Clifford also used, had always been clean; Clifford had little piles of notes on the desk, each one held down by a small paperweight. McNamara made quick decisions; Clifford pondered. Bob talked; Clark listened. McNamara had answers; Clifford asked questions. McNamara looked up at his clock on the wall to signal that time was running short; Clifford seemed to have plenty of time for business, and even some left over for small talk.

One of the first encounters I had with the new secretary illustrated the differences between the two men. The Navy was anxious to gain approval for a couple of nuclear-powered frigates that had been strongly endorsed by key members of Congress. McNamara and Alain Enthoven opposed them because they cost more than conventionally powered ones. I thought we needed a mix of both types but had been unable to convince McNamara. I succeeded with Clifford. Congressional support for the ships was a significant factor for him. He was much more sensitive than McNamara to congressional opinion, spent more time with influential members, and spoke with them at a leisurely pace compared with McNamara's staccato pronouncements.

Many people have told me that the job of secretary of the Navy is the best one in Washington. I suspect they have in mind the opportunity it affords for travel to interesting places. One such place was Brazil. The State Department wanted me to make an official visit because a principal figure in the military government was a Brazilian admiral. Nan, looking glamorous, accompanied several officers and me to Rio. We were put up at a fancy hotel and chauffeured around town with an ostentatious police escort until I asked that it be stopped. Several months later, I hosted a return visit for the admiral and his wife. He presented Nan with a beautiful aquamarine jewel as big as a plum that we deposited with the State Department as required, as soon as the admiral and his lady had left town.

There was also the necessary and informative visit to the Sixth Fleet in the Mediterranean, going from ship to ship, meeting with the skipper, and eating in the crew's mess. The visit also included a stopover in Rota, Spain, where the Navy had an important submarine base, and two days in Madrid for talks with naval and governmental leaders.

A trip to Southeast Asia in October 1968 was the most important and busiest one. With the war still raging, I wanted to see for myself how the men and the equipment were performing. I stopped briefly in Hawaii and Japan for talks with our naval commanders but spent most of my time in Vietnam and at sea aboard Seventh Fleet ships.

In Saigon, I stayed at General Abrams's house, somewhat to the surprise of the naval leaders who had expected that I would stay with them. Abe had reoriented the war effort after taking over from Westy. Instead of measuring progress by the infamous "body count," Abe put his emphasis on protecting the South Vietnamese people and working toward a more stable environment. One can only speculate how his approach, if emphasized from the outset, might have affected the ultimate outcome.

Abe praised Admiral Zumwalt and made arrangements for me to visit him and his units in the Delta area. Zumwalt believed we should help the Vietnamese to take greater responsibility for the war. He obtained equipment more suitable for their use and started English language classes to improve communication. He was beginning a program of "Vietnamization" before the term was coined and the concept expanded under Melvin Laird, Clifford's successor as defense secretary.

From the Delta I went to the north to meet with Marine Corps commanders who had fought some of the bloodiest battles of the war. The most alarming one was the siege of Khe Sanh where twenty thousand North Vietnamese troops had pinned down five thousand marines. They had cut the roads to Khe Sanh, and supplies and ammunition had to be delivered by air. Marine Corps losses were heavy. U.S. officials, including President Johnson, feared that Khe Sanh might become another Dien Bien Phu, the 1954 battle where the French Army had met disaster at the hands of the Vietnamese General Vo Nguyen Giap. The gallant marines held out and avoided a similar fate.

The battleship USS *Missouri* had joined the Seventh Fleet, and its 16-inch guns pounded enemy installations. Capt. Ed Snyder, an officer who had served on my staff, commanded the ship. In company with Vice Adm. William "Bush" Bringle, the fleet commander, I spent a day on the "Mighty Mo," scene of the surrender of the Japanese that ended World War II. After a deafening salvo had been fired, I asked Captain Snyder how targets were acquired and what the big guns were hitting. He said the target was a military facility. The land area of the country was largely rural, and I wondered just what kind of facility he was talking about and whether it was worthy of so formidable a ship.

When it was time for me to leave Saigon, General Abrams drove me to the airport in his Jeep. I thanked him for his hospitality, shook his hand, and wished him well. Abe was silent for a moment. Then he said, matter-of-factly, that U.S. intelligence had picked up a report that a team of assassins was moving down from North Vietnam to try to kill him. I couldn't think of anything useful to say. Neither could Abe. We shook hands again, I gave him a bear hug, and wondered if this was the last time I would see my friend alive. He was finally done in, not by assassins, but by cancer after returning to the United States to become chief of staff of the Army.

Ceremonial Duties

Ceremonial duties came with the job. They ranged from perfunctory ones like showing up at social functions or naval anniversaries to profound ones like awarding the congressional Medal of Honor. In between were ship launchings and speeches to the public or Navy groups.

One speech gave me special pleasure. It was in San Diego, a great Navy town where many senior officers lived in retirement. In the audience was Fitzhugh Lee, my old skipper from the USS *Manila Bay*, the small aircraft carrier on which I had served during World War II. Lee had retired as a vice admiral and was living in nearby La Jolla. I'm sure he never believed that one of his young lieutenants might end up some day as secretary of the Navy. I told the audience what a great captain Lee had been, how he had won two Navy Crosses on the *Manila Bay*, and how much I learned about the Navy while serving under his command.

Other memorable occasions included a ship launching and a ship commissioning ceremony. My wife was chosen to strike the bottle of champagne on the hull of the USS *Seahorse*, a nuclear-powered attack submarine, when it slid into the water at Groton, Connecticut. It was a family affair, with our young daughter Amy serving as Nan's "maid of honor," me giving the obligatory speech, and my father from California watching it all with pride. We had a nice, old-fashioned clambake when it was over, with the assembled notables and many of our friends from Massachusetts and Washington.

The commissioning of the USS *John F. Kennedy* in 1968 was another memorable event. The *JFK* was a large aircraft carrier, conventionally powered because McNamara and his systems analysts, over the strong objections of the Navy, opposed nuclear propulsion. Jackie Kennedy, her daughter Caroline, and son John Jr. were among the many members of the extended Kennedy family who had traveled to Newport News for the ceremony. The speaker was Robert S. McNamara, by then president of the World Bank.

When McNamara stepped up to the speaker's platform, he handed me a copy of his remarks and whispered that I might have to complete them for him. I understood what he meant when he began his recollections of the fallen president. "For a bright, blazing moment, his youth made us all feel young again," he said, his voice faltering. "Though brief was his voyage, those of us who knew him will never be quite the same again." He coughed, cleared his throat and then resumed. "No one expects our lives to be easy, not in this decade and not in this century," he said. Then he stopped abruptly and left the platform to sit among the Kennedys.

The most profound moments of my time in office occurred when I was privileged to award congressional Medals of Honor to seven Marine Corps and three U.S. Navy men, some posthumously to a wife, parent, or other family member. The medal is given for conspicuous gallantry and intrepidity at the risk of one's life, above and beyond the call of duty. Here are brief accounts of the incredible heroism of these men.

I presented the congressional Medal of Honor to Capt. William L. McGonagle, the commanding officer of the intelligence ship *Liberty*, which was attacked by Israeli warplanes and torpedo boats on June 8, 1967. McGonagle kept his heavily damaged ship under control for seventeen hours despite his own serious wounds, saving the lives of many of his men and preserving his ship. The *Liberty* was gathering sensitive information when it was attacked off Sinai during the brief Arab-Israeli war, killing thirty-four men and wounding seventy-five others. Israel later said the attack was a mistake. Though in great pain and weak from loss of blood, McGonagle stayed on the bridge, maneuvering his ship and seeing to the care of his wounded men. He wiped away his tears when the medal was presented to him.

Private First Class James Anderson Jr. was the first marine of African American heritage to win the Medal of Honor. Anderson was killed in

Vietnam when he snatched an enemy grenade that had landed in the midst of his comrades and smothered it with his body. His parents, Mr. and Mrs. James Anderson Sr., received the medal for their son.

Mr. and Mrs. George P. Singleton of Memphis, Tennessee, alternately held hands or wiped tears from their eyes as I spoke about their son, Marine Sgt. Walter K. Singleton, killed in action in Vietnam. Singleton left a relatively safe position in the rear and moved to the forward point of the attack where he repeatedly dragged men out of danger. Then he grabbed a machine gun and fired at the enemy concentration before losing his life.

Lance Cpl. Roy M. Wheat was another marine who hurled himself on an explosive to save his comrades. The most poignant moment in the award ceremony was when the mother of the dead marine hugged Cpl. Vernon Sorenson of Albany, California, one of the two marines her son had saved.

Mrs. Janice Graham, the widow of Marine Capt. James A. Graham of Forestville, Maryland, received her husband's Medal of Honor. Graham died in Vietnam while commanding a company under intense fire. Though wounded, he accounted for fifteen enemy killed. When his marines ran out of ammunition, Graham ordered them to withdraw while he remained with one man too seriously wounded to be moved. He died when twenty-five enemy troops assaulted his position.

Another marine, Private First Class Gary M. Martini, received the medal posthumously for braving enemy fire to pull two wounded comrades to safety. The men he saved, Sgt. David G. Messer and Lance Cpl. William R. Boudreau, attended the ceremony. Martini was seriously wounded when he saved the first man. Then he returned through enemy fire to save the second one, dying from his wounds before he himself could be saved. His parents, Mr. and Mrs. William M. Martini of Charleston, West Virginia, received the award.

Twenty-year-old Private First Class Douglas E. Dickey's Marine Corps' unit was pinned down by enemy gunfire. Someone yelled "Grenade!" and Dickey dived onto the explosive, saving the lives of four fellow marines. His parents, Mr. and Mrs. Harold Dickey of Rossburg, Ohio, were presented with the medal.

Despite murderous enemy gunfire, Marine Corps Lt. John P. Bobo of Niagara Falls, New York, organized a hasty defense, inspiring his out-numbered comrades. When an enemy mortar blew away his right leg below the knee, he refused evacuation. He was mortally wounded while firing his weapon into the main point of the attack. His parents, Mr. and Mrs. Paul A. Bobo, received the medal on behalf of their dead son.

Navy Seaman David G. Oullet's parents, Mr. and Mrs. Chester J. Oullet of Wellesley, Massachusetts, received his Medal of Honor, which was awarded to him for saving the lives of his shipmates. Oullet was a forward machine gunner on a patrol boat on the Mekong River. An enemy grenade landed toward the stern of the boat. He raced the full length of the speeding ship, shouting to the others to take cover, and then absorbed the exploding grenade with his own body.

A Navy chaplain, Lt. Vincent R. Capodonno of Staten Island, New York, received the congressional medal posthumously for comforting wounded marines under heavy enemy fire. He went from man to man, ministering to each of them, then ran to a wounded medical corpsman in the direct line of fire, making the ultimate sacrifice. His brother James received the medal. Father Capodonno was the second chaplain to receive the Medal of Honor in the Vietnam War and the sixth in U.S. military history.

The Vietnam War

More than fifty-eight thousand Americans were killed in the Vietnam War and many, many others were wounded, physically and psycholog-ically. Not all of them were self-sacrificing heroes like the Medal of Honor winners. All those who fought there, willingly or unwillingly, merit the nation's compassion and respect. "He deserved a better war," Robert Shaplen said of Gen. Creighton Abrams in a 1969 *New Yorker* article. So did the soldiers, sailors, airmen, and marines of Amer-ica's longest war.

When President Kennedy decided in 1961 to increase the number of U.S. military advisors to assist the South Vietnamese, I thought he did the right thing. We had stood by while Laos slid into uncertain circumstances. Vietnam was different. It wasn't a landlocked place like Laos, and its people seemed more willing to make war than the Laotians, who were supposed to prefer making love. There was also a general agreement among administration and congressional leaders that unless we took a stand in Vietnam, Southeast Asian countries such as Thailand and Cambodia, and perhaps even the Philippines, would fall like dominoes. The new form of warfare was below the threshold of more familiar wars like Korea, where an aggressor invaded another country. Now, wars of national liberation were the preferred method for overthrowing governments, with small-unit guerrilla actions replacing battles between regiments. The U.S. special forces—the Green Berets—were trained and equipped for this new kind of warfare, and Vietnam was a likely place to employ them.

Vietnam occurred in the context of the Cold War, the forty-year struggle to contain communist expansion and to deter the Soviet Union from general war. We mounted a sustained, comprehensive, and successful effort using military power, economic influence, diplomacy, and the dark arts of covert action. We were fighting against an ideological enemy—Communism—and blocking a major power that had massive conventional forces along with nuclear weapons aimed at the United States.

Domestic issues influence international events, and the Democrats were sensitive to the Republican charge that they had "lost" China to the Communists. President Kennedy didn't want to lose another country to communism. That is why he opposed Fidel Castro in Cuba and Ho Chi Minh in Vietnam. "We will pay any price, bear any burden," President Kennedy had said in his inaugural address. The press, the Congress, and the American people overwhelmingly approved his actions to prevent a Communist takeover in Vietnam.

In the early stages of the Vietnam War—from 1961 through 1964— I had no troubling thoughts about what we were doing. I was absorbed in my work helping to reorganize Army logistics and to improve the management of the business functions of defense—procurement, supply, maintenance, and transportation. I remember once asking at an

Army policy council meeting why *their* Vietnamese seemed to be fighting with greater commitment than *our* Vietnamese, but I never went much beyond that.

When we began to deploy large numbers of combat units in 1965, I was so caught up with the responsibility of ensuring that they were adequately supported that I seldom thought about fundamental questions of why we were there. By the time of the Tet offensive, as I said earlier, I questioned the wisdom of sending larger numbers of U.S. troops to what had become an American war, not a war where Americans were helping the South Vietnamese to fight their war. Clark Clifford performed a valuable public service, I thought, when he encouraged President Johnson to seek a diplomatic solution to the conflict.

As 1968 was drawing to a close and my career in government was coming to an end, I looked expectantly at the peace talks struggling to get under way in Paris. I hoped that ambassador Averell Harriman and Cyrus Vance, the leaders of the U.S. side, would find a way to bring the long war to an honorable conclusion.

Time to Go

In a close race, Hubert Humphrey, the Democrat, lost to the Republican, Richard Nixon. The final weeks of President Johnson's administration concentrated on getting the peace talks started and on internal arguments over whether a halt in U.S. bombing would speed a negotiated settlement. The talks in Paris were hampered by procedural difficulties among Hanoi, Saigon, and Washington. The parties seemed unable to agree on the shape of the table and on who should sit where. Additionally, the Saigon government was stalling, presumably in the belief that it could get a better deal with the new president than with the departing Johnson. LBJ was insistent that the talks begin in earnest before Inauguration Day, January 20. The South Vietnamese continued to stall until January 25, when a formal meeting was finally scheduled. By this time, Ambassador Harriman had said good-bye and been replaced by Henry Cabot Lodge Jr., a prominent Republican who had been ambassador to South Vietnam from 1963 to 1967.

My last few days were largely spent perusing the many interesting jobs that came my way. The usual parties and pleasantries took place at term's end. Admiral Moorer gave me the Navy's Distinguished Public Service Award, and I reciprocated by awarding Distinguished Service Medals to him and to the commandant, General Chapman. Moorer and I were a good example of how two quite different people can unite in a common cause—in this case, furthering the interests of the United States Navy. Moorer was an intensely conservative person and I wasn't, but we didn't let our differences get in the way of accomplishing our shared purposes. Moorer acknowledged this in a laudatory letter he sent to me on my departure. He was most impressed with the many new programs for which we had obtained approval. They included the LHA, an amphibious assault ship; the *Los Angeles*–class attack submarine; the electric submarine; a new antisubmarine attack plane, the S-3; a new fighter, the F-14; and the additional nuclear-powered frigates.

Nan and I had scheduled a three-week vacation in the Caribbean starting immediately after President Nixon's inauguration. We had taken very little time off in the previous eight years and were looking forward to the sun and sandy beaches of St. John and St. Croix. A phone call caused a delay. Melvin Laird, the new secretary of defense, asked me to stay on for several more weeks. The new Navy secretary, John Chafee, had been a late selection, and unless I remained for a while, he wouldn't have the benefit of an orderly transition. Chafee had called me from Providence, where he had been governor of Rhode Island, before accepting the Navy offer, and I took an instant liking to him. He was serious-minded but had a nice sense of humor. I wanted to help if I could and agreed to stay on with him for one week. That was time enough because he could then lean on the knowledgeable Sally Moser who would remain at her desk as his secretary. One of my last and most pleasant duties was giving her the Navy's Superior Civilian Service Award.

My wife had enjoyed her time with the Navy as much as I had. She participated in the many social activities and wrote a couple of articles for Navy journals. She also found the time to work on a master's degree in international relations at American University. She helped me every step of the way, especially one evening when I came home angry and sullen over something that had gone wrong during the day. She listened to me complain at inordinate length, and when I finished she said, "But remember, you're entitled to a nineteen-gun salute."

Seven

Troubled Waters

A NUMBER OF INTERESTING CAREER OPPORTUNITIES OPENED UP when my government service ended. Of the several offers, I chose the one that turned out to be a painful experience for me and for my employer, the Washington Post Company.

Not unexpectedly, companies that produced defense hardware expressed an interest in hiring me. One of them, Boeing, was the world's leading manufacturer of commercial airplanes and an important defense contractor. Its CEO, Bill Allen, was a man I knew and respected. Allen said he wanted me to join Boeing in a high-level position. I liked the idea of working with Bill but never followed up on his proposal because I believed someone with an engineering background was better suited to be a leader at Boeing. Allen pointed out that he was a lawyer, but I thought he was a special case.

William Miller, the chief executive of Textron, had been a lawyer at the Cravath firm in New York before moving to Providence, Rhode Island, to head the first and one of the most successful conglomerates. Textron made a variety of products for the civilian market but also owned Bell Aircraft, manufacturer of the UH-1 Huey helicopter. Miller said he wanted to leave Textron at some point, that he regarded me as a candidate to succeed him, and that meanwhile I should get started by heading Bell Aircraft. I gave serious thought to his offer, visited the company, and looked for possible places to live in the Providence area. I decided against Miller's proposal because after so many years on the government's side of the table, I knew I would feel uncomfortable on the contractor's side. Miller later became secretary of the treasury during the Carter administration.

Ben Heineman was the head of Burlington and Northern in Chicago. Though principally a railroad company, it had broadened its interests under Heineman's dynamic leadership. He came to Washington to spend a day with me. He wanted to devote his time to diversifying the company and proposed that I take over day-to-day operations. The two of us got along easily, and I was tempted by his offer.

Gordon Richardson (later, Sir Gordon Richardson, head of the Bank of England) was in charge of J. Henry Schroeder-Wag Ltd., the venerable London merchant bank. He wanted to make Schroeder's a more imposing presence in the United States and thought the way to do this was with the three Pauls—Nitze, Warnke, and Ignatius. Nitze would work part time on strategic issues, Warnke would handle international matters, and I would run the operation from New York. Gordon offered me all that I might want in salary, living arrangements, and fringe benefits. Nitze was enthusiastic about the concept, but Warnke had already decided to form a law firm with Clark Clifford. I put the Schroeder proposal high on the list, along with the Heineman offer.

Bill McCormick wanted me to join Cresap, McCormick and Paget, the management consulting firm where Tom Morris had worked. He made an intriguing offer. I could live in the United States or abroad, work on projects that interested me, and expect to be compensated at a high level. There were two drawbacks from my point of view. First, I didn't want to be away from home for long periods, a necessity in management consulting work. Second, I had found from my government experience that I liked being in charge of something, as opposed to playing the consultant's role of giving advice.

In addition to these solid proposals, there were several "feelers" that never led to valid offers. Among them was a meeting with John Rockefeller in New York about the position of head of the Lincoln Center for the Performing Arts and a discussion with Charles Luce about joining him at Consolidated Edison, the large New York public utility. Finally, there was the Washington Post Company, not a "feeler" but a serious proposition from the first encounter.

John Sweeterman, who had recently announced his retirement, made the initial contact. A tall, serious, somewhat humorless person, he had been hired from the *Dayton Journal-Herald* to be the *Post*'s business manager, and eventually became the publisher. Sweeterman seemed mainly interested in whether someone who had dealt with national security matters would be happy soliciting ads from local department stores.

Next, there were meetings in Washington and New York with Frederick S. "Fritz" Beebe. He had been the lawyer from the Cravath firm who handled the details when publisher Philip Graham acquired *Newsweek* for the Washington Post Company. When the transaction was completed, Graham asked Beebe to leave the law firm and become chairman of the board of the Washington Post Company, while looking after *Newsweek* from New York. Beebe was one of the most appealing people I had ever met. He was warm, funny, urbane, and smart, with a merry face and a generous waistline accommodated by expert tailoring. He smoked Don Diego cigars and gave me one at our first encounter and at the others that followed. Beebe was impressed by my record in government and said he thought I would bring modern management to the company.

Finally, I met with Katharine (Kay) Graham at her home in Georgetown. She was the daughter of Eugene Meyer, the wealthy industrialist and banker who had bought the paper at auction in 1933, and the widow of Philip Graham, the brilliant *Post* publisher who died by his own hand in 1963. Kay was tall, tastefully dressed, wore a long gold necklace, and spoke with a curious combination of hesitancy and certainty. She said she was ready to hire me. When I mentioned one or two things I wanted clarified, she told me "not to pick the lint off the offer." She had gone to her close friend Bob McNamara for suggestions on people to consider for the Sweeterman position, and he had enthusiastically recommended me. I suspect Bob's judgment was uppermost in her mind when she asked me to become president of the

Washington Post and executive vice-president of the Washington Post Company.

The details were handled in later meetings with Fritz Beebe. We agreed on terms that included a salary of $125,000, of which $25,000 was deferred until retirement, a year's pay if my employment was terminated, membership on the board of directors, a car and a driver, and a grant of twelve thousand shares of *Washington Post* stock that would become mine progressively over a ten-year period. He suggested that the eminent lawyer Lloyd Cutler draw up the formal contract.

I learned from my conversations with Fritz that in addition to the newspaper and *Newsweek*, the Washington Post Company owned three television stations as well as radio stations in Washington, D.C., and Cincinnati. The company also owned 49 percent of Bowaters Mersey, a paper mill in Nova Scotia that was the major supplier of the *Post*'s newsprint.

The newspaper was the flagship of the company. It employed around two thousand people, most of whom were represented by eleven labor unions under collective bargaining agreements. Weekday circulation was about 500,000, with Sunday copies around 650,000. It ranked fifth among U.S. newspapers in the amount of its advertising revenue.

Fritz told me a lot about Katharine Graham. He was extremely fond of her and valued her friendship. He had known her and her late husband for many years and had served as the family lawyer for the Grahams and for Kay's parents, the Meyers. He said Kay had gotten back on her feet after the shock of her husband's suicide. She was determined to play a major role in the paper and the company as a whole, but had known nothing about business management. She was learning fast, he said, and had great curiosity about everything and a fine mind. She had decided that she wanted the title of publisher, and that was why my title would be president. Then he said, off-handedly, almost as an aside, that I should let him know if I thought Kay was about to do something that seemed questionable from a business standpoint. His remark took me by surprise and I wasn't sure what to make of it. Perhaps it was simply an observation that, as one trained in business administration, I should keep an eye on someone just beginning to find her way in the business world. Maybe he was intimating that he was the ultimate authority, even though neither he nor Kay had specified which of them was the chief executive. Whatever the reason, I tended to think that Fritz, not Kay, was my boss. It was a mistake.

I accepted the *Post* offer over the others for many reasons. First, it was a distinguished newspaper that covered the city, the country, and the nations of the world. Though it was an "independent" voice, it was regarded by most people as being on the liberal side, in keeping with my own predilections. (My conservative partner in running the Navy, Adm. Tom Moorer, stared at me in disbelief when I told him of my decision.) The newspaper business was an exciting one with some of the characteristics of the public service that had meant so much to me. Beebe was a high-minded type of person like Vance, Nitze, McNamara, and others at the Pentagon, and it appeared that I would be working closely with him. Not least, the job was in Washington. My family had become rooted in the city over the past eight years. Nan was busy with many worthwhile activities at the Washington National Cathedral and at St. Albans, the school both our sons attended. Sarah and Amy were at fine girls' schools in the city. I had many friends for tennis games and social occasions. For all these reasons, the *Post* was the job for me, and I approached it with eagerness and high expectations.

Building Relationships

I couldn't have asked for a more cordial introduction to the newspaper business when I began work in March 1969. Fritz and Kay announced that I was a "proven executive after eight years in top Pentagon jobs and eleven years running a management consulting company. We needed just such a man." Kay gave me a tour of the premises and introduced me to the editors. Ben Bradlee had only recently moved into the top slot of executive editor, and he was happy to have someone on board who had served in the Navy, as he had, and had worked for the president, John F. Kennedy, whom he admired above all others.

My immediate priority, Fritz said, should be to review the new building project and recommend what should be done. The *Post* was running out of production capacity to produce enough newspapers to meet its growing circulation. A contract had been awarded to the distinguished architect I. M. Pei to design a new building. The design work was far behind schedule and the cost estimates for the building kept rising. Both Kay and Fritz were afraid the project might jeopardize the company's financial stability. Meanwhile, expensive new presses were sitting in a warehouse in Virginia.

Kay wanted to give the city of Washington a memorable architectural landmark. I. M. Pei had designed the striking new East Wing of the Mellon Art Gallery and the Kennedy Library in Boston. Although justly famous for his elegant buildings, Pei had limited experience with structures like a newspaper plant, a manufacturing facility with the systems and equipment for producing hundreds of thousands of newspapers every day, seven days a week. Pei's office lacked the needed engineering experience and depended on outside consultants for technical assistance. In addition, Pei's design was complex, with a cantilevered observation deck and other innovative features. The delay in completing the design, the emerging production shortage, and the money tied up in the stored presses caused much concern.

When I dug into the details, I found that in 1965 the paper had considered a plan to enlarge its present building rather than construct a new one. The plan had been developed by Detroit architect Sol King, who was noted for industrial plants. I studied the plan carefully, concentrating on its ability to meet the growing production requirements. It appeared to provide enough capacity to meet the paper's needs for a ten-year period, that is, until about 1980. Future growth could be accommodated by enlarging the main plant or by building satellite plants in Maryland and northern Virginia, where circulation was growing more rapidly than in the central city. By managing the project on an accelerated basis, with concurrent design and construction—the technique we had followed for critical military needs—the entire task could be completed in two years. Our cost studies showed that we could bring it in for $25 million, compared with at least $42 million for the Pei building.

In July, after completing the review, I submitted a detailed memorandum to Fritz Beebe that compared the Pei building with the alternative plan, and showed how daily and Sunday production needs would be met. The key management, production, and circulation officials at the paper unanimously preferred the alternative plan. I recommended that it be adopted.

After studying the memorandum and discussing it with Kay and me, Fritz gave his approval. Kay went along with the decision but was disappointed not to be able to leave the city with an architectural monument. Instead, there would be a serviceable but undistinguished building facing on 15th Street. She was relieved, however, that the alternative plan would save a substantial amount of money and meet the urgent need for new capacity.

It remained for Fritz and me to face the painful task of informing Pei of our decision. We met at Pei's offices in New York, and Fritz explained why it was necessary to terminate his work. We had reimbursed Pei for $1.3 million of his $2 million fee, and would owe him an additional $400,000 in termination charges.

The new architect said our twenty-four-month schedule for design and construction was the tightest one he had seen since building war plants in the 1940s. A construction contract was awarded to a Washington firm that eventually became the Clark Construction Company, one of the nation's largest and most accomplished builders of commercial properties. The project boss was young Jim Clark, his first time out as the man in charge of a major program. I organized a project office like the ones we used for urgent military programs. Each week, all the parties—construction contractor, subcontractors, equipment suppliers, and *Post* production personnel—met in my office. Potential delays were identified, solutions developed, and responsibilities assigned. One of the most critical needs was assuring that construction did not interfere with daily production of the newspaper. The situation was not unlike that of a busy airport where airplanes take off and land while new runways and terminals are being built.

Having seen how useful helicopters had been for supply missions in Vietnam, I insisted on a capability to operate helicopters from the roof of the building. It turned out to be a valuable asset several years later when the *Post* was embattled with its striking pressmen and struggling to produce a paper despite the angry picket lines surrounding the building. Helicopters delivered page proofs to outlying printing plants and enabled technicians to enter the building without confronting the pickets.

The building was completed on time and at the initial cost estimates at the end of 1971. I give a lot of the credit to Jim Clark and to the *Post* technical personnel who worked closely with the contractor and the equipment suppliers.

The Newspaper Business

Although the building project was my immediate priority, I was hired, after all, to run the business side of a great newspaper, not to oversee a construction job. I began to learn as much as I could about the business. Newspapers were in a period of intense technological innovation after decades of reliance on familiar production processes. The electronics revolution was changing the newspaper industry along with the other sectors of the U.S. economy. Its impact on newspapers was particularly severe because the new technologies were upsetting the traditional jurisdictions of the solidly entrenched labor unions, each guarding its own turf.

The rapidly changing technology was similar to what had occurred in newspapers after the Civil War, when the stereotype process, the linotype machine, photoengraving, and the web press—the fundamental production processes—were introduced. These techniques, revolutionary in their day, had replaced the handset type. For roughly six decades, from around 1890 to the middle 1950s, there were no significant changes in the post–Civil War technology. Now a quick walk through the *Post* composing room showed what was beginning to happen. Next to a linotype machine turning out several lines of print a minute were tape-fed linotypes turning out 10 lines, a Photon producing 30 lines, and Linotron 505s churning out 150. Nearby were IBM computers that tidied things up with hyphenated and justified formats along with a correction routine. And these were just the beginning of what was in store. Automation of the composing room, which had already occurred at some papers, promised gains that dwarfed those represented by the Linotron over the linotype.

In June 1970, I was invited to make the keynote address on production technology at a meeting of the Research Institute of the American Newspaper Publishers Association. For the executives in the audience, I posed some of the questions that faced us at the *Post* and at other papers: How fast should we move into the promising new world? Who in the managerial ranks should direct the effort? How could we be sure that the anticipated savings would be realized?

It was easier to pose questions than to find the right answers. The *Post* had moved slowly in adopting the new technology compared with many newspapers that had progressed from "hot lead" to "cold type." Even the *Washington Star,* running second to the *Post* in advertising, circulation, and influence, was ahead of it in the application of the new processes.

With all this in mind, we joined several other newspapers in an IBM study of the newspaper of the future. It anticipated a bold leap from where we were to a full-page composition system driven by computers that linked the editorial desks to the production equipment, in short, the entire publishing process. It was too big a jump for us at the *Post.* Our management, including me, didn't know enough to make intelligent judgments about so major a change. Additionally, it was not at all clear how we would handle the certain opposition of the labor unions to techniques that eliminated many jobs and substantially altered others. Until we knew more and could persuade the unions to

accept the inevitability of technological change, it was better to proceed with caution rather than attempt a fundamental makeover of the
business.

Business Management at the *Post*

Fritz and Kay had told me at the beginning that the *Post* needed more
modern management. The management team had been put in place by
John Sweeterman, and he had run a tight ship, making decisions with
little interference from Phil Graham, and after his death, from Kay.
Like Sweeterman, the *Post* managers were experienced newspaper
people. The general manager, Jim Daly, was a Sweeterman favorite
who had been promoted from the advertising department. Joe Lynch,
the advertising director, was a good businessman who met or exceeded
his departmental goals. Production of the paper was in the hands of
"Bud" Eberle. The new building occupied much of Eberle's time,
diverting his attention from the problems of getting out the paper each
day. Circulation was handled by a real pro, Harry Gladstein. Nobody
ever second-guessed Gladstein because he never failed to increase circulation, even when the price of the paper was raised. Labor relations
were Larry Kennelly's responsibility. He and Daly tended to accommodate union demands in order to avoid a strike and depended
unduly on input from union leaders in formulating *Post* negotiating
objectives.

It soon became apparent that some management changes were
needed. Daly, like Eberle, was overburdened and needed someone to
help get out the paper on time. Personnel administration, including
employee communications, was a barren area without clear direction.
There was a respected treasurer who concentrated on companywide
finances but no one to devote full time to the comptroller functions of
budgeting, accounting, and cost studies. Finally, the organization
needed to become more formalized, with everyone's responsibilities
clearly defined.

Kay and I talked often about individual managers and her well-founded belief that more forceful leadership was required to deal with the increasingly assertive unions. There were slowdowns in the composing room and unexplained breakdowns in the pressroom. When she blamed Eberle, for example, when a production deadline was missed, I would explain how important he was for getting the new production equipment installed. She correctly put her finger on the sorry state of labor relations, but I said much more was needed than simply sacking Larry Kennelly. When she expressed dissatisfaction with Joe Lynch, I showed her data on our growing advertising revenues. Our meetings were becoming argumentative, and I am sure she thought I was too anxious to defend our managers.

Within a few months, we brought in the new people we needed. *Newsweek* made available a Wharton School graduate to be our comptroller. We hired a personnel director who immediately went to work on employee relations and a training program for company foremen. A man from a smaller newspaper was hired as Daly's assistant for production control. A new organization chart was issued that put Daly in charge of operations, with advertising, promotion, and personnel administration reporting to me.

The *Post* managers were more secure in their jobs when they worked for John Sweeterman. He was a tough, experienced newspaperman who brooked no interference from anyone. With me, it was a different ball game. I hadn't grown up in the newspaper business. I was close to Kay and Fritz. The managers weren't sure whether I was there to lead and support them or to get rid of them. There were times, in all honesty, when I wasn't sure myself.

My most difficult moments were when Eberle or Lynch complained to me about Kay. They said she criticized them on the basis of comments from people outside the paper or from employees in their departments. Her concerns were well meaning, part of her desire to learn about the business side of the paper and to improve it, but the unintended effect was increased self-doubt for managers already uncertain of their status. Kay acknowledged the problem in her

Pulitzer Prize–winning autobiography, *Personal History:* "What people really need is rational, logical leadership, but when I had to decide something I asked the advice of everyone I could, often irritating those closest to me, who felt, understandably, that I should trust their judgment."

I handled one of these situations quite poorly when Kay criticized Daly and said the *Star* was doing a better job than we were. I jumped to Daly's defense and offended her by the vigor of my response. Incidents like this prompted her to send me a revealing hand-written note. I reproduce portions of it here because it portrays what was becoming a serious problem for me—a failure to get along comfortably with the proud and forceful woman who owned the paper:

> What I want to say is this. I believe very much in what you are doing and how you are doing it. I also have a strong feeling that life is too short for people not to enjoy working—to really have fun at it. When problems are big and tough, as this one is, it's more important, therefore, to enjoy doing it together. There is nothing worse in the world than going home in the evening feeling you have been lying on a bed of nails all day.
>
> An old friend of mine had a variety of slogans for different circumstances, one of which was "shut up and be attractive." I will embroider this on my new white walls for the future.
>
> Don't answer this. It doesn't need any until we see it in action.

Social Notes from All Over

Katharine Graham was Washington's most prominent hostess. She entertained frequently at her spacious house in Georgetown, mixing government officials, media celebrities, society matrons, and business leaders at her receptions and dinners. She included Nan and me in many of these gatherings.

Kay always included her top editors and columnists in her guest lists—Ben Bradlee, Joe Alsop, Rowland Evans, Art Buchwald—so they could exchange views with her business and government guests. On one occasion, Kay gave a dinner for the incoming and outgoing British ambassadors and for Walter Annenberg, the newly appointed U.S. ambassador to the Court of St. James. After dinner, Rowland Evans and I got into a conversation with Annenberg. Rowly said he had heard rumors that Annenberg had also been considered for secretary of the Navy. "What," Annenberg said, "me take that errand-boy job!" Annenberg wasn't sure who I was, so Rowly obligingly introduced me as the former secretary of the Navy.

Lyndon Johnson was the star attraction at another of Kay's dinners. Her late husband, Phil Graham, had helped Johnson become vice president by supporting his candidacy in influential political circles, from which position he had become president after John Kennedy's assassination. Nobody was duller on television or more animated in person than President Johnson. He flirted with Kay and dominated the conversation in the dining and drawing rooms. Johnson was one of many presidents who dined at Kay's house. She also knew foreign leaders. Fritz Beebe told me that once when he and Kay were in Mexico, she showed up late for a meeting with him, explaining that she had stayed too long at an impromptu breakfast with her good friend, the president of Mexico.

Early on, Kay invited me occasionally to share a meal with her at her house on R Street. She told me a lot about her family and the difficulties of growing up under Agnes Meyer, the demanding mother she could never seem to please. Many of the things she said were later described in *Personal History*. I saw at first hand what she had been up against at a luncheon at her mother's splendid mansion near 16th Street. Informed people like the columnist Joe Kraft were also guests, but Mrs. Meyer had the last word on every subject. When the conversation turned to China, Nan, who had just received an MA with a thesis on Chinese diplomatic history, spoke up. Mrs. Meyer interrupted her and quickly summoned a maid to fetch one of her priceless Shang bronzes. She said it was she who interested Charles Freer in collecting the Chinese art that is now the pride of the Smithsonian's Freer Gallery. When I told Kay about this, she laughed and said her mother had a good head for value. "When Pa was buying copper mines in South America," she said, "Ma was buying Cézannes."

Toward the end of my first year at the *Post*, in January 1970, Kay and Fritz thought I should make a trip to Europe to visit the *Post* and *Newsweek* bureaus and to get to know the foreign correspondents. They also thought I should meet with the press lords in England and the leading publishers in France and Germany. Kay was on good terms with all of them and sent letters ahead introducing Nan and me. Fritz wrote the *Newsweek* people, explaining that, as a member of the board of directors, it would be useful for me to gain a better understanding of the magazine's overseas operations. We had meetings, lunches, or dinners in London with the *Daily Telegraph, Financial Times, Guardian, Observer,* and the *Economist.* There was also a lunch with Sir Martin Ritchie, chairman of Bowater's, co-owners with the *Post* of the newsprint mill in Nova Scotia. Everyone wanted to know about Kay. They also wanted to hear what I, as a newcomer to the business, had to say. I talked mostly about the new technology and the difficulties with the trade unions.

The merry-go-round continued in Paris with discussions at *France Soir* and *L'Express.* There was more shoptalk at the *International Herald Tribune,* owned jointly by the *Post,* the *New York Times,* and Whitney Communications, where my son, David, incidentally, later became the executive editor. Gen. Fred Weyand, a good friend from Pentagon days, was in Paris as a member of the U.S. delegation to the Vietnam peace negotiations, and he and his colleague from the State Department, Phil Habib, joined Nan and me for dinner. Fred said that Phil knew the Vietnamese so well that he could tell what they were going to say just by watching when they tapped their feet or drummed their fingers. Another pleasant experience was lunch with U.S. ambassador Sargent Shriver.

After Paris, we went to Bonn for discussions with bureau chiefs and correspondents about cost and personnel matters and relationships with the host countries. Then on to Geneva where we were met by Arnaud de Borchgrave, *Newsweek*'s colorful foreign correspondent.

Nan and I had always felt a sense of impermanence during my years in government, not knowing for sure where we would live when those years came to an end. Now that we were here to stay, we started doing things that Washingtonians did. The Chevy Chase Club was nearby and in time we became members. I agreed to join the Federal City Council, a business group started by Phil Graham to assist local government to accomplish needed community improvements. Nan became more involved with work at the Washington National Cathedral. She also formed an environmental group, Concern, Inc., with four other women, and served as its president for many years. Concern led the way in promoting activities that are now commonplace, like recycling waste and avoiding environmentally harmful consumer products. Our kids had attended private schools in Washington, after six years of public schooling, and were now in college—David at Harvard, Sarah at Stanford, Amy at Oberlin and then Wisconsin, and Adi soon to enter Haverford.

Many of our friends had second homes in nearby Maryland, Virginia, or West Virginia for weekends or vacations. Kay had a fine place in The Plains, near Middleburg, Virginia. Ben Bradlee had a mountain cabin in West Virginia, and John Sweeterman had a beach house in Rehoboth. Our good friends Russ and Aileen Train had a farm on the eastern shore of Maryland, and Steve and Nellie Ailes spent weekends at their farm near Martinsburg, West Virginia. As guests of the Aileses one weekend in the summer of 1970, we learned that a farm called Spring Hill, fifteen miles away in Bunker Hill, was for sale. For seven generations, it had been owned by the Henshaw family. Much of the original land had been sold, but sixty-five acres remained, with three barns, a smokehouse, and a springhouse. The large main house was built in 1785. Mill Creek, in front of the main house, had provided water power for generating electricity, and the old waterwheel was still in place. We fell in love with the farm and purchased it within a week for $55,000.

Spring Hill farm was only eighty miles from Washington, and we spent weekends there whenever we could. After a few months, we started a small "cow and calf" operation with a Hereford bull and some cows. We had horses for the kids and me to ride, and we built a tennis court. I installed a hotline directly to the *Post* so that I could keep in touch.

Kay worried when I bought the farm because she recognized, quite rightly, that I would want to spend weekends there rather than in Washington dealing with problems with Sunday production, which was becoming more erratic. After eight years of punishing time demands at the Pentagon, where personal and family interests had to be subordinated to national security needs, I thought that I owed my family and myself the pleasures the farm offered. We enjoyed it for almost thirty years, finally selling it to a local physician.

Labor Problems

The labor situation at the *Post* was a complex and difficult business challenge. Although I made some progress in bringing it under control, several years passed before it was fully solved. The first of many complications was the large number of unions, representing crafts such as typesetting, stereotyping, and engraving, and production areas such as the pressroom and the mailroom. Eight hundred employees, including most of those in the newsroom, were represented by the powerful American Newspaper Guild.

Each union controlled its jurisdictional area as a territorial imperative. In the composing room, for example, the printers would stop work immediately if an "outsider," including members of management, touched a piece of type. The atmosphere in the pressroom was sullen, and the pressmen found ways to delay the completion of pressruns when they wanted to show their opposition to something they disliked.

A further complication was the different termination dates of the labor contracts. This meant that the paper faced the possibility of a strike many times during the year, as each contract expired. It also encouraged competition among the unions, with each one striving to make a better settlement than the one before it.

Finally, the new printing technologies were threatening jurisdictional boundaries and job security. The unions were typically resistant to change, but when they thought their members' jobs were at risk, they dug in their heels even deeper.

Newspapers feared strikes because they were especially vulnerable targets. A company that made lightbulbs, for example, could ride out a strike for a period of time by selling bulbs from previously manufactured inventory. In the newspaper business a new product—today's newspaper hot off the presses—was created each day. There was no such thing as a previously printed stack of papers to cushion the cost of a strike. Moreover, the principal source of revenue was the advertising space the newspapers had for sale. If a paper was on strike, there was no space to sell. An ad unsold today could not be sold tomorrow; once gone, the revenue was gone forever. Moreover, during a strike advertisers could switch to other media, such as television or radio, and never come back to the paper after the strike ended.

Because strikes were so costly, *Post* management sought to avoid them. Often, this meant giving in to unwarranted demands, settling at higher than market rates, and accepting practices that inhibited management's ability to control costs. The union leaders, of course, knew this and were ready to take advantage of the situation when they thought it served their interests.

The labor situation was even worse in New York, where the *Times* and the other dailies struggled unsuccessfully to free themselves from the tyranny of union domination. In 1962, the International Typographical Union (ITU) led a 114-day strike against the *Times*, the *Daily News*, the *Journal-American*, and the *World Telegram & Sun*. As Susan E. Tifft and Alex S. Jones explain in *The Trust*, "The siege sounded the death knell for New York journalism. Within several years of the strike's conclusion, the number of newspapers in the city dwindled from seven to three—the *Times* and two tabloids, the *New York Post* and the *Daily News*."

Several years later, in 1970, the *Times* acceded to the ITU's costly demands in order to avoid the devastating impact of another strike. The *Times* had hoped to gain some leeway from the union to begin automating the composing room. The union won a huge wage increase without giving up an inch of its opposition to the new technologies.

"Bogus" Type in the Composing Room

At the *Post*, a battle with the ITU arose over a "make-work" practice called "reproduce" or "bogus."

The composing room was the place where the printers prepared the materials for the news and advertising columns. The ITU contract contained a clause on "reproduce" or "bogus," as it was also called. The reproduce clause was a job protection measure of many years' standing that the printers believed would enable them to keep working in the event of layoffs. The clause required that local advertisements run in a newspaper had to be set by the employees of that paper. If the mat for an ad was furnished by a department store, for example, and the *Post* put the mat into production, it had to reset or "reproduce" the ad even though there was no need for a new mat. It was a costly and wasteful practice.

The reproduce obligation at the *Post* had reached alarming levels during the 1960s. The paper was so busy handling its rapidly growing volume of ads that it was unable to keep up with the mindless task of reproducing unnecessary copy. In 1968, for example, it set only 780 pages of an obligation to set 4,066. The cumulative obligation by May 1970 was 17,814 pages. The other Washington papers were doing much better—the *Star* had no backlog at all, and the *News* was only a few pages behind.

The upcoming negotiations with the ITU in September 1970 offered an opportunity for getting rid of reproduce because the international union had decided to let its locals substitute beneficial contractual provisions in lieu of the reproduce clause. These provisions included such things as a shorter work week, unemployment benefits, and contributions to a pension fund or to an automation fund for training printers to handle computers, photocomposition equipment, and the other new technologies.

The automation fund appealed to me as a statesmanlike way to solve the reproduce problem. Working with the other two Washington papers, we began to develop a plan that we hoped might serve everyone's best interests. The printers faced a dismal future if all they could do was work on outmoded machinery. The publishers needed flexibility and labor support to reap the benefits of automation. The solution was to persuade the local to cancel the reproduce backlog in return for a $1 million contribution from the *Post* to form the Washington Printing and Technology Center. The center would be operated jointly by the ITU local and the publishers. The three papers would make annual contributions to meet the center's operating costs, estimated to be $500,000 a year. The concept would facilitate the transition from the old world of hot lead to the new world of cold type, protecting the printers from technological obsolescence and enabling the publishers to run a more profitable operation.

I worked hard to shape the terms of the proposal and to sell it to the ITU international, where I made good progress, and to the local, where the leaders were skeptical from the outset. The local traditionalists, in the end, clung to their view that the backlog would provide jobs in hard times. They simply weren't willing to give up their security blanket for a training center. An opportunity was lost and the wasteful practice continued for several more years.

A Common Expiration Date for Labor Contracts

During 1971, seven of the union contracts were due to expire between May and December. Each one could result in a work stoppage at great cost to the paper and to the union employees. Everyone would gain if the exposure to strikes were lessened. What was needed was a common expiration date and a common economic package for joint bargaining. A target date of October 1, 1972, was established for planning purposes.

The unions seemed as anxious as we were to reach a common date. Moreover, our research showed that the pay differentials among the various crafts had stayed fairly constant since 1952, so we thought a joint economic package was feasible. A precedent for what we had in mind was a joint settlement like the unions made with San Francisco newspapers, reached under the auspices of labor arbitrator Sam Kagel.

We invited Kagel to meet with us in Washington in April 1971. Kay, Fritz, and I, along with Jim Daly and Larry Kennelly, hammered out a schedule with Kagel's help for extending the craft contracts to October of the following year. We hoped to include the Newspaper Guild contract in our plan if Brian Flores, the local president, agreed. Daly and Kennelly were authorized to open discussions with the craft unions and Flores. There were weeks of detailed work ahead of us to extend the contracts, bring the Guild on board, and develop a common economic package. With Kagel's help, we thought we might succeed. It turned out that we were overly optimistic. Meanwhile, a new development occupied *Post* officials and the nation.

The Pentagon Papers

Katharine Graham has provided a full and fascinating account of the Pentagon Papers case in her autobiography, and there is little I can add except for a few personal touches. The affair took place in June 1971 at a time when the Washington Post Company had decided to go public and offer shares of its stock to investors.

The Pentagon Papers was the name given to the massive accumulation of sensitive documents on the Vietnam War assembled on the order of Robert McNamara. The project was cloaked in secrecy with only a few people knowing of its existence. (I was not one of them.) McNamara's purpose was to provide a complete record of decision-making on Vietnam for future historical analysis. The *New York Times* had surreptitiously obtained a copy of the sensitive material and, after due deliberation, decided to publish it. The first story appeared June 13. The government asked the *Times* to suspend publication and said it would seek an injunction against the paper if it refused. The *Times* declined. On June 16, the *Post* secretly obtained more than four thousand pages of the papers, and the editors, secluded at Ben Bradlee's house, were going through the pile of documents, preparing to publish their first story.

On the afternoon of June 17, Kay gave a farewell party at her house for Harry Gladstein, who had retired after a long career as the *Post*'s circulation and business manager. Beebe had flown down from New York to attend the party, but he was diverted to Bradlee's house nearby to meet with the editors and two of the *Post*'s lawyers. The editors insisted on publishing the material despite the temporary restraining order against the *Times*.

The lawyers opposed publication, certainly before a decision was reached on a preliminary injunction. Beebe sided with the lawyers. He was worried that the *Post*'s stock offering might be jeopardized if it appeared that the paper was defying a court order.

The phone rang at Kay's house just as she was offering a toast to Gladstein. I stood next to her as she talked to Bradlee. He said he and the other editors were determined to publish the story as an act of journalistic conscience. I told Kay more than once to wait a day for the decision on the injunction against the *Times*. When she asked Beebe if he thought the *Post* should publish, he said, "I guess I wouldn't." He said she would have to make the decision.

As she described the dramatic situation in her book, Kay took a big gulp of air and said: "Go ahead, go ahead, go ahead. Let's go. Let's publish." Then she hung up the phone and returned to the party.

The government filed suit against the *Post* as it had against the *Times*. After several more judicial proceedings, the case reached the Supreme Court on June 26. The government case was presented by the solicitor general, Erwin Griswold, the former dean of the Harvard Law School. Kay, Fritz, and I were among the many people in the crowded chamber. When the session ended, Fritz drove with me to our farm. We spent the evening going over the case and the responsibilities of newspapers as both private businesses and public institutions protected by the First Amendment. With us as fascinated participants was our son David and his girlfriend, both hoping to become journalists after college. Several days later, on June 30, the Supreme Court announced in a 6–3 decision that the government had failed to prove its case that continued publication would harm the security of the United States. It was a great victory for freedom of the press and a personal victory for Katharine Graham.

I talked recently with Tony Essaye, one of the *Post* lawyers at Bradlee's house who had opposed publication. I asked him how the case looked to him today, after the passage of more than thirty years. He said that from a legal standpoint the advice he had given was correct. From a broader public policy standpoint, he added, you could look at it differently. Then he asked what I thought. I said I had given Kay the correct business advice. "But she did the right thing," I said. "I'm certain in my mind about that."

I have thought a lot about why Katharine Graham went ahead in spite of both legal and business warnings. I think she reacted from the gut, like President Harry Truman when he was certain intuitively that he was doing the right thing. Her courageous decision to publish helped to make Ben Bradlee's dream a reality—that when U.S. newspapers were discussed, the *New York Times* and the *Washington Post* would be mentioned in the same breath.

I probably should have stayed out of the whole Pentagon Papers matter. My input wasn't all that important; the views of the lawyers and the editors carried more weight. After eight years in the Pentagon, I had a certain mind-set about the release of classified information. I couldn't help but wonder what my uniformed colleagues would have thought if I had urged publication in defiance of a court order. It was an uncomfortable position that I could have avoided by standing aside.

The Labor Situation Worsens

The problems with the printers grew more serious as the weeks went by. They delayed publication by misspelling words, slowing down work, or dumping type "accidentally" that had already been set. When foremen tried to discipline them, they threatened to stop work. Even worse, printers from other cities who had lost their jobs had to be hired at the *Post* because there was "work" to be done, namely, the pile of reproduce.

The pressmen, always hostile, resisted efforts by managers to penalize those found asleep on the job or those who had deliberately damaged newsprint to cause delays. The *Post*'s independent dealers, who handled delivery of the paper, had to wait in the alley, sometimes for hours, for bundles of papers to load onto their trucks. This problem had serious implications. The *Post* had never wanted to see the delivery of the paper in the hands of a union. If the delays continued, the dealers might seek relief by forming a circulation union.

Kay was desperate, Fritz was worried, and I was frustrated. The nagging reproduce problem had grown more serious over the years, but no one at the *Post* had paid much attention to it until I disclosed its full impact. Having identified the problem, I had been unable to solve it. I even equipped a special room just to work down the backlog, but the printers had no incentive to reset the old ads, and the backlog increased.

When I was a student in Professor Sumner Slichter's labor economics course at the Harvard Business School, I became acquainted with his young assistant, John Dunlop. In the intervening years, Dunlop had become a national authority on labor relations. I invited him to meet with Kay and me to discuss our problems at the *Post*. Dunlop emphasized what we already knew to be so true—there was an absence of effective communication between labor and management.

Dunlop was right about our long-term need for better communications, and we had begun efforts to improve our situation. In the meantime, we faced the immediate problem of unions that controlled the production of the paper and had the power to enforce their will. Beebe and I believed that we could redress the imbalance through more effective negotiating strategies and tougher bargaining. Neither of us gave serious thought to training nonunion employees to operate production equipment in order to keep going during a strike. Daly and Kennelly, the ones most directly responsible for dealing with the unions, preferred private meetings and private understandings with the union leaders to direct confrontation.

Kay had a better understanding than the rest of us of the true nature of the problem. She had learned from the experience in New York that repeated concessions to labor's unwarranted demands had emasculated management and led to the death of once great newspapers like the *New York Herald Tribune*. She wasn't sure how to do it, but she knew that the *Post* had to free itself from labor's control.

Our eyes were focused on the October 1972 deadline for negotiating a common economic package with the craft unions and the Guild. As the work went forward, I sensed that both Fritz and Kay were losing confidence in my ability to resolve the labor situation. I continued to work with and through Daly and Kennelly, but Fritz and Kay had little respect for either of them. Because I had been unable to come up with a solution to our problems, I thought the proper thing was to resign. I prepared a draft of a letter of resignation, but before I made a decision to submit it, Fritz asked to meet with me. He said it would be better for all of us if I were to resign. That was a polite way of saying that I was being fired. Kay joined us and said she was sorry it had come to this.

Fritz, with Lloyd Cutler as the lawyer for both the *Post* and me, prepared a termination agreement. In accordance with my contract, I was entitled to a year's pay. I had to turn in my twelve thousand shares of Washington Post Company stock, but I received a cash settlement for a portion of it. Kay quickly hired a newspaperman with a good record—John Prescott—to succeed me, and he started work on the first of January, 1972. I gave Kay a plan I had developed to meet future growth through production plants in Maryland and northern Virginia, and a set of objectives for the next year. Then we shook hands and said good-bye.

The *New York Times* had said in an article on August 5, 1967, that I "had the ability to solve any problem . . . that is quite rare in this town." That may or may not have been true at the time it was written, but it wasn't true on the day I left the *Post*. The unresolved labor problems were now in the hands of others.

Epilogue

The labor situation worsened over the next few years before *Post* management established its authority over the unions. John Prescott had to deal with a wildcat strike. His successor, Mark Meagher, oversaw the production of the newspaper by nonunion employees when the pressmen set fire to one press and damaged the others. Things began to improve when Meagher's successor, Richard Simmons, was hired. He and Kay worked together as partners and friends. Kay's oldest son, Donald Graham, joined the paper and was a steady and effective leader from the moment he came on board. Fritz Beebe died of cancer, but Warren Buffett appeared on the scene as Kay's confidant and wise business counselor. Ben Bradlee, the *Post*'s great editor, was succeeded by Leonard Downie but remains on hand as vice president at large. 'Bo' Jones, Donald Graham's close friend and the *Post*'s senior counsel, eventually became the publisher under Graham's overall leadership as the company's chief executive.

Kay and I remained on friendly terms, though I saw her only occasionally until her death in 2001. She had weathered the early storms in her struggle to become a successful executive and ended up as the most respected person in American journalism.

Eight

A New Flight Plan

Failing at something is difficult for anyone, but it is harder to bear for someone accustomed to success. Since boyhood, things had come easily to me, and I went from class presidencies in school and college to high positions in the government. To this day I think about what I might have done differently at the *Washington Post* and occasionally have troubling dreams about the experience.

Because I thought then and continue to believe that there were unusual circumstances at the newspaper not of my making and beyond my control, I didn't lose confidence in myself or in my ability to tackle a new assignment. Fortunately, prospective employers knocked at my door.

One of the first was Bill Miller, the head of Textron, who had wanted me to join his company at the end of my Pentagon career. He was as enthusiastic about my prospects with the firm as he had been earlier. Harry Hague asked me to return to Harbridge House, the company that he and Sterling Livingston and I had started in 1950. Peter Temple, who joined Harbridge House at my invitation and later founded a highly successful management consulting firm of his own, wanted me to join him in managing Temple, Barker, and Sloane.

While I was considering these and other possibilities, the president of the Air Transport Association (ATA), Stuart Tipton, called. He was looking for an executive vice president. My friend Steve Ailes had told him to get in touch with me.

ATA and hundreds of trade associations in the Washington area represented the chemical, petroleum, steel, and other U.S. industries in issues before the government. ATA was one of the largest, with several hundred highly qualified professionals who understood the complexities of aircraft engines, airport construction, air traffic control systems, and bilateral treaties that affected international aviation. The major U.S. air carriers and the two leading Canadian airlines made up its membership. Tipton had been ATA's general counsel for many years and succeeded to the presidency after two outsiders failed to provide effective leadership during their brief terms of office.

I had been in love with airplanes since boyhood. I'd seen Lindbergh at my hometown airport, rode in an early model Ford trimotor, and read thrillers like *Tom Swift and His Flying Machine* and Lucky Lindy's account of his solo flight to Paris. I also knew a lot about aircraft operations from my wartime experience with an air squadron and on an aircraft carrier, and from my consulting and government experience with the aircraft manufacturing industry. If I was hesitant about joining ATA, it was because of a belief that as a trade association official I would be spending all of my time roaming the halls of Congress looking for someone to lobby.

I decided to bring my concerns to a friend, John Gardner, one of the authentic wise men of the period. Gardner, the founder of Common Cause, the citizens' organization, had been secretary of health, education, and welfare under President Johnson, and he knew about the airlines from his experience as a director of one of the largest, American Airlines.

Gardner said most trade associations had rather narrow objectives that offered little in the way of intellectual challenge. ATA was different, he said, because the industry was regulated and ATA had to forge industry views on complex operational and safety issues. Additionally, the airlines were an indispensable element of the U.S. and world economy, and they depended on ATA for informing the public, the Congress, and the administration about matters that affected personal and business travel and the shipment of mail and commercial products. He said there was more than enough at ATA to keep the mind alive and encouraged me to pursue Tipton's initiative.

I met again with Tipton and this time the talk was mostly about congressional relationships and the need to make campaign contributions in order to assure access to influential political figures. Talk like this made me apprehensive, so I decided to consult with my lawyer, Lloyd Cutler. Like Gardner, Cutler knew the airline industry from years of representing airline clients. Cutler told me that ATA was an important organization that would offer a real challenge. I said my only concern was whether I would face compromising questions about congressional fund-raising. "Don't worry about the political aspects of the job," he said. "Do what you always did in the government, and stay away from anything that raises an ethical question in your mind."

With Cutler's and Gardner's encouragement, I decided that I wanted the ATA job and got down to details with Tipton. He said the starting salary would be $75,000, and that I could count on periodic increases. In addition to the usual pension and health benefits, I would have what amounted to a lifetime pass to ride free on the airlines. He offered me the job contingent on the approval of ATA's executive committee.

The half dozen or so committee members were airline chief executives. Two of them—Edward Carlson, the newly appointed head of United, and Harding Lawrence, the Braniff CEO—were unable to attend the meeting. With the others I had a full and cordial discussion, and at the end of it they welcomed me as the new executive vice president. I thanked them but said I wanted to meet with both Carlson and Lawrence to make sure that they also wanted me. There was some risk in this since I had already been offered the job, but I thought it was important to have the support of the full committee.

The meetings with the two airline chiefs illustrated how different individual airline executives could be. Eddie Carlson was folksy, without ego, a highly competent hotel executive who had begun his career as an elevator boy. As a member of United's board of directors, he was asked to take over the leadership of the airline when the prior chief departed. "We can learn the business together," he said, "and I look forward to working with you."

Harding Lawrence was self-confident to the point of cockiness. Handsome and expensively tailored, he was married to a prominent New York advertising executive. Lawrence made some uncharitable comments about some of his fellow airline executives and suggested that I would be well advised to heed his views when considering industry policy questions. He wished me well in the job.

I began work at ATA in March 1972. Within a year, my title was changed to president, with Tipton becoming the chairman. After a short while, the directors designated me as the chief executive officer, and some months later, Tipton, who had given years of devoted service to the airlines, retired. I remained as the head of ATA until my own retirement in 1986. As Tipton had indicated, my salary was raised periodically, reaching $250,000 in my final year.

John Gardner was right when he said ATA would be an intellectual challenge. Five major problem areas dominated my period of service: hijacking and airline security; the air traffic controllers' strike; fuel cost increases arising from the Arab oil embargo in 1973 and the Iranian Revolution in 1979; the battle over airline deregulation; and the persistent shortages of airport and airways capacity.

The Airline Industry

Air transportation is a hybrid industry, consisting of private companies—the airlines—and government at the national, state, and local levels. The airlines operate the *airplanes*. The federal government owns and operates the *airways*. State and local governments own and operate the *airports*.

The federal government carries out many functions essential to air transportation. Through the Federal Aviation Administration (FAA), it regulates airline safety. The FAA also employs some seventeen thousand air traffic controllers who assign flight paths and govern air movement. The Department of State negotiates bilateral treaties providing for the exchange of air rights with the hundred or so aviation nations of the world. Finally, many of the advances in aircraft technology have come from research efforts of the National Aeronautics and Space

Administration (NASA) and its predecessors. Commercial aviation has also benefited from military aircraft development and production.

The airline industry has several defining characteristics. First, it is *capital intensive*, with $131 billion invested in flight and ground equipment. A modern Boeing 777 jet costs almost $200 million, and the U.S. fleet consists of 4,478 jet aircraft of various sizes. Even smaller regional jets cost over $25 million, more than the cost of a factory for many manufacturing companies.

The airlines are also *labor intensive*, with some 512,000 highly skilled, well-paid employees. They are heavily unionized, and the unions have great bargaining power. The situation is not unlike that of the newspaper industry. If an airline goes out on strike, there are no seats to sell and the lost revenue cannot be recovered at a later date. As a result, airline management has tended to accede to labor's demands, very much like the publishers anxious to avoid nonrecoverable advertising losses.

The industry is also *time urgent*. Schedules, interconnections, and on-time departures and arrivals demand intensive management attention. Airlines cannot afford to have too many late passengers or late shipments.

The airline industry is *pervasive*. It covers most of the country with more than twenty-four thousand flights per day. The cities of the United States and those of most of the world are linked in a comprehensive network of scheduled flights. The flight patterns are concentrated, with perhaps 70 percent of the U.S. passengers originating at twenty-five airports.

Airlines are a *vital* industry. Nine out of every ten intercity letters move by air. Air cargo enables overnight shipment, permitting manufacturers to operate with smaller inventory investments, restaurants in Los Angeles to serve Maine lobsters, and fashion boutiques to restock quickly a hot item that sold out yesterday. The industry is closely tied to national defense through the Civil Reserve Aircraft Fleet, a program that makes airline aircraft available in times of need to augment the air force's organic aircraft.

Finally, the industry is *safe*. The rapid growth of air transportation is the direct result of the industry's highest priority, the commitment to safety. Through the efforts of the FAA and the National Transportation Safety Board (NTSB), along with the aircraft manufacturers and the airlines themselves, a remarkable safety record has been achieved. It is safer to fly than to drive a car or take the bus. The airlines compete in many ways, but never where safety is concerned; each one is dedicated to safety above all other considerations.

The airline industry is a young one that traces its beginnings to the historic flights of the Wright brothers at Kitty Hawk, North Carolina, in 1903. In a period of only thirty years, aviation progressed from a manned kite with bicycle wheels and a four-cylinder motor that flew for twelve seconds to the Douglas DC-3 in 1933, the all-metal, enclosed airplane that popularized air travel. Only twenty-five years later, in 1958, the first U.S. jet-powered airplane, the Boeing 707, entered service, inaugurating what has become a mass transportation system in the air, with 643 million U.S. passengers in 2003 flying 655 billion passenger miles. International travel, in particular, benefited from the jets, and ordinary Americans in large numbers made trips abroad that only the favored few could enjoy in earlier times. The jet engine democratized air travel.

Early aviation history breaks down into two periods of roughly equal length. In the *formative period* from 1903 to 1938, the airplane was invented and perfected. It was a time of adventure and innovation that produced more powerful engines, reliable instruments and navigational aids, and larger, more comfortable airplanes. In World War I, the airplane demonstrated its usefulness for military purposes. After the war, a fledgling industry began to emerge with mail subsidies serving as the means for commercializing air transportation.

The second period, the *regulated period*, ran from 1938 to 1978. In 1938, Congress enacted the Civil Aeronautics Act that established the Civil Aeronautics Board (CAB) to regulate the airlines as quasi-public utilities. CAB regulation ended in 1978 with the passage of the Airline Deregulation Act. Under regulation, the airlines became what many considered to be the best transportation system in the world, with the characteristics of pervasiveness, vitality, and safety already described. The CAB determined the fares that air carriers could charge and the cities to which they could fly. The board shielded the carriers from the full effects of competition, and weakened management's hand in labor negotiations by accepting increased labor costs in the base for determining fares. The sheltered existence under regulation led to incipient managerial and economic problems that were masked by the extraordinary productivity of the jet engine and the phenomenal growth of air travel.

In 1978, by an overwhelming vote, Congress deregulated the airline industry. Overnight, the airlines were transformed from public utilities to market-oriented, highly competitive enterprises. Never before in U.S. business history had an industry been changed as fundamentally in such a short period of time. After deregulation, an airline could go anywhere it wished in the United States. It no longer needed CAB approval for what it could charge; indeed, the CAB went out of existence. The transition was a wrenching experience for airline management. Like some stars of the silent screen who couldn't cope with the "talkies," many senior executives were unable to function in the changed environment. Deregulation produced some new airlines and services and some bargain fares. It also produced some airline bankruptcies, in marked contrast to the earlier period in which a failing airline was protected by the CAB's benevolent hand and allowed to merge with a healthy airline.

Whether because of or in spite of CAB regulation, air transportation was a spectacular success. As ABC news commentator Harry Reasoner said one night: "I suppose, all things considered, that no human enterprise in history has done as well as the commercial aviation of this century."

The Air Transport Association

ATA began life in 1936, two years before the Civil Aeronautics Board was established by the Congress to regulate fares and routes for U.S. carriers. In those early days, four airlines—United, American, Eastern, and TWA—accounted for more than 80 percent of passenger revenue. By 1970, they still dominated the domestic scene, but their combined share had declined to 60 percent, as other carriers gained prominence. Pan American was the world leader in the international arena.

The airline chiefs were the pioneers of commercial aviation. At American, C. R. Smith, a straight-talking man, never wasted words. When an interior decorator showed him some sample upholstery fabrics and asked what he wanted to see on the airplane seats, Smith said, bluntly, "Asses." At Eastern, the head man was Eddie Rickenbacker, a Medal of Honor winner in World War I and the leading ace who shot down twenty-six enemy planes. At United, "Pat" Patterson guided the airline from its inception in 1934 until 1966. Juan Trippe, the legendary founder of Pan American, who had engaged Charles Lindbergh to lay out his international routes, headed the great overseas airline for decades.

These industry pioneers were no longer active at the time I joined ATA. Their successors, though less formidable, were nevertheless an imposing lot. Najeeb Halaby, a celebrated test pilot and former head of the FAA, had replaced Juan Trippe at Pan Am. American had another blunt, straight talker in Bob Crandall. Don Nyrop, the flinty head of Northwest Airlines, operated out of a windowless office in Minneapolis and thought up ways to save money such as using worn carpet from the aisles of his airplanes to cover the floors of his offices.

The airline chief executives met periodically at ATA's offices in Washington to discuss industry problems and develop policy in areas of common interest. The meetings were lively, with sometimes rancorous conversation between an aggressive Bob Crandall and a soft-spoken but influential Ed Colodny of USAir (now U.S. Airways). Harding Lawrence typically sat at the end of the table reading the *Wall Street Journal* while his compatriots discussed the agenda. Dave Garrett, the Delta chief, spoke up only when he sensed that a conciliatory remark would resolve a contentious issue.

Leading their deliberations was always a challenging job for me. They were tough-minded men anxious to protect their turf. Each one of them was my boss so I had to maintain strict neutrality even though, in many instances, I had my own ideas about the preferred course of action. Two general rules helped me to keep them together and focused on the objective. First, I emphasized that ATA discussions were limited to those aims that could be achieved only by the airlines working together, not by a single carrier acting alone. Therefore, it was in the individual airline's best interests to help to find an industry solution. Second, in the fifteen years that I presided over the boardroom discussions, I never asked for a vote to settle a question. I preferred to let the airline chiefs argue the issues until I sensed that a working consensus had been reached. Then, I summarized the discussion and declared that we had reached sufficient agreement for ATA to go forward on behalf of the industry, even though others and I realized that there were still some minor differences around the edges. This approach was more useful than a vote of, say, twenty-one to eleven, a clear majority that decided the question but also identified eleven of my thirty-two constituents in opposition.

The real work of ATA was not done in the boardroom but rather in industry committees led by ATA staff members. The operations and technical department was headed by Clifton F. von Kann, a retired Army general, and his staff included experts in such areas as aircraft noise reduction, pilot fatigue, landing and take-off procedures, and airport runway construction. The legal staff, headed by Jim Landry, an expert in international law, was one of the busiest parts of the organization. A bedrock responsibility was to ensure that all discussions avoided anything that might run afoul of antitrust regulations. Litigation over aircraft noise, a persistent problem, was handled for ATA by top-flight lawyers such as Warren Christopher, a future secretary of state.

The traffic department dealt with bread-and- butter issues affecting the movement of passengers and cargo, like procedures for handling people with disabilities or special privileges for military personnel. If a person wanted to become a travel agent, the first step was to submit information to ATA's Air Traffic Conference. Because an agent could sell tickets for a single trip for travel on more than one airline, ATC oversaw a vital clearinghouse function to determine what each airline was owed.

Legislative issues at both the federal and state house levels occupied the half dozen or so members of ATA's legislative affairs depart-

ment, headed by Leo Seybold. Each airline had its own legislative representative in Washington who looked after company interests and
who joined with the others in a combined ATA effort when important
industry matters arose. Congressional hearings required testimony on
a wide variety of subjects including aircraft noise, airline security, the
investment tax credit, regulatory reform, and international and military issues.

Although I handled most of the testimony, I depended on Seybold
and his staff to do the lobbying and to attend the many congressional
fund-raisers.

One morning Seybold said that he had something important to tell
me. He had received a phone call from a former ATA political consultant who had been questioned by special prosecutor Leon Jaworski.
The consultant had been paid a fee of $10,000 in 1970 to help achieve
a legislative objective. After the conversation I asked Stuart Tipton,
Seybold, and Norman Philion, an esteemed industry veteran whom I
had recruited from United Airlines to be the ATA executive vice president, to meet with me. I asked Seybold if he thought that part of the
consultant's fee had been used for political contributions to one or
more legislators. He replied: "Since you have asked me directly, I'll
tell you. Some of the fee was used for political contributions." When I
asked how many political consultants we had on retainer today he said
there were four of them with annual fees ranging from $5,000 to
$25,000. He stated emphatically that none of the money paid to them
was used for political contributions. "What accounted for the change
from 1970?" I asked him. "You," he replied. The meeting ended after
a brief conversation about the difficulty that Seybold's people faced in
finding money to attend the many $100 fund-raisers held on so many
evenings on Capitol Hill. There was a short but inconclusive discussion as to whether ATA should form a political action committee to
handle the contribution problem. I never was comfortable with the
whole area of political contributions and managed to stay clear of it.

In addition to its other responsibilities, ATA was the primary
source of data on the scope of the industry's operations and its financial
circumstances. Under the direction of an economist, George James,
ATA published statistical information on passenger miles flown by the

carriers each year, the number and types of aircraft in service, accidents, if any, and other data. Every effort was made to assure the accuracy and reliability of the information. Indeed, I told James one day that if two lawyers on opposite sides of an airline dispute entered the courtroom, I would hope that both of them would carry the ATA data book as the best and most authoritative source of industry data.

To help get the job done, I persuaded two stars from my Pentagon days to join me at ATA. One was the indispensable secretary and administrative assistant, Sally Moser. The other was Dan Henkin, an assistant secretary of defense who had ably handled public information for the department and who would now be the ATA spokesperson.

Hijacking and Security

For many years, beginning as far back as 1961, U.S. aircraft had been hijacked to unintended locations. The first one, in May of that year, was diverted to Cuba. Six other hijacked flights to Cuba followed through 1967. The pace quickened in the next four years, 1968 to 1971, with seventy-three of the eighty-one hijackings ending in Cuba. Some of the hijackers were homesick Cubans, others were committed leftists, and a few were insane. The prevailing wisdom was to avoid the use of force and to comply with the hijacker's demands in order to prevent harm to passengers and crew. Pilots used to joke that a hijacking simply meant a weekend in Havana.

The situation became much more serious in 1972. There were many more hijackings than in the previous year, with the destinations shifting from Cuba to other locations. More ominously, they were carried out for political purposes with passengers held hostage in order to secure a huge ransom. In some cases, aircraft were destroyed on the ground. A Delta flight, for example, was commandeered by a group that demanded passage to Algiers and a ransom of $1 million. The event occurred at a time when government and airline officials were debating whether sterner measures were needed, including the use of force. The importance of the debate was highlighted when influential

Life magazine devoted the cover story of its August 11, 1972, issue to hijacking. The story reported that some hijacking experts, including David G. Hubbard, opposed the use of force because it posed an attractive challenge to the hijacker. "These people look normal but they're not," Hubbard said. "They're all crazy and they're all dangerous."

I had just joined ATA at the time this was happening and became involved in the discussions of what to do. An immediate need was to define more clearly the respective roles during a hijacking of the FAA, the FBI, the pilot in command, and airline management. Another need was to set up a communications net and command post at the FAA. ATA's security officer, a former FBI agent, worked closely with his airline counterparts and helped to formulate the new procedures.

Despite the doubts of Hubbard and many airline pilots, the FAA and the FBI adopted a tougher line. FBI agents were authorized to storm airplanes on the ground. Metal detectors were installed at the nation's airports. In January 1973 the FAA ordered the airlines to screen passengers and to search carry-on baggage. Airline officials worried at first that the new procedures would delay flights and inconvenience passengers. Industry lawyers were concerned that the searches might run afoul of the guarantee against unreasonable searches embodied in the Fourth Amendment to the Constitution. It quickly became apparent that passengers were willing to accept the new regime but were eager to let the airlines know when they thought not enough was done to protect them.

In 1974, Congress enacted a comprehensive antihijacking law that made it a crime punishable by twenty years in prison or, if a death occurred, by life imprisonment or the death penalty. It authorized the airlines to forbid transportation to anyone who refused to be searched. It also empowered the president to deny the entry into the United States of an airline from a country that aided or abetted terrorists.

Unfortunately, the new security procedures were no match for determined terrorists with political objectives in mind. In 1985, for example, Islamic Jihad hijacked TWA flight 847 to compel Israel to release some Shiite Muslim prisoners. Pan Am's flight 103 was blown up over Scotland by terrorists acting on behalf of Libya. None of these events, horrible as they were, approached the bestiality of the attacks on September 11, 2001, on the World Trade Center and the Pentagon, which killed three thousand innocent people. The airplane itself had become a weapon in the hands of al Qaeda.

The Oil Shocks of the 1970s

Modern airliners are powered by jet fuel, a petroleum distillate similar to kerosene. For years its price seldom exceeded ten cents a gallon. As a result of the oil shocks of the 1970s, the price of jet fuel was catapulted from a dime to a dollar, and many in the industry feared it might continue its upward climb to as high as two dollars. The surge in the price of fuel caused a fundamental change in the economics of operating an airline. Suddenly, the variable cost of jet fuel assumed an importance usually accorded to fixed costs, primarily the enormous investment in aircraft. Now it was no longer possible to serve a thinly traveled market or a small community, because the yield in passenger revenue was hardly enough to cover the cost of the fuel.

The first oil shock occurred in October 1973 as a consequence of the so-called Yom Kippur War when Syria and Egypt invaded Israel on its holiest of days. The United States stepped in to assist Israel, which was on the verge of defeat, with arms and supplies. In retaliation, Saudi Arabia and most of the Arab states used oil as a weapon, raising its price by 70 percent or more and stopping shipments to the United States and other countries.

The effects on the airlines were overwhelming. The cost of fuel tripled, reaching a level of 30 percent of operating costs, close to the cost of the industry's large and well-paid workforce. The airlines took immediate steps to get the most out of each gallon of the now precious liquid. Cross-country flights operated at somewhat slower speeds to conserve fuel. Pilots taxied planes without all engines running. Unnecessary items in the cabins were removed to save weight and lessen fuel consumption.

In the following year, because of conservation measures across the economy and increased production of oil, prices began to fall and the Arab oil embargo ended in March 1974. There was more than enough oil to meet worldwide demand. Although supply and demand determined the price of imported oil, domestic oil pricing was controlled by measures instituted by President Nixon in 1971.

The second oil shock in less than a decade was a consequence of the revolution in Iran and the removal of the shah of Iran from power in 1979. As Daniel Yergin states in *The Prize*, "Iranians from every sector of national life were losing patience with the Shah's regime and the pell-mell rush to modernization. Grasping for some certitude in the melee, they increasingly heeded the call of traditional Islam and of an even more fervent fundamentalism." Ayatollah Ruholla Khomeini, an elderly Muslim cleric and longtime opponent of the shah, established an Islamic republic. The United States was branded as "the Great Satan."

Iran had been exporting 4.5 million barrels a day from its total output of 5.5 million barrels. By December 1978, the export of Iranian oil came to an end. Once again, the price of oil skyrocketed, from around $13 a barrel to $34, and even higher on the so-called spot market. The effect on the airlines was devastating. Each penny increase in the price of a gallon of jet fuel raised the airlines' annual fuel bill by $110 million. The carriers' total fuel bill was $1.4 billion in 1973, $4.2 billion in 1978, and $6.4 billion in 1979. It rose to almost $10 billion in 1980, even though the industry used several hundred million fewer gallons than in the previous year.

The high price of oil was accompanied by shortages of petroleum products for industry and the public. Long lines at gas stations throughout the country were a familiar sight. Everyone was angry. Daniel Yergin describes a vivid example: "On the way to the White House one morning, Eisenstadt [Stuart Eisenstadt, a high official in President Carter's administration] had sat for 45 minutes in a gas line at his local Amoco station on Connecticut Avenue, and he had found himself seized by the same almost uncontrollable rage that was affecting his fellow citizens from one end of the country to the other."

ATA did what it could to lessen the effect of high prices and scarce product. In one instance, the Federal Energy Office diverted jet fuel from military stocks to the airlines. The CAB, in response to an industry filing, permitted the airlines to raise fares to account for some of the added costs. Additionally, ATA's lawyers recovered several million dollars in cases where domestic oil prices exceeded Nixon's price controls.

The country was up in arms about the energy crisis and the dependence on foreign oil. The oil industry became a target for the public's wrath, and was blamed for creating artificial shortages. Senator Henry Jackson summoned the oil industry chiefs to an unfriendly hearing where he and other senators demanded answers to why the shortages arose and who was to blame. President Carter, in an effort to normalize the situation, decontrolled the price of domestic oil, but called for a windfall profits tax to recover "excess" profits from the oil industry. Newspaper editorials called for a broad energy policy that included conservation, increased domestic production, and less dependence on foreign sources, particularly from the troubled Middle East. The Navy sent ships to the Persian Gulf to guard against the possibility of attacks on oil tankers or threats to block the Strait of Hormuz, the narrow passage in the Persian Gulf that tankers traversed to get to the open seas. More than anything, the United States hoped to free itself from the monopoly power of the oil cartel, OPEC, the Organization of Petroleum Exporting Countries, that held the world in economic bondage.

A Bold Plan

In the midst of the energy crisis in 1979 that preoccupied President Carter and the American public, I unexpectedly found myself a part of the effort to find a solution. It began quite by chance in a luncheon conversation with my old friend, Eugene Zuckert, from the Harvard Business School and the Pentagon. Zuckert had returned to the practice of law (he had a joint business and law degree) after leaving his post as secretary of the air force, and his office was located just a few blocks from mine.

During our luncheon we talked about synthetic fuels, the effort to obtain liquid fuel from coal or oil shale deposits. In an article in the July 30 *Washington Star* reporter John J. Fialka wrote about our conversation: "What they discussed and what happened afterward is now viewed at the White House and on Capitol Hill as having 'greased the skids' for the massive energy legislation now moving through the Congress. It is also credited with helping embolden the White House to propose spending $88 billion over 10 years to develop new sources of energy to blunt the monopoly power of the Organization of Petroleum Exporting Countries."

Here is a recounting of our conversation and how it led to "massive energy legislation." Both of us knew from our Defense Department experience that the United States could achieve production miracles, such as getting the Polaris missile to sea, when it set its mind to the task. We knew also that after the attack on Pearl Harbor in 1941 almost all of the world's natural rubber facilities came under enemy control. We knew in addition that by the end of the war, almost all the rubber consumed in the United States was synthetic, produced in government-owned plants operated by private industry. We were familiar also with the tremendous expansion of aluminum capacity during the Korean War by means of guaranteed contracts with private industry. Finally, both of us remembered that Germany fought World War II with synthetic fuel, an indication that the technical know-how was well understood. Why couldn't the United States develop a government-industry program today, based on these precedents, that would free us from OPEC bondage? We ended our conversation determined to come up with a feasible program.

First, however, we needed to do more research. I looked into the details of the synthetic rubber effort to understand more about how it was financed. I called some of my friends with scientific and engineering experience, such as John Foster, the former head of the Pentagon's research and development program who was now an executive with

TRW, to learn more about the liquefaction of coal and shale. From another friend, Charles DiBona, a petroleum expert, I learned about oil industry efforts to pursue synthetic fuels. Meanwhile, Zuckert investigated a major effort in South Africa, aided by U.S. companies, to build a large synthetic fuels plant. Zuckert also studied proposals Vice President Nelson Rockefeller made in 1975 to undertake a large-scale government-industry program not unlike what we had in mind.

I needed more expertise on financing mechanisms and called Lloyd Cutler for help. When I told Cutler what Zuckert and I were up to, he said he had developed some similar ideas after the 1973 oil shock. I suggested that he join us in preparing our proposals. He agreed, and we welcomed aboard one of Washington's most eminent lawyers.

By April we were far enough along to send a memo on our plan to the White House Domestic Council and several members of Congress. We proposed the creation of a synthetic fuels industry capable of producing five million barrels a day within a five- to ten-year period. The fuels would be derived from sources such as shale, coal, tar sands, and heavy oils, but also perhaps from agricultural products. It would be a joint government-industry effort that drew on financial mechanisms employed earlier to deal with the rubber and aluminum shortages.

Our proposal was premised on our energy predicament. We pointed out that half of our imports came from the Middle East. Our heavy dependence on these sources made us highly vulnerable to sudden upward price movements resulting from interruptions to supply. We said no one could be certain that this oil would continue to flow uninterruptedly to our shores—political changes, terrorist activities, overt military action, and natural disasters could lead to a reduction in or even a halt to deliveries. Each time one of these contingencies occurred, the stress on the economic and social fabric of the industrial democracies would be enormous. We concluded that the "risks of not trying to correct the situation were too great to bear."

The reception to our memo was polite but lukewarm. We decided to go public with it to see whether we could drum up more interest. Cutler got it into the hands of several leading columnists—James

Reston and Leonard Silk of the *New York Times* and Joseph Kraft and Hobart Rowan of the *Washington Post*. I tried to get it placed on the op-ed page of the *Wall Street Journal* but was told that the *Journal* was already committed to a piece in some ways similar to our proposal that had been developed by President Johnson's national security advisor, Walt Rostow.

Joe Kraft was the first to hit the press with our proposal. On May 29 he wrote that "thanks to the gas lines and soaring fuel prices, the irresistible power of an idea whose time has come is now on the verge of asserting itself in the American approach to the energy problem. The idea is government partnership with industry in the production of synthetic gasoline." Leonard Silk's economics column on June 6 was devoted to our plan: "With OPEC now free to manipulate the world oil price and arrest supplies, the program could actually mean net savings as well as far less vulnerability." "Scotty" Reston, probably the leading journalist of his generation, rang in on June 8: "There are not many miraculous new ideas around here for solving the energy crisis, but there is one old idea that is beginning to get thoughtful consideration. This is that the United States government should create a financing institution like the Reconstruction Finance Corporation of World War II days to help private industry produce five million barrels of synthetic oil a day—over 20% of our current needs—within five to ten years."

Roscoe Drummond in the *Christian Science Monitor* said that "three old Washington hands, working together . . . uninhibited by the clutter of bureaucracy—have devised ways and means to relieve the oil shortage and reduce such dependence on the Middle East."

On June 10, the *Washington Post* printed our entire memorandum as a feature article in its Sunday "Outlook" section. In the same issue, its economics columnist, Hobart Rowan, fretted about the energy crisis and said "one of the most promising ideas comes from three members of the Washington Establishment with close ties to the top corporate structure of the country." In its lead editorial on June 15, the *Post* said that "the case for a large-scale effort to make oil and gas out of coal has become overwhelming."

The flurry of press interest sparked the interest of the White House. Cutler, Zuckert, and I were invited to meet with Vice President Walter Mondale and senior members of the administration. Representative William J. Moorhead placed our "Outlook" article in the *Congressional Record* and later introduced a bill that authorized the plan we had recommended.

On July 17, the three of us were invited to testify before the Senate Governmental Affairs Committee, and several days later before the Senate Banking, Housing and Urban Affairs Committee. In the banking committee hearing, we were joined by Felix G. Rohatyn, chairman of the New York Municipal Assistance Corp., who was known as "the financial savior of New York City." In his remarks, Rohatyn said that "the current situation presents potentially the greatest threat to our system since World War II, . . . namely, our over-dependence on foreign sources of energy. Only a major national effort involving the Federal Government and the private sector, involving new production and conservation, can bring about a solution. The proposal to consider a Government-owned corporation . . . to create additional capacity for synthetics is, in my judgment, worthy of serious support."

Not all the press articles were favorable. A week after ours ran, Representative Dave Stockman of Michigan wrote his own "Outlook" piece, "The Senseless Stampede to Synfuels." He pointed out some of the technical problems that would have to be solved and was generally pessimistic about the outcome. Several articles said we had overlooked adverse environmental consequences. A Harvard Business School study said the nation could save more energy through conservation than it would gain through a synthetic fuels program. The study was probably right, but then, as now, there was unfortunately very little political support for a major conservation effort. The American people are too much in love with gas-guzzling automobiles.

Despite the concerns about a large-scale synfuels program, the proposal had gained so much momentum that President Carter adopted it as the centerpiece of his energy policy, which was announced in July. Carter proposed an objective of 2.5 million barrels a day. (Daniel Yergin says in *The Prize* that Carter wanted a five-million barrel level, but his staff talked him out of it.) In 1980, Congress passed the Energy Security Act, which established the U.S. Synthetic Fuels Corporation and provided $20 million in loan guarantees to get the program rolling.

Many oil companies opposed government meddling in their industry, but one of the largest, Exxon, welcomed the new initiative. The Exxon chairman, Clifford C. Garvin Jr., said in the *New York Times* on July 29 that synthetic fuels were "the best hope for a successful transition to the age of non-depletable energy."

Then, as Exxon, Union, Occidental, and other oil companies were hard at work on their different technical approaches for wresting liquid fuel from oil and shale, the price of oil dropped from its stratospheric levels, just as it had after the Arab oil embargo in 1973. With an abundance of oil at more reasonable prices, the enthusiasm for producing the more expensive synthetic product began to wane. West Texas crude was available at $10 a barrel compared to $30 earlier. You could buy some barrels of Persian Gulf crude for only $6. Synthetic fuels were simply not competitive at those prices. When Ronald Reagan became president, he appointed as head of the Synthetic Fuels Corporation an individual who had chaired his energy transition team and who had advised the new president to kill the program.

In August 1985, a *Washington Post* editorial said Congress was likely to terminate the synfuels corporation, "a good idea whose time never came. . . . The world market is too weak and the budget too tight to justify the effort any longer." In April of the next year, the *Post* said in another editorial that "with hardly an audible gurgle the U.S. Synfuels Corporation died a few days ago." It went on to say that "there was a useful and sensible idea in the concept of federal support for synthetic fuel development. It got buried under all the hype, the muddle, and the incompetence that came to characterize the operation."

What is one to make of all this? First, I should emphasize that my efforts were made entirely on my own initiative without any involvement by ATA or airline executives.

Second, I was amazed then and to this day at how fast our ideas caught on and moved forward. The time was ripe for an affirmative effort to disengage ourselves from dependence on Middle Eastern oil.

The plan was propelled by the power of the press and the favorable publicity of influential commentators.

The drop in the price of oil and the availability of more of it was perplexing, coming so soon after high prices and scarce product. The oil companies were criticized, probably unfairly, for manipulating the market and creating inventory shortages to drive up the price and reap larger profits. A more likely explanation is that prices for oil and gasoline are especially sensitive to current demand, existing inventories, and anticipated production. When there is uncertainty about future supply levels, the price rises quickly. When the expected shortage, real or imagined, is relieved, prices drop almost as quickly.

Although I don't believe the oil companies conspired to take advantage of the energy crises in the 1970s, I do believe that they held back on their oil resources when the price of domestic oil was controlled by President Nixon. You can't blame them, I suppose, for wanting to get the most from their holdings.

Last, though the shortages disappeared and the prices returned to more normal levels, I wish we had continued with the government-industry program to develop synthetic fuels, at least to the point where working plants demonstrated feasible technologies. It would have given us greater assurance of our ability to deal with future crises. It would also have provided a laboratory for determining whether the environmental problems were as serious as some contended. The Canadians pursued their synthetic fuels program with dependable leadership and successful results. A successful U.S. program would have helped to safeguard the country from terrorist threats to Middle Eastern oil resources.

Those who argue against programs in which the government is involved with industry forget how effective such programs can be when they are well conceived and properly managed. We would not have the Internet today were it not for the initial impetus from the Department of Defense's Advanced Research Projects Agency. The airline industry would not have made its enormous strides in such a short time were it not for the participation of the National Advisory

Committee on Aeronautics (now absorbed by NASA). Clearly, in our economic system we are far better off leaving industrial tasks to private industry, but sometimes government has a role to play. The synfuels program was one such case.

The Air Traffic Controllers' Strike

When Ronald Reagan was beginning to assemble his cabinet in 1981 after defeating Jimmy Carter for the presidency, I noticed in the paper one morning that he intended to nominate Drew Lewis, the chief executive of Union Pacific railroad, to be his secretary of transportation. The major component of the Transportation Department was the FAA and its seventeen thousand air traffic controllers. I didn't know Lewis but decided to call him anyway. I told him that within a few months the new president was likely to face a domestic crisis and that the transportation secretary would be the crisis manager and key advisor. Lewis agreed to meet me for lunch.

The crisis I had in mind was a possible strike by the controllers that, if allowed to happen, could shut down the air transportation system, not only for U.S. carriers but also for foreign carriers flying into and out of U.S. airspace. The cost to the airlines and to the economy from the shutdown could total hundreds of million dollars. Passengers would be inconvenienced, critical overnight shipments would stop, and the delivery of mail would be delayed.

The controllers were represented by the Professional Air Traffic Controllers Organization (PATCO). The PATCO president, Robert Poli, thought that a controller's income should approximate that of an airline pilot because, like a pilot, a controller was responsible for the safety of the flight. In speeches to his members he had raised their expectations that a large increase in pay, a shorter work week, and other benefits would soon be theirs.

Like postal workers, air traffic controllers were public employees permitted to bargain on terms of employment but not to strike. On many occasions, however, they engaged in disruptive job actions to coerce acceptance of their demands. In March and April of 1970, for example, some three thousand controllers participated in a "sickout" that interfered with airline operations. ATA took legal action and filed for an injunction against PATCO and for $50 million in damages. PATCO consented to a permanent injunction in return for an agreement by the airlines to drop the $50 million claim. Under the court ruling, they were permanently barred from any "strike, slowdown, sickout, or other concerted action." A permanent injunction is rarely granted, and it proved to be a valuable weapon for ATA as difficulties with the controllers worsened.

In 1978, ATA asked a federal court to hold PATCO in contempt for violating the injunction by engaging in a four-day slowdown. The judge required PATCO to pay ATA $100,000. PATCO appealed the decision and lost, and the Supreme Court declined to review the matter. Despite its failure on the legal front, PATCO pressed its case with the FAA to the point where the agency believed the controllers might walk off the job if their demands were not met in the 1981 contract negotiations.

During the election campaign in 1980, PATCO president Poli played a political card. He agreed to endorse Ronald Reagan for president in return for his support for PATCO's demands for a shorter work week, increased pay, replacement of outdated equipment, and a right to veto Reagan's nominee for FAA administrator. In a carefully worded letter to Poli on October 20, 1980, Reagan said he had been briefed by his staff on "the deplorable state of the nation's air traffic control system" and pledged to take whatever steps were "necessary to provide our air traffic controllers with the most modern equipment available and to adjust staff levels and work days so that they are commensurate with achieving a maximum degree of public safety." He did not address PATCO's insistence on a veto power, but pledged that his "administration will work closely with you to bring about a spirit of cooperative behavior between the President and the air traffic controllers."

Poli believed that the president's assurances gave him additional clout, and his words and actions became more aggressive. Concerned about the situation, I invited Poli to lunch in September 1980 for a discussion of his intentions. He said without qualification that he would not initiate a strike in 1981. He made the same assertion in Senate and House hearings and before the public in a television interview in August with Jim Lehrer. On May 28, 1981, I reminded Poli of this in a letter that urged him to retract a recent statement that PATCO intended to initiate a strike or other unlawful actions on June 22, 1981, when the current labor contract expired.

My relationship with Drew Lewis, the transportation secretary, was on a solid footing in part because I had forewarned him in our initial encounter of what he was likely to face. He kept me informed on virtually a daily basis of the tense negotiations between PATCO and the government. He told me on June 16, for example, what the president would say in his press conference later that day and, on an extremely confidential basis, revealed the wage increase he was prepared to accept. The next day, he told me that Poli had walked out of a meeting in his office and it wasn't clear whether he would return. He said further that the government would hang tough and "play brinkmanship over the weekend." He expected the airlines to support his tough policy and not cut and run in order to avoid the financial losses a strike would entail. I assured him, on the basis of my frequent phone calls with the airline chiefs, that they were anxious to settle the PATCO problem once and for all and would stay the course.

On June 17, with the negotiations at a crisis point, Lewis issued a press release that outlined the government offer to raise controller pay and grant many of their demands. He regretted that the offer had not been accepted and that negotiations had broken down. "A strike would cause millions of dollars in economic loss to the airlines and to air commerce," he said, and warned that it would be "an illegal action, with PATCO—and individual controllers—subject to criminal liability."

PATCO and the government, under the auspices of a federal mediator, resumed their negotiations. In the early hours of the morning on June 22, the initial strike deadline, Poli accepted an offer that would assure the controllers of a pay increase of over 11 percent. Poli said he believed that his members would ratify the agreement, but then he reversed himself when some of the more vocal controllers reminded him that the offer was far below what Poli had earlier led them to expect.

The parties returned to the negotiating table but with little hope of reaching an agreement. The government had gone as far as it could with its offer, which was valued at $40 million or more. PATCO's many demands could amount to some $600 million in federal tax dollars, a totally unrealistic figure. Lewis said to me that "this nonsense has got to stop."

At 2:45 AM on Monday, August 3, the talks reached an impasse. At 4 AM, Poli held a press conference and said a strike would commence with the day shift that morning. The Department of Justice sought a restraining order, and ATA initiated contempt proceedings under the permanent injunction. The FAA immediately invoked the "flow control" plan it had developed with the airlines some time earlier. Under this plan, air movements would be centrally controlled and limited to only those that could be handled safely. Additionally, trailing distances between aircraft in flight would be lengthened.

The focus now moved to what the president should say and when he should say it. Dick Ferris, Eddie Carlson's successor, and Justin Dart, a United Airlines director and one of the Los Angeles businessmen who brought Ronald Reagan to national attention, had called the president before the strike and urged him to say that controllers who struck would be fired and never hired back. Lewis was concerned about this, telling me on August 2 that it would take three years to train new controllers and that we would be in a mess. The controllers were on a "high," he said, that could not be relieved without a brief strike. He intimated that the president might make a strong statement soon. "Paul, we have only one cannon here and we don't want to fire it too soon," he said. "Once he makes up his mind to do this, he comes on strong."

Lewis was right; President Reagan came on strong. He said the government would fire air traffic controllers who failed to return to work the following day. The leading newspapers praised Reagan for not caving in. The *Washington Post* said on August 4 that "the air traffic controllers' strike was a wildly misconceived venture that deserves the government's extraordinarily severe response." The *New York Times* said on the same day that "President Reagan's tough threat to fire the workers who are not back to work by Wednesday is appropriate." The *Wall Street Journal* said the decision to fire the controllers was mild under the circumstances. "The issue," it said, "has become a question of whether a union has the power to flout the law."

Now the FAA and the airlines had to cope with an unprecedented situation. Twelve thousand of the seventeen thousand PATCO members had walked out August 3, and their employment was subsequently terminated when they refused to return to work. The air traffic control system was left with five thousand controllers and three hundred supervisors who were not PATCO members. Within hours, one hundred military air controllers were airlifted to critical centers, and within three weeks an additional three hundred were added. Some three hundred retired controllers were recalled to help out. A forty-eight-hour work week was instituted, additional overtime was authorized, and vacations were cancelled. FAA's flow control system, which tailored traffic to available capacity, enabled 75 to 80 percent of the previously planned flights to operate safely. In testimony September 10, I assured the Congress that "the U.S. air traffic control system was as safe today as it was prior to the strike."

Although air transportation was safe, the reduced traffic was costly for the airlines, particularly in the first days of the strike. On August 3, the revenue loss exceeded thirty to forty million dollars. During the first four weeks, the losses exceeded two hundred million dollars. The public was confused about which flights would be permitted to operate, and there were large-scale cancellations of both business and vacation travel. Under a revised FAA plan, it became possible to publish reliable schedules at a level of about 75 percent of normal. The FAA estimated that it would take at least twenty-one months to rebuild the system.

The Congress, the press, and the public continued to applaud President Reagan's strong leadership, but by early fall in 1981 a difficult new issue arose. Should the fired air traffic controllers be rehired?

Favoring their return was concern about the long working hours of the controller force, the reduced level of airline operations, and the cost to hire and train new controllers to fill the many vacancies. In an editorial on August 30, the *New York Times* suggested that rehiring the strikers, perhaps with penalties such as loss of some of their benefits, might be preferable to a twenty-one-month period to restore full capacity. "The decision to fire the strikers was justified," the editorial stated. "Now with victory in hand, there is every reason to temper justice with mercy." In September the president was urged by some members of Congress to negotiate a settlement that would return the experienced controllers to their former jobs, and a bill was introduced that required their reemployment.

The president, Secretary Lewis, and FAA Administrator Lynn Helms opposed rehiring the strikers. Helms said their return would jeopardize safety. He pointed out that safely handling airplanes is a team effort that would be compromised by the bad blood between those who struck and those who stayed on the job. I agreed with Helms. The strikers were never rehired; instead, the system was patiently rebuilt by hiring and training new people.

The ATA continued to litigate for the harm caused by the illegal strike. In U.S. district court in Brooklyn, ATA was awarded $4.5 million in coercive fines and penalties, and fourteen of its member airlines were awarded $29 million in compensatory damages for losses in the first three days of the strike. In Washington, ATA succeeded in attaching PATCO's cash assets, amounting to about $4 million. PATCO filed for Chapter 11 bankruptcy. ATA's lawyers believed there was no way that PATCO could be reorganized, and it soon went under. A new union was formed to represent the controllers and it continues in existence to the present day. The $4 million obtained by ATA was distributed to its member carriers.

The air traffic controllers are an indispensable part of the system that makes air transportation the safest form of travel. Their work requires skill, concentration, and clear-headedness under pressure. They are highly trained and well paid. Today, they enjoy a productive relationship with the FAA in marked contrast to the earlier time when their illegal behavior caused the demise of their union and the suffering of the members who lost their jobs.

The strike required a sustained effort by ATA and long hours of work. Along with several other senior members, I slept in our offices during the critical periods. The operations department helped to devise the flow control procedures that assured safety in flight. The legal department added to its long record of success in dealing with PATCO's slowdowns and other job actions. Many staff members, including some with low-level jobs, took on additional responsibilities and demonstrated talents that led to their advancement.

Deregulating the Airlines

The gossip in the aviation community was that it all began when Teddy Kennedy flew from Boston to a midwestern city and paid a fare that he thought was much too high. Since he was not a member of the Senate Commerce Committee, which had jurisdiction over aviation matters, he held an investigation of CAB regulation of the airlines through the Subcommittee on Administrative Practice and Procedure, which he chaired.

Senator Kennedy's 1975 hearings were organized by a staff director specially engaged for the purpose, Stephen G. Breyer, a Harvard law professor later appointed by President Clinton to the U.S. Supreme Court. Breyer has written a thoughtful account of the seven-day hearing in his book, *Regulation and Its Reform*. Like the good lawyer he certainly was, he arranged the order of the witnesses so that ATA, representing the airlines, was on the defensive when faced with Senator Kennedy's probing questions. The hearing raised fundamental issues about the nature of the airlines—were they natural monopolies requiring regulation or ordinary businesses that should function in a free market environment?

The Federal Aviation Act of 1938 regarded the airlines as natural monopolies similar to electric-power-generating companies that required regulation to prevent monopoly power. The CAB was responsible under

the act for keeping prices at a low, competitive level but also for promoting the expansion of the industry. It decided which routes to award
and selected the airlines that could serve them. The board's decisions
were made after lengthy hearings conducted by administrative law
judges that included pleadings from the affected communities and their
governmental representatives. Once the route decisions had been
made, the CAB controlled the fares that could be charged through its
legislative mandate to set "just and reasonable" prices.

The initial witnesses in the Kennedy hearings were independent
economists and representatives of government agencies, including the
departments of transportation and justice and the Council of Economic Advisors and Council of Wage and Price Stability. Without
exception they contended that CAB regulation had produced exces-
sive prices and more service than was needed. Since the airlines could
not compete on price, they competed on the basis of service, offering
more flights, more frills, specially catered meals, and even piano
lounges. With more flights than the market warranted, load factors (the
percentage of seats occupied by paying passengers) suffered; in 1971,
for example, as Breyer states in his book, transcontinental load factors
averaged only 39 percent.

The hearings contrasted the higher fares and lower load factors of
the CAB-regulated airlines with the lower fares and higher load factors
of unregulated airlines in Texas and California. It was pointed out, for
example, that Pacific Southwest, an unregulated California carrier, put
158 seats in a Boeing 727-200 with a 60 percent load factor compared
with the same plane with 121 seats flown by American with a 55 percent load factor. As Breyer reported: "In 1976, the 456-mile, 1 hour and
5-minute flight from San Diego to San Francisco cost $26.21, while the
399-mile, 1 hour and 7-minute flight from Boston to Washington, D.C.
cost $41.67. American Airlines data showed that if it had put 158 seats
in its 727-200's and flew 60% full, it could have covered its one-way
costs by charging $32 versus $42."

The CAB-regulated carriers—ATA members—were proud of
what they had accomplished ("no human enterprise in history has
done as well") and, with one exception, opposed deregulation. The

single exception was United Airlines, the largest of the carriers. Because the CAB protected the weaker carriers at the expense of the stronger ones, United knew that under CAB regulation it was unlikely to gain additional routes. The other carriers, always fearful of United, welcomed the regulated environment.

ATA's senior staff members such as George James and Jim Landry strongly favored the regulatory regime as did their mentor, Stuart Tipton, who had been on hand at the birth of the CAB. Tipton believed that in an unregulated environment the carriers would destroy themselves by predatory pricing to maintain market share. In short, the CAB was needed to protect the carriers from devouring one another. Breyer recognized that predatory pricing and ruinous scheduling were possible outcomes of deregulation, but he believed that "the anti-trust laws are capable of dealing with this problem."

After the testimony against regulation from the economists and the governmental witnesses, it was ATA's turn on the witness stand. Because ATA's case for defending regulation was somewhat technical, the principal witness was its economist, George James, supported by its general counsel, Jim Landry. James argued that the pervasive network of flights to small towns and large cities depended on "cross subsidy," that is, the support of less remunerative routes by those that were profitable. A great many deserving communities would lose air service, he said, if the airlines were deregulated and the system of cross subsidy were supplanted by concentration on only the profitable routes.

James was challenged by Senator Kennedy and Stephen Breyer to produce evidence that the unprofitable routes would be abandoned. In response, ATA commissioned a computer simulation from Lockheed that was later given to the committee. The Lockheed simulation indicated that 373 nonstop route segments would lose air service if regulation came to an end. The committee staff then asked the independent economists for comments on the study. They argued that it was a flawed effort because it assumed that the air transport system was operated by a single carrier, whose aim was to maximize profits, not by carriers competing against one another. Breyer wrote that "ATA could muster no respectable support for the conclusions it drew from the study. . . . Thus, the study weakened rather than strengthened the industry position."

The Kennedy hearings were widely publicized and brought great pressure on Congress to eliminate or substantially reduce CAB regulation. It now became necessary for the committee with legislative jurisdiction, the Aviation Subcommittee of the Senate Commerce Committee, chaired by Senator Howard Cannon of Nevada, to take up the issue. Meanwhile, President Gerald Ford sent a letter of congratulations on the hearings to Senator Kennedy. President Ford also appointed a new CAB chairman, John Robson, who introduced reforms before the new legislation was enacted. On the campaign trail, Jimmy Carter advocated airline deregulation and later, as president, helped to bring it about.

Unlike James, Landry, and Tipton, I had no strong feelings in favor of CAB regulation. My training in business administration had led me to believe that the airlines would be strengthened by the rigors of competition and that the public would be the ultimate benefactor. Safety would continue to be regulated by the FAA so I had no concern that economic deregulation would jeopardize the airlines' superb safety record. Since the industry, except for United Airlines, continued to support the regulatory regime, I had to keep my personal views pretty much to myself.

As part of our preparation for Senator Cannon's hearings, where I would be the principal witness, I asked several airline officials to meet informally with me to describe what they thought would happen if the airlines were deregulated. They were quite certain that they would suffer when new carriers appeared in an environment previously closed by the CAB to new entry. The new carriers would have nonunion workforces compensated at lower wage levels. Their employees could be used flexibly, free from the rigidities imposed by union jurisdictions. In short, they thought that regulated carriers would be modern-day dinosaurs unable to survive against the low-cost, no-frills entrants.

The airline unions, like the airlines, opposed deregulation, as did business travelers. The unions were afraid that jobs would be lost and wages lowered as a result of the pressure of competition and the emergence of new, low-cost carriers. Business travelers liked the abundance of flights currently available to meet their needs.

The public increasingly favored lower fares. Air travel had become democratized. In the bygone days, men and women wore hats and gloves as they boarded the plane and waved good-bye to friends who had come to the airport to wish them "bon voyage." Now, everyone wanted to get on an airplane—never mind the hats and gloves—and see Los Angeles or Las Vegas or London, but they needed low fares to get there. The time was ripe for the argument that removing the bonds of regulation would lead to lower fares.

When I appeared before Senator Cannon, I testified against deregulation but advocated greater freedom for the airlines to adjust fares within a "zone of reasonableness." This was the position adopted by the ATA board in vigorous discussions before my appearance. Although most of the airline chiefs opposed a fundamental change in a regulatory regime they knew and understood, some doubts were beginning to appear. A particularly significant moment occurred when Al Feldman, the head of Frontier Airlines, told his fellow CEOs that he was having trouble explaining to his wife just why it was that the industry opposed greater freedom of action.

In 1978, the Airline Deregulation Act, cosponsored by Senators Cannon and Kennedy, became the law of the land by a wide margin. It gradually phased out price and entry controls and eventually abolished the Civil Aeronautics Board. Much of what the new legislation required had already been accomplished by a more liberal CAB under chairman Robson and his successor, Alfred Kahn, who took steps to end regulatory control of price and entry. In many respects, the new act simply codified what had already taken place.

The effects of deregulation were immediate. Harding Lawrence plucked so many new routes that he plunged his airline, Braniff, into bankruptcy. Contrary to some of the carriers' earlier fears, United did not become the six-hundred-pound gorilla, gobbling up everything in sight. There were a number of significant changes in the structure of the industry. Pan Am acquired National in an attempt to establish a

domestic network to complement its international routes. Delta
acquired Western. Northwest acquired Republic. United purchased
Pan Am's Pacific routes when the great international carrier met financial difficulties. TWA acquired Ozark, and many years later, American
acquired TWA.

While the established airlines were rearranging themselves through
acquisitions and mergers, new airlines such as People's Express, New
York Air, and Midway appeared on the scene, offering low fares and
spartan service. John Meyer and Clinton Oster in *Deregulation and the
Future of Intercity Passenger Travel* provide a good description of how the
new carriers operated:

> The new entrants typically achieved lower costs than the old estab-
> lished carriers in a variety of ways, including being less unionized
> and paying lower wages with less restrictive work rules, flying their
> aircraft more hours per day, allowing more managerial discretion in
> making labor assignments, using less expensive satellite airports or
> terminals, eliminating "unnecessary" service frills, encouraging
> travelers to carry their own luggage (sometimes even quoting spe-
> cial charges for luggage that was checked), eliminating meal serv-
> ices, and using less comfortable and more closely spaced seats.

To the surprise of many, the established airlines did not follow the
dinosaurs into extinction. During the regulated era, individuals with
legal and political skills tended to run the airlines. Deregulation ush-
ered in more business-oriented executives, enabling management to
manage or, as Al Feldman once told me, "to run my operation like a
business, not like an airline." (One indication of the new businesslike
approach was the loss of my lifetime pass privileges.) Hubs were
formed at strategically located airports where incoming passengers
were sorted out for flights to their ultimate destinations. Computers
were harnessed to permit lower fares without displacing passengers
willing to pay more, a process known as "yield management." It
worked like this. Data stored in the computer enabled an accurate
forecast of how many passengers would pay full fare on a flight, say
from Boston to Cleveland on a Tuesday morning in August. The air-

line could then fill otherwise empty seats by offering substantially reduced fares to entice new passengers to fly on that particular Tuesday. The number of discount seats was limited to those expected to be empty. Previously an airline discounted the fares of all the seats, causing a loss of revenue from those passengers willing to pay more.

American Airlines, in particular, under Bob Crandall's leadership, responded with entrepreneurial vigor. Crandall perfected the techniques of yield management, pioneered in the development of computer reservation systems, developed a two-tier wage structure in which incoming workers were paid less than those with seniority, and launched the frequent flyer concept. Airlines traditionally offered an undifferentiated product. They flew the same planes, served what many passengers called the same lousy meals, and enjoyed at best "brand preference" but not "brand loyalty." Brand loyalty was what Chevrolet, for example, enjoyed when loyal customers turned in their old Chevies for the new model. A person might prefer a particular airline but typically chose the one that departed at the most convenient time. The frequent flyer program changed all that. It conferred brand loyalty on an undifferentiated product by offering the enticement of free trips as airline miles accumulated.

Meyer and Oster summarized the results of deregulation:

Passenger airfares unquestionably have been lower on average because of deregulation.

Service has probably improved for the majority of travelers with typically more flights on each route and more airlines serving each city. The airlines have also become more productive and cut costs.

Most post-deregulation concerns about adverse social impacts also do not seem to have materialized. By most measures, service to small communities is now at least as good, and probably better, than under regulation and the subsidy cost to the government is dramatically lower.

Airline safety had also apparently not been degraded; indeed, the industry has amassed a slightly better safety record since deregulation than in the comparable period before.

Deregulation was not an unalloyed success. Familiar names—Pan Am, TWA, Eastern—disappeared. More seats were added to already crowded coach sections, making travel less comfortable. New fares appeared in such bewildering abundance that no one could be sure whether he or she got a bargain or paid too much. The *New York Times*, in a March 25, 1983, editorial, had fun with what it called "The Air Fare Carnival": "Flying to Los Angeles? That will be $198 round trip. . . . Not until April 3? Oh, then it's $318, provided you pay seven days in advance and stay between seven and 14 days. . . . Not long enough? Well, the unrestricted fare is $499 one way and $539 if you stop en route. But hold on! Some new fares are coming over the computer now."

In 1982, following several years of economic losses by the airlines, Senator Howard Cannon appeared as a guest at an ATA board of directors meeting. He wanted to know whether deregulation was the cause of the dire financial straits and, if so, whether Congress should consider reregulating the airlines. The airlines represented in the room were the same ones, with the exception of United, that had opposed deregulation. The chief executives responded individually to the senator. Not a single one of them wanted to see the airlines reregulated, though one thought some minor adjustments might be helpful. The current financial difficulties arose from a sluggish economy and high fuel prices, they said, not deregulation. Trying now to reimpose regulation would result in chaos.

The airline chiefs were realists and had come full circle. Deregulation was the law of the land, one of them said, so let's get on with it. There is bound to be a shakeout after so fundamental a change, another said, and each carrier will have to find its place in the new market. Another said he no longer opposed deregulation: "We much prefer to be in control of our destiny."

The battle for deregulation had come to an end. But twenty years later some of the old worries about the fate of the unregulated industry began to arise as big carriers such as United and U.S. Airways operated under bankruptcy protection and others such as American and Delta struggled to avoid financial collapse. What had led to the crisis? First, there was a sharp drop in passenger revenue after the terrorists attacked the World Trade Center and the Pentagon with hijacked United and American Airlines aircraft. A lagging economy caused many businesses to curtail travel plans or to shift from premium seats to economy fares. The cost of fuel, a major part of operating costs, rose to a new high as the price of a barrel of oil climbed from around $25 to more than $60 in 2005. Finally, traditionally low-cost carriers such as Southwest and new ones such as Jet Blue offered dependable flights at fares the full-service carriers could match only by operating at a loss. In the four years since 2000, the big carriers lost a staggering $30 billion. Southwest and Jet Blue were buffeted by the same headwinds, but they were better able to cope with the system because of their lower cost structure.

In an effort to stave off financial collapse, the big carriers laid off thousands of employees, forced large pay cuts, grounded aircraft, reduced the number of flights, eliminated meals and other amenities, and charged for some services previously offered at no cost. Still, the ultimate survival of some carriers remained in doubt. Not everyone thought the public would suffer. "I don't see it as dark, foreboding, and black," Southwest's chairman, Herbert D. Kelleher, said in an October 30, 2004, *New York Times* article. Perhaps the dynamics of the marketplace will sort things out and assure an adequate level of air transportation for the public and for business. If not, there will be a rising clamor for some sort of regulated regime. A country as large as the United States simply cannot function without a dependable air transportation system.

Airport and Airways Constraints

The ATA staff spent much of its time trying to relieve airport and airways constraints. Persistent shortages of airport capacity were mainly the result of the phenomenal growth of air travel. Is it possible to find a major airport anywhere that is not hobbled by expansion projects, with building cranes, detour signs, and temporary entrances impeding easy access? ("Please pardon our dust while we build for your future.")

Because the airports are owned by local government, the decision-making process for modernization or expansion must involve the citizenry and is usually agonizingly slow. For years it was apparent that National Airport in Washington, D.C., built in the 1930s, was wholly unsuited to modern needs. I once said that if Franklin D. Roosevelt had somehow reappeared in the Washington so vastly changed from his time, the only thing he would recognize would be the old, shopworn airport. Yet it took years for all the constituents to agree to modernize it.

Building a new airport is a huge undertaking. St. Louis spent years trying to decide where to site a new airport. Much the same thing happened in Denver. Environmental impact was always a central concern. In this regard, the airlines are a "clean" form of transport compared with cars and trucks, which are major polluters of the air. The airlines' environmental problem is noise. Despite successful efforts to reduce the volume and irritable characteristics of engine noise, a modern jetliner climbing into the skies can be a noisy intruder. ATA's lawyers and technical engineers manned their battle stations fighting the imposition of nighttime curfews, limitations on the number of permitted flights, and nuisance suits claiming that aircraft noise at night interfered with conjugal enjoyment. One of ATA's most effective projects was a careful analysis of the causes of delays at twenty-two major airports and the development of corrective measures at each one.

Airways constraints were equally serious, perhaps more so, and they arose from the failure of the Federal Aviation Administration to replace its ancient equipment in a timely fashion. The traffic control computers, based on stone-age vacuum tube technology, were often older than the men and women who operated them. When a computer broke down and needed a repair part, the buyers searched their supplier lists trying to find a part no longer being made. Aircraft were slowed down or rerouted and separation distances widened until the computer was fixed.

During the 1980s, the FAA finally proposed its long overdue airways modernization plan. It was a gigantic undertaking from the standpoint of cost and complexity, not unlike national defense projects to design and build the Polaris missile and submarine. What the FAA lacked was the managerial expertise to bring such a challenging venture to completion. There was no one at FAA such as Adm. "Red" Raborn or Adm. Levering Smith with their technical staffs and resources to oversee the project. Moreover, the proposal lacked adequate definition of the technical parameters and likely costs, with the result that no one could be sure when it would be completed and how much it would cost. To overcome its managerial deficiencies, the FAA turned over project management to Lockheed-Martin.

The airlines were not the only users of the airports and airways. There are over 216,000 private planes owned by individuals or corporations that travel the country for business or personal reasons. These aircraft typically carry only a handful of people compared with the hundreds on an airliner, but they take up as much airspace and as much time to land as a large airliner. Accordingly, I thought we should apply in the air the principles we follow on the ground during peak hours when resources are overtaxed. On the ground, you can travel in the fast lane if you have another passenger with you, or use a specially designated lane if you commute by bus. These common-sense principles do not apply where air travel is concerned. Everyone is handled equally on a first-come, first-served basis. When I suggested once in congressional testimony that we do in the air what we do on the ground, I was shot down at once by the powerful private plane lobby. I was equally unsuccessful in suggesting that we should employ measures such as peak-hour pricing to ration scarce resources, just as theaters and restaurants do. A ticket for a Wednesday matinee costs less than one for Saturday night. You can get a bargain-priced dinner if you're willing to eat it between 5 PM and 7 PM. In recent years, some of these economic incentives have been adopted.

If there are even more severe airway and airport constraints in future years, we may have to adopt transportation policies that optimize the inherent advantages of the various transportation modes. The airplane has the unmatched advantage for trips of five hundred miles or more. For a short trip, you burn a lot of kerosene climbing to twenty-eight-thousand feet, only to begin descending a few minutes later to complete your one-hour flight. It doesn't take much more time to travel by train from Washington to New York—portal to portal— than it does to fly, and it costs less.

Time to Go

When a person at ATA reached the age of sixty-five, it was time to go. That time for me came in 1985. I had prepared for it by making Norm Philion the president and assuming the title of chairman for myself. Philion was superbly qualified to take over by virtue of experience, hard work, good judgment, and the respect of the industry and the ATA staff.

Shortly before my time of departure, tragedy struck. Norm and I and our wives had been at an airline party at the Air and Space Museum in Washington. Driving home to his house in Great Falls, he suffered a severe heart attack and died almost immediately. He was still a relatively young man and seemed to be in good health, though we always worried about his smoking and eating habits. He consumed a couple of packs a day, usually skipped lunch, and ate a big dinner when he got home. Perhaps this regimen brought on his untimely death. He is still remembered around ATA as one of the finest practitioners the industry has ever produced.

I was asked to stay on for an additional six months to keep the ship afloat and find a successor. With the help of ATA's executive committee, we considered a number of candidates. We decided to hire a man who had been the assistant postmaster general and knew the ways of Washington, supported by a retired air force general expected to succeed him after a couple of years. It seemed like a good plan at the time but it didn't work out. The ATA board then turned to its general counsel, Jim Landry, and like the earlier general counsel, Stuart Tipton, he brought informed leadership to the presidency. When Landry retired, the board elected a talented woman, Carol Hallett, who served ably for many years.

ATA gave me a lovely present on my retirement on June 11, 1986. It was a beautifully crafted coffee table with the wings of each airline over the facsimile signatures of the respective chief executives. It is today, I suppose, something of a museum piece. Most of the airlines whose proud wings embellish the table are now gone—Eastern, Pan Am, Republic, TWA, Frontier, Western, Ozark, Flying Tigers, Braniff, Piedmont—and none of the chiefs who signed their names below the wings is still active.

I got more satisfaction from my years at ATA than I had expected. With the help of outstanding professionals, we built what I believe was the finest trade association in Washington, able to deal with the inevitable petty matters but fully capable of handling crises like the threat of terrorism, the illegal strike of the air traffic controllers, the oil shocks of the 1970s, and the upheaval occasioned by deregulation of the airlines. The time went faster than a jet airplane, and my bosses from the industry and my associates at ATA were good people to have along for the ride.

Nine

Nonprofit Rewards

I WASN'T SURE WHAT I WANTED TO DO AFTER RETIRING FROM THE Air Transport Association. The main question for me, as for so many others who have had executive responsibility, was whether to seek another time at bat or do something useful in a "retirement" status. I thought that getting out of town and focusing on entirely different matters would help me decide. Nan and I saw an advertisement for a three-week summer study program at Oxford University and decided at once that we should head for England. The program was scheduled to start in July, about a month after my retirement party at ATA on June 11, 1986.

Worcester College, where the summer students were housed, is one of the oldest colleges at Oxford. Our room was snug, with barely enough space for a bed, two small desks, and a washstand. (Toilets and showers were down the hall.) I expected the food to be sitting in steam tables—mostly soggy Brussels sprouts left over from the Norman Conquest in 1066. We had fresh fruit and salads every day, but the meat at dinner time was a puzzle. Was it beef, lamb, or pork? Perhaps chicken? It looked about the same each night and tasted as lifeless as it looked.

Deciding which subject to study was as difficult as deciphering the origin of the meat; all the courses sounded interesting, but we could

246

take only one. Nan chose the Evolution of Darwinism, which was taught by a brilliant young biologist with an unpronounceable Polish name. When she discovered that her classmates were science majors and that the course was highly technical, she tried to get out, but the instructor persuaded her to stick with it. She did, and gained what has become a lifelong interest in the theory of evolution and the point at which science and religion intersect.

I wanted to take British Attitudes on the American Revolution but it was oversubscribed so I settled on Shakespeare's Tragedies. We read, discussed, and wrote analytical papers on *Hamlet, King Lear, Macbeth,* and *Othello.* For someone who had been immersed in airways constraints and the price of jet fuel, it was a welcome and enjoyable change. Why *did* Othello trust Iago, a person of "motiveless malignity," more than his devoted wife? Was Macbeth's hand that held the dagger guided by Lady Macbeth or his own dark impulses? I look at one of the essays I wrote then and recall the pleasure of Shakespeare: "No longer can the Fool say of Lear that 'thou shouldst not have been old till thou hadst been wise.' Lear, to paraphrase Eugene O'Neill, has made a 'long night's journey into day,' and prepared for the death that awaits him momentarily because the truth has lighted his way."

Beyond the intellectual pleasure was tennis—lawn tennis—on Worcester College's courts. The English weather cooperated and we played almost every day. Weekends in London and a side trip to Stratford-upon-Avon to see *The Winter's Tale* rounded out our Oxford experience. Education was too precious, someone said, to confine to the young, and it was no accident that several years later we returned for a second Oxford experience.

The respite from day-to-day preoccupations made me realize that I didn't want another full-time job. I had enough income from my ATA and government pensions and from Social Security to live comfortably. (Several years later I gained additional income from the appreciation of stock options in an information technology company on whose board I had served for six years.) I decided I would concentrate on community and public service activities in nonprofit organizations. I would also do the things that pleased me most—read, write, play tennis, spend weekends at our farm, and travel, particularly to where our children and grandchildren lived.

Many men go to pieces when they retire. They miss the sense of importance that a big job confers, the perquisites of office, the demanding schedules that fill their days. None of this troubled me because my work was not the only thing in my life. What I missed most of all was a good secretary, but I bought a used IBM typewriter from ATA and got by with the help of its handy correction tape. I found that nonprofit community activities offered management challenges every bit as absorbing as those one found in business.

The National Symphony Orchestra

The National Symphony Orchestra was founded in 1931 and performs regularly at the Kennedy Center in Washington, D.C., on U.S. and foreign tours, and at special events such as presidential inaugurations and national holidays. Through the efforts of its board members, it has money to hire top-flight conductors and musicians and an able administrative staff. It is one of the best symphony orchestras in the United States.

I joined the symphony board in 1970 when I was president of the *Washington Post* and continued as a member for more than twenty-five years before deciding to resign and make room for someone else. Board members included active businessmen and women—heads of banks and local companies—along with prominent lawyers and real estate developers, socially ambitious men and women, and even several people thoroughly schooled in symphonic music. A great many people sought to become members of boards such as this one because it enhanced their social standing in the community.

The board's principal function was raising money. Prospective members were informed that they were expected to give or get $10,000 a year. Many gave far more. The concert program for the 2002 season, for example, lists nineteen individuals or married couples who had contributed $250,000 each.

The board played a role in determining the quality of the orchestra. It hired the music director, obtaining during my tenure such luminaries as Mstislav Rostropovich and Leonard Slatkin. It also studied major policy questions. In 1977, I drafted the committee report of one of these studies that charted the course for the future. The report's major conclusion was that the NSO could become one of the world's great musical institutions if the board was willing to raise enough money. We were already running deficits that were likely to grow larger in the coming years. We thought that the only way to reverse this trend was to become a great orchestra, to fill the hall for each concert, to raise ticket prices, and to attract a broader base of individual and corporate support. In short, we believed that high quality would bring high income.

As a first step, we recommended an increase from 96 to 106 musicians, the recognized level for a fully staffed symphonic orchestra. Next, we needed funds to help orchestra members to acquire the best musical instruments. More money was needed for touring, recordings, and television tapings to enhance the prestige of the orchestra. A great world capital without a superior symphony orchestra would be unthinkable, we said. I ended the sixty-seven-page report with the following paragraph: "There is a single word in the Chinese language that means at once both crisis and opportunity. No word could more aptly describe the circumstances facing the National Symphony Orchestra. It cannot stand still; it dare not retreat. It must go forward, seizing the opportunity for musical greatness within its reach as the means of averting the financial crisis that otherwise will be its fate."

The board's decision to go forward was not unlike commitments by corporate boards. There is a saying in business that you have to grow or you will stagnate. You cannot stand still while others adapt to change. But there are risks in going forward. The NSO board took on the risk, and its reward was an orchestra of surpassing accomplishment.

The vision of a top-quality orchestra playing to full houses was not fully realized until Leonard Slatkin became the music director in 1994. I sent him a memo prior to his arrival that discussed board matters but also ventured into verboten territory for a board member—programming, the virtually exclusive domain of the music director. I was concerned about our graying audiences and had some ideas that I thought might help to attract younger patrons:

> There are many musicians in the orchestra who like to play jazz. Why not feature them occasionally in jazz concerts? Why not do programs on movie music, perhaps multimedia in nature, showing how music enhances drama, and showcasing motion picture scores by Sergei Prokofiev, Erich Korngold, Virgil Thompson, and others? Why not—especially—recognize the great composer from our own city, Duke Ellington, and develop programs from both his well-known and lesser-known works?
>
> What can we do to make the Kennedy Center and the concert hall more inviting? . . . Our lounges are off-limits except for those who contribute $1,000 or more. We need places where people can crowd together before a concert and during the intermission for a drink and a snack. We need to warm up the concert hall. Would flowers help? A new podium? Large works of art like those at Lincoln Center? The Kennedy Center, indoors and on its fine outdoor pavilion, offers many locations for incidental entertainment, dancing, and civility that we should use more often.

Slatkin did many of the things I suggested and a whole lot more. He is one of the world's foremost music directors, but he isn't stuffy. He loves baseball along with Bach, Beethoven, and Brahms. The audiences now include younger men and women along with the faithful gray-haired regulars.

The George C. Marshall Foundation

General of the Army George Catlett Marshall was the architect of victory in World War II; the greatest man of the century, President Truman thought; "the last great American," in Winston Churchill's words. Marshall served the country as secretary of state after his military career and proposed the plan that came to bear his name for rebuilding war-torn Europe. He was awarded the Nobel Peace Prize in 1953.

At President Truman's urging, a library and museum in Marshall's honor were established on the parade grounds of the Virginia Military Institute where he had been the cadet captain in 1901. The museum contains his wartime maps, and memorabilia from his distinguished career. At the library, Forrest C. Pogue wrote his multivolume biography of Marshall, and other scholars continue to publish books and articles on his achievements.

The early board members of the Marshall Foundation were men who had served on his wartime staff or with him at the State Department. As these men grew old or died, they were replaced by men and women who admired Marshall but never served with him. I was one of these newer directors when I joined the board in 1987. The closest I ever came to Marshall was when I sat in my seat in Harvard Yard in front of the platform where he delivered the "Marshall Plan" speech in June 1947.

The purpose of the foundation is to preserve Marshall's legacy and to inspire future generations with the example of his character and selfless service. One of its long-standing efforts is a four-day seminar each year for the outstanding cadets from each of the colleges offering Reserve Officer Training Corps (ROTC) programs. Here is how General Colin Powell described Marshall when he spoke to the cadets in 1993:

> There were no pearl-handled revolvers or corncob pipes or crusty anecdotes to spice up the legend of Marshall, and there were no hand grenades strapped to his chest. He never wrote a book to tell his story. He never ran for election to public office. He never sought popularity. He never exploited his fame. He never asked for recognition or favors. He was a man driven more than anything else by a sense of duty, by the powerful, overpowering obligation of service.

We cannot all hope to be as dedicated as Marshall, but his example is instructive at a time like the present when personal ambition seems to have triumphed over selfless service. How should the Marshall Foundation keep his example alive beyond what it is accomplishing through the ROTC seminar? One attempt is a new program to develop leadership skills for participants in the high school Junior ROTC. Another is an educational effort in the middle schools of Virginia that uses Marshall and other eminent Virginians, such as athlete-activist Arthur Ashe, as role models worthy of emulation. We hope to adapt this program for use in other states by selecting outstanding natives of the states for inspiration and study. We have conducted a seminar for young men and women with an interest in public service, but it has not yet become a permanent feature of our program structure. On two occasions we have cosponsored with the World Bank conferences on rebuilding the economies of the Balkan nations. The archival material at the library is being digitized to make it available to a much wider audience.

I joined the Marshall board because I believed that public service was a high calling, and that anyone privileged to serve his country was a fortunate person. Marshall exemplified the meaning of public service to me. Long after he had paid his debt to his country, he responded to further calls—to mediate the civil war in China, to serve as secretary of state and then as secretary of defense—at a time when he had earned the right to spend his final years with Mrs. Marshall, devoting himself to gentle tasks such as the gardening he loved.

I hope others will be motivated by Marshall's example, as I am. Everyone seems to know about the Marshall Plan—it's what you need when there's a big job to be done. Most people have forgotten about George Marshall himself. Our foundation needs to do more to make the man and his peerless character better known.

The Logistics Management Institute

In an earlier chapter I described how Tom Morris, with my participation, developed the concept of a small outside-management analysis and research organization to augment the work of the military and civilian logistics staffs in the Pentagon. Secretary McNamara immediately recognized the benefits of Morris's plan and quickly obtained

President Kennedy's approval to launch the Logistics Management Institute in 1961.

LMI was a government-chartered FFRDC (Federally Funded Research and Development Center), a nonprofit organization like the RAND Corporation or the Institute for Defense Analyses. It worked exclusively for the Defense Department but later took on projects for civilian agencies. It performed no private sector work.

During the 1960s, LMI was at the center of Secretary McNamara's efforts to reform military procurement and rationalize the relationship between the department and the contractors who supplied its weapons and equipment. Its work was overseen by Morris, and by me when I replaced Morris as an assistant secretary of defense. Because its size and resources were limited, it undertook only high-priority projects for the senior members of the department. McNamara met frequently with the LMI president and with the chairman of its board, Charles Kellstadt, the former head of Sears, Roebuck.

In 1986, long after I had left the Department of Defense, I was invited by Roger Lewis, who had succeeded Kellstadt, to become an LMI board member. I accepted because I had been present at the creation of LMI and understood the special nature of its work. What I found when I came on board surprised me. LMI had become a "body shop" with a much larger staff that provided manpower to prepare the endless studies and reports that were an inevitable aspect of the department's vast undertakings. Instead of working on high-level projects where its independent point of view could influence logistics policy, LMI was burdened with routine assignments better done by departmental personnel.

A short while after I joined the board, Roger Lewis died and I was asked to chair the board. I welcomed the assignment because I hoped to return the institute to its original concept. The first step was to replace the president with a more dynamic leader. The person we chose was a retired air force general, Robert Pursley, a unique officer who had been the military assistant to three secretaries of defense—Robert McNamara, Clark Clifford, and Melvin Laird. Pursley was a West Pointer with a master's degree from the Harvard Business

School. He had taught economics along the way at the Air Force Academy, served as commanding general of U.S. forces in Japan, and was a partner after his retirement in the venture capital firm of J. H. Whitney & Company. I had worked with Pursley in the Pentagon and believed that there was no one better qualified to rebuild LMI.

The next step was to reinvigorate the board. Too many of the board members had served in their positions for too long a time. We established seventy-two as the mandatory retirement age, freeing up several openings for new members. We obtained some highly qualified replacements—Ed Pratt, the chairman of Pfizer, Inc.; Gen. Bernard Rogers, the former NATO commander and a Rhodes scholar; Dr. John Foster, the former head of the Pentagon's research and development work; and another Rhodes scholar, Charles DiBona, who had distinguished himself in both government and private sector positions.

LMI had traditionally faced difficulties in the job market because its salary structure was based on civil service levels, while companies such as McKinsey and Booz Allen, which sought the same type of people, could pay more. After a detailed study, the LMI board approved a new salary schedule that made LMI more competitive. Salary was the most significant element of compensation because, as a nonprofit institute, LMI could not offer inducements such as stock options or profit-sharing bonuses.

Meanwhile Pursley met in off-site sessions with his staff to discuss needed changes in organization and management. He hired a consultant to help the staff to write concise, well-argued reports. He instituted a lecture series with distinguished speakers from government, industry, and academia. Finally, he and I met on a regular basis with the top civilian and military leaders of the Pentagon to reacquaint them with LMI and the ways it could help them to carry out their responsibilities.

Two things happened as a result of all this. First, LMI began to undertake once again the important logistics policy studies for which it had been established. Second, the volume of work increased so much that the institute was forced to move to a large new building in northern Virginia.

Pursley had agreed to stay for three years at the time he was hired, but he later agreed to stay for one more. When I reached the mandatory retirement age of seventy-two, the board extended me for a year until 1993, so that Pursley and I would not leave at the same time. We recruited a new president to replace Pursley, a retired four-star Army general and logistics expert, William Tuttle, who, like Pursley, had a Harvard MBA.

LMI continued to grow under Tuttle's leadership. By 2004, its annual volume of work totaled more than $100 million, compared to $12 million at the time I joined the board. The staff numbered over five hundred professionals, and the share of work was 60 percent for national security and 40 percent for the civilian agencies.

LMI named a conference room for me when I retired in 1993. Charles DiBona assumed the chairmanship and, with Bill Tuttle, provided strong leadership. Under its current head, Adm. Donald Pilling, a former vice chief of naval operations. LMI continues to grow because its expertise in the world of logistics is at the heart of the revolutionary changes occasioned by the Internet and the information-based economy. Its understanding of government organizations has helped to improve public-sector management.

The Washington Tennis and Education Foundation

Since its beginning in 1955, this foundation has had three different names. The name changes reflect the progress toward its ultimate goal of improving the lifetime prospects for Washington youth, particularly those from low-income communities. It does this through tennis and educational activities that teach discipline, build self-esteem, and sharpen academic performance.

Originally, it was called the Washington Area Tennis Patrons Foundation. It was a small, somewhat elite group of mostly white, socially prominent individuals who played tennis at country clubs and private courts, and raised modest amounts of money to send promising young players to regional tournaments. One of these young players was Donald Dell, destined to become a Davis Cup captain and the founder of ProServ, a pioneering sports management firm that represented athletic stars such as the legendary Arthur Ashe.

Through his extensive tennis connections, Dell obtained the right to schedule a men's tennis championship in Washington. He wanted to hold it in a public park to get away from the "white flannels" image that had characterized tennis for so long. Working with tennis foundation officials, Dell made arrangements for the foundation to own the tournament and for ProServ to manage it.

Dell needed a financial sponsor and approached me when I was president of the *Washington Post*, offering to name the tournament for the paper in return for a sponsorship fee of $25,000. I was very much in favor of the proposition, but others at the paper objected. They remembered the time when the *Post* had sponsored a golf tournament that distracted its executives from their jobs. Dell went to the rival newspaper and the tournament was named for the *Washington Star*. It was first held in 1969 at Rock Creek Park, with the spectators sitting in temporary grandstands and the players showering in portable bathrooms. Like the foundation, the tournament has gone through several name changes; it is now called the Legg Mason Classic.

Tennis was a big deal in Washington. Teddy Roosevelt played tennis on the White House court with members of his cabinet and several foreign ambassadors whom he favored. At the St. Albans Tennis Club, located below the towering Washington Cathedral, there were sometimes enough senators on the courts to constitute a quorum for transacting business. Count Wilhelm Wachmeister, the Swedish ambassador, used his court for tennis with government leaders and media heavies, and was a regular at the White House in games with President George H. W. Bush. Encouraged by Wachmeister's success and not to be outdone, the Australian ambassador built a grass court, the only one in Washington, on the grounds of his residence.

Washington's interest in tennis helped to make the *Star* tournament a financial success, benefiting the foundation. In some years, the foundation's share of the profits exceeded $300,000, more than enough to fund its then quite modest programs.

Tennis had always been an important part of my life. My grandfather had his own tennis court in California where my mother and her brothers played. They taught me the game, and I played on my high school team and on the freshman squad at the University of Southern California. In 1970, when I was asked to join the foundation board, I accepted with enthusiasm. I worked hard on its programs and after several years was elected its president.

Television turned sports into show business, and tennis pros such as John McEnroe and Jimmy Connors became matinee idols. With their star status, they expected more than the temporary toilets and showers of the Washington tournament. They also wanted a larger stadium for more paying customers to meet their demands for more prize and expense money. Dell told the foundation that it would lose the tournament unless a larger facility was built. With a founding grant of $1 million from a board member and tennis enthusiast, William H. G. FitzGerald, the foundation embarked on a successful campaign to raise the $8 million thought to be necessary. The stadium, seating 7,500, ended up costing $11 million, with the shortfall financed by a bank loan to the foundation.

The foundation's executive director in the mid-1980s, when the new stadium was being constructed, was a young man named Dwight Mosley. An African American, Mosley felt a kinship with the poor black kids in Washington and thought that the foundation, through tennis, could improve their lot. Tennis, like any difficult sport, requires discipline and concentration. The disadvantaged kids, mostly from single-parent households, needed to develop these attributes if they were going to succeed in life. Tennis was a means toward that end. The foundation under Mosley's leadership enlarged its efforts and enrolled thousands of young boys and girls, mostly from the black community, in afternoon, weekend, and summer tennis activities. Because the foundation's name sounded patronizing, it was changed from "the Patrons" to the Washington Tennis Foundation. The cost of Mosley's expanded programs together with the interest payments on the bank loan caused serious financial problems for the foundation, and there were even a few times when we had difficulty meeting the payroll. Moreover, for the moment at least, tennis tournaments throughout the country had lost some of their luster, and box office receipts tumbled. With income down and expenses up, the take from the tournament was far below what the foundation needed. There were even several years when the tournament ended up in the red, with ProServ absorbing the losses.

Something needed to be done to broaden the financial base. I was asked to look into the problem and suggest some remedies. What was immediately evident was our need for a different kind of board. We needed more members with an interest in raising money and with contacts in corporations and foundations that would produce grants for our programs. Additionally, our governance structure needed to be simplified; we had what amounted to two boards, one of them honorary, with no clear understanding of what each was expected to do. I agreed to serve as president for a second time to put the recommended changes into effect.

New board members such as former FBI director William Webster and longtime ones such as William FitzGerald tapped new sources of money. My tennis-playing brother mentioned our program to another senior player, Jerome Kohlberg, who became a generous and faithful supporter. Lady luck smiled on us again when I met D. D. Eisenberg at a cocktail party. She had recently moved from Philadelphia because her husband had been appointed as a professor of medicine at Georgetown University. D. D. said her main interest was sports programs for kids and agreed to join our board. She duplicated in Washington what she had originated in Philadelphia—a spectacular tennis event with celebrity players and a fabulous auction. It became the foundation's major source of funds, netting as much as a half million dollars annually.

Meanwhile, the emphasis in our tennis program was shifting to education. The bellwether effort was one we named after Arthur Ashe. The Ashe program was conducted after school four afternoons a week in some of the most blighted areas of the nation's capital. Two afternoons were reserved for tennis and the other two for educational purposes. More primary and junior high schools were added each year, reaching a total of twenty-two. Specially selected teachers were engaged by the foundation to handle the educational responsibilities.

While all this was going forward, tragedy struck. Dwight Mosley developed a brain tumor and died within a year. The young man who had propelled us toward the goal of improving children's lives was no longer there to guide our efforts.

By the greatest good fortune, I learned about a young woman named Jennifer Brown Simon. I couldn't believe her résumé. She was a graduate of Yale University where she had captained the women's tennis team. She went on to earn an MBA from Harvard. She had worked during summer vacations on development programs in Africa and South America, and knew the Washington scene from a stint as a congressional aide. She was a rising star at McKinsey & Co. but wanted to work in the nonprofit sector with kids who needed help. I dropped everything I was doing and spent two weeks persuading Jennifer to become our executive director.

Building on Dwight Mosley's efforts, Jennifer extended our educational reach to the point where it became necessary once again to change the foundation's name. We now called ourselves the Washington Tennis and Education Foundation. We converted several of the corporate suites at the stadium, where our offices were located, to learning centers for our kids. An expert on college preparation was added to the staff to lead classes for high schoolers, sometimes accompanied by a parent. It is called the Center for Excellence and had an unparalleled record during its first four years, with 100 percent of its high school seniors gaining admission to college and receiving more than $1.3 million in tennis and academic scholarships.

Jennifer, with her business background, upgraded the foundation's management. One grantor that had somewhat reluctantly backed us at a level of $10,000 annually upped its contribution to $50,000 when learning about the management changes. The foundation placed second in the *Washington Post*'s competition for the best managed nonprofit organization in Washington, D.C. In 1999, the United States Tennis Association selected the Washington Tennis and Education Foundation as the top tennis organization in the country. Two women—D. D. and Jennifer—and one gifted young man, Dwight, made it happen. Jennifer resigned in 2000 to become a special assistant to the mayor of Washington. In a farewell letter to her, I said that adding the word "education" to our name during her tenure was a fitting memorial to what she had accomplished.

The tennis foundation continues to grow under new leadership. I am still on the board after thirty-five forty years of involvement, but less active each year. It's about time for me to move on. Of my several nonprofit activities, the one that has given me the greatest satisfaction has been the tennis foundation. Partly it was a pleasure for an old guy to work productively with young talent like Dwight and Jennifer. Partly it was knowing that we were doing some good for children who needed help. Partly it was realizing how many people—board members and volunteers—were eager to give their time, energy, and money to a worthwhile effort. These are the rewards that come from labor in the nonprofit sector, and they are hard to match in the world of business.

Ten

Some Final Thoughts

I HAVE LIVED A LONG AND HAPPY LIFE THROUGH PERIODS OF momentous change. Looking back, some things seem especially important. I want to write about my heritage, my marriage and our children, my brother and sister, some of the changes that have occurred during my lifetime, major events such as the Great Depression, World War II, the Cold War, and Vietnam, and a link across four generations of my family.

Writing a chapter such as this one is not easy. Humorists do a better job than the rest of us when called upon to isolate significant events. For example, when James Thurber was asked in 1950 to describe how the world looked at mid-century, he said that women were gaining on men and the dog was about holding its own. Mel Brooks, as the two-thousand-year-old man in the classic recording, responds immediately when asked to name the greatest invention of the last two thousand years: "Saran Wrap! You can look right through it. It clings. You can wrap up olives in it."

I want to look right through what I have described in earlier chapters, find out what clings, and wrap it all up, not with olives, but with some concluding thoughts.

My Armenian Background

Both my parents were Armenians born in the Anatolian highlands in present-day Turkey, ancestral home of the Armenian people. My mother's family came from Armenia by way of Manchester, England, where they lived for twenty years, arriving in the United States in 1911 aboard the ocean liner *Lusitania*. My father came from the old country in 1904 as a young man of nineteen aboard a more spartan ship.

The Armenians were a Christian nationality in the largely Islamic Ottoman Empire, which feared they might agitate for autonomy or independence. Both my mother's family and my father left Armenia to escape Turkish persecution, which culminated in the 1915 genocide of more than one million Armenians.

My maternal grandfather was one of the first graduates of Euphrates College, which had been founded by American missionaries. He spoke and wrote English, and translated Milton's *Paradise Lost* into Armenian. After the Turks arrested him for writing poems that contained dreaded words like "freedom" and "liberty," his family sent him to England to avoid further persecution. He was followed a year later by his wife and my mother, Elisa, the oldest of what became six children. My grandfather started a prosperous company that exported English cotton goods to the Middle East and became a British citizen. His children attended good English schools, where, among other things, they learned how to play tennis.

In 1895, three years after my grandfather left Armenia, Turks and Kurds went into many Armenian villages and massacred the adult males, including my grandfather's brother, his uncle, the uncle's sons, and my grandmother's father. In all, some three hundred thousand Armenians were killed.

My father's family was not harmed, but among those who emigrated to the United States after the massacres were my father's four older brothers. My father, Hovsep, was the youngest of six children. Like my mother's family, they lived in the Kharpert area, and my father graduated from Euphrates College. The brothers, who had settled in Pittsburgh, dropped the patronymic "ian" from their last name, Ignatiosian. My father joined them in 1904, attended a business college, and became office manager of a West Virginia manufacturing company. He became an American citizen in 1911, the same year my mother arrived from England, when her family moved to Glendale, California. On a trip to Los Angeles in 1912, my father looked up my grandfather (known to him from his articles and poems in Armenian American newspapers), met my mother, moved west, and married her in 1919. I was born a year later. My sister, Helen Mary, known as Miggs, was two years younger, and my brother, Joe, five years younger.

My mother's father and my own were businessmen.

When my maternal grandfather arrived in the United States he was rich enough to retire, but bad investments left him with little but a soap factory, a business of which he knew little, but which became the family firm, where he and his sons worked. My father established an Oriental rug and importing business, which prospered until the 1929 crash.

My mother, Elisa, was the free spirit in the family and one of the most cultivated people I've ever known. A talented pianist, she also was an idealist, and opposed war of any kind. My mother encouraged me in whatever I did. She taught me the importance of music, painting, and the value of human life. She played the piano for us and took us to classical concerts and the ballet. I took piano lessons, but gave it up for sports. My mother died in 1957 from complications following the onset of diabetes.

My father was a leader of the Armenians in Southern California, in effect their consul general. His office was the meeting place where civic, religious, and charitable issues were settled. Prominent writers (including William Saroyan), artists, and musicians were frequent visitors at our home. My father helped establish an Armenian old folks' home, was co-founder with my mother of the Armenian Allied Arts Association, and was the toastmaster at events honoring prominent Armenians. He was a handsome, influential man who charmed women, excelled at card games and backgammon, and was the dominant figure in our lives until his death in 1971.

My father had one foot in the Armenian world, where he was Hovsep, and one in the Los Angeles business world, where he was Joe. Unlike my father, I had both feet planted in the middle-class world of public schools, athletic events, and school activities. I acted in school plays, was class president twice, and president of the student body in my senior year. There were no Armenians at Hoover High School except for my siblings and me. I could not speak Armenian and my parents never urged me to learn. I was baptized in the Armenian Church but did not attend Sunday School. We never talked about how the tragic events in Armenia had affected my ancestors, and I learned of them only years later. My mother talked fondly about life in England, but not about Armenia, which she left as a small child. She was less Armenian than my father and not so preoccupied with Armenian affairs. My parents wanted me to know something about Armenian history and culture but not enough to hinder me from becoming a well-rounded American boy. They wanted me to take my place in the new country they had adopted but not forget the place from where they came.

My wife was pleased to marry someone with a background different from her own because it added an interesting dimension to the relationship. She learned to cook Armenian dishes and traveled to Armenia in 1983 with a group from the Washington National Cathedral. Because of me, she studied Armenian history, and, as a graduate student, wrote a paper on the treaties of Sevres and Lausanne involving the disposition of Armenian questions after World War I. She gave a copy to my father on his seventy-fifth birthday, and he told her it was the most precious gift he could possibly have received.

My son David visited Armenia in 1990 and met with political and intellectual leaders. My younger son Adi has been urging me to visit Armenia with him. I think we might go in a year or so. He wants to see where at least a part of him originated. Like my other children, he is intrigued with his Armenian background. Their mother's background also has been of great interest to them. A New Englander, one of her ancestors came over on the *Mayflower*, and another, Conrad Weiser, was an early Pennsylvanian who fostered harmonious relations with the Native American tribes.

My father spent a great deal of his time on Armenian matters, but until recently I spent very little at all. As I grew older I became intensely interested in Armenian history and in current events affecting the new Republic of Armenia. I spoke at a symposium in 2001 celebrating the

seventeen-hundredth anniversary of the founding of the Armenian
Apostolic Orthodox Church. I am proud to be a member of a nation
that was the first to adopt Christianity as its religion and that has maintained its identity while many other early civilizations have vanished.
The University of Southern California has asked me to help them
secure support for a center of Armenian studies. My father, who
helped raise funds for similar centers at Harvard and UCLA, would
have been pleased. I value my heritage and am grateful to my parents
and the extended family that raised me.

My grandfather's and my father's families suffered terribly at the
hands of the Ottoman Turks in 1895 and 1915, with half a dozen members killed and others deported from their ancestral homeland. My
father's sister Ahvni and her two young sons were among the thousands herded across the desert to Aleppo, Syria, during the 1915 massacres. She and her sons survived the ordeal, as she once told me,
because of her faith in God. (Two of our grandchildren are named
Ahvni after her.) I cannot for the life of me understand why the modern Republic of Turkey doesn't acknowledge what its Ottoman predecessors did and apologize to the Armenian people. Great nations are
capable of such gestures. The Germans have come to terms with their
Nazi past and hold their heads high once again among the nations of
the world. The United States has apologized to its citizens of Japanese
ancestry for the internment of the Japanese Americans during World
War II. Why can't the Turks do the same thing?

Marriage and Children

I gave my wife a gyroscope on our fifty-second wedding anniversary a
few years ago. A gyroscope is a child's toy. I had one when I was a boy.
It is more than a toy, however. It has many useful applications in navigation, aviation, and military science. The gyroscope's characteristics
also help to sustain a marriage.

A gyroscope is a rapidly spinning wheel mounted in a framework
that permits it to tilt freely in any direction. It retains its original attitude when the framework is tilted because of the momentum of the

spinning wheel. If the speed of the wheel decreases, the rotor begins to wobble. If a perpendicular force is applied to it, the gyroscope "precesses," that is, it moves at right angles to the direction of the force.

A good marriage needs to maintain its original attitude. Fifty years after taking their vows, the married couple should care as much about each other as they did when they first fell in love. This can happen only if they keep up the speed and maintain the momentum. Otherwise, like the gyro, they will begin to wobble. Momentum imparted at the outset of the romance by the sense of wonder, the anticipation of a shared voyage, and the spirit of adventure must not be lost. "Maintain speed," the sign in the tunnel warns drivers. A sign next to it should say, "Keep up the momentum or you will wobble."

A marriage must be able to withstand all kinds of perpendicular forces. Some of these forces come from the outside—a death, a disappointment, a financial reversal. Others are self-generated—a caustic remark, an unworthy act, a refusal to understand what is being said. Here it is necessary to precess, to move at right angles to the direction of the force in order to keep going in the original direction. That's what a nicely spinning gyroscope does, and that's how a long marriage can continue to be a happy one.

My marriage and the four children it produced is the most rewarding aspect of my life. There is simply no doubt about it. I think that the basic building block in the human enterprise is two people in love who decide to make a go of it for the long haul. Everything else depends on that commitment. The family is the nucleus for the larger aggregations of community life. The essence of the democratic ideal in the United States is the social compact—the willingness of a person to recognize a common good without the loss of individual identity. This is also the essence of marriage. When it works right, individual fulfillment is enlarged by the reciprocal fulfillment of the other person. The larger purpose is to create a protective environment where the passion of love produces one or more children.

I am struck by how much good fortune has come my way as a result of fortuitous events. I was privileged to serve in the government for eight years because Tom Morris happened to tell Elvis Stahr about me. Steve Ailes mentioned my name to Stuart Tipton at lunch one day and I ended up spending fifteen eventful years at the Air Transport Association. Most important of all, my sister Miggs told me about a girl in her class, and fifty-seven years later I'm still married to Nancy Sharpless Weiser. She has been the good wife, the good mother, the good friend and companion, and the good influence on our four children and me.

In the evolution of the women's movement, Nan was a transitional figure. You can trace the stages of the movement over the past hundred years through the women of her immediate family. Her grandmother devoted what free time she had to the Congregational church in Holyoke, Massachusetts. Her mother took the next step. She became the quintessential community activist, fully engaged in uncompensated work on behalf of the hospital, the school, the community chest, and many other worthwhile endeavors. If she had been paid even a small salary for these various jobs, she would have been a wealthy woman.

Nan has had a foot in both camps. She volunteered her time for churches and schools, as her mother and grandmother did, but also enjoyed a professional career for a period of time. Because of her pioneering work in a nonprofit environmental organization that she and several women friends founded, she was hired by the Department of Energy as a GS-13 civil servant. Over a four-year period she prepared analytical and instructional materials on innovative ways to conserve energy and lessen dependence on uncertain foreign sources of oil. Her professional career was cut short because of the lingering effects of a hepatitis infection. After regaining her strength, she went back to work as a consultant for the Environmental Protection Agency, and later on resumed her community work.

Our two daughters, Sarah and Amy, exemplify modern women at the completion of the cycle from volunteerism to full career status. Both went to law school and have practiced law in both private firms and public agencies. Somehow, like so many other modern women, they have been able to raise families while coping with their demanding work schedules.

Nan's work outside the home really didn't begin until our children were able to look out for themselves a bit. Before that, she confined her extracurricular activities to occasional university courses—at Harvard when we lived in Cambridge, at UCLA when California was our home, and at American University when we moved to Washington. Looking after four small children was full-time work. Though she read Dr. Spock's book, as other young mothers of her time did, she learned how to raise children by doing the job. Her New England background had taught her the importance of discipline, and she set limits and boundaries for the children. They had to come to dinner on time, go to bed at a reasonable hour, do their homework, and stay away from the TV set except for permitted periods. To relieve the stress, she gave them five minutes every evening, from 4:55 to 5 PM, to complain about their treatment. They could call her a big oaf or a pumpkin head, but only for five minutes.

The kids did well in school and later life and deserve the credit for their accomplishments. Nan and I gave them a good start. I was away a lot on consulting assignments when they were young, and the main burden fell on Nan. During the Pentagon years, I spent almost as much time in my office as I did at home. Still, I think I contributed to their development in several ways. My interest in public service made them realize that there was more to life than making money. Since we had very little money in the early years, they were not burdened with expensive gifts, expensive activities and lessons of all sorts, or an expectation that inherited wealth would bail them out of any later difficulties. My Armenian background interested them and provided pleasant and sometimes hilarious conversations at leisurely Sunday breakfasts. David developed a remarkable relationship with my father, and the old man and the young boy would converse for hours on weighty subjects. Sarah became close to my Uncle Nicholas during the last years of his life.

Finally, the fact that Nan and I respected and cherished one another must have had a good influence on the kids. As adults, the four of them are doing worthwhile work. David, after a career with the *Wall*

Street Journal, held several senior editorial positions with the *Washington Post* before becoming the executive editor of the *International Herald Tribune* in Paris. He now writes an influential op-ed column for the *Post* and is the author of five novels. Adi, like David, worked for the *Wall Street Journal*, serving as bureau chief in Beijing and then in Moscow. He is now an executive editor at *Time* magazine. Sarah, a passionate believer in human rights, left a promising career with a private law firm to head PAIR, a nonprofit organization in Boston that arranges for pro-bono assistance from lawyers for people from repressive countries who are seeking political asylum in the United States. Amy, with a stern sense of right and wrong, is sometimes called the conscience of the family. She was an assistant attorney general of New Hampshire and is now the general counsel of the state's Public Utility Commission. Nan and I have been blessed by our children, doubly so because they have given us nine wonderful grandchildren.

My Sister and Brother

If Hillary Clinton, a graduate of Wellesley College, runs for president, my sister could claim to have foreseen it sixty years ago. Miggs wrote the book for the Wellesley class of 1947's junior show, a musical about a Wellesley graduate who runs for president.

Despite serious illness in her final months in college and at various times in her life, my sister raised a family of three children, maintained her talent as a pianist, and worked from time to time as an editor or writer. After college she became editor of *The Californian*, a magazine of fashion and cultural events. She got the job by creating on her own an entire issue of the magazine, writing the suggested articles and indicating the accompanying artwork. The publisher, astonished at what she had done, hired her on the spot.

Miggs lived abroad most of her life, in England, Iran, and Saudi Arabia, where her husband, an engineer, designed and managed large-scale petroleum projects. She died peacefully on August 14, 2005.

My brother Joe was told by his junior high school counselor that he was not "college material" and should concentrate on vocational courses, perhaps carpentry or auto repair. He finished high school with top academic and athletic honors and went to Stanford University, where he earned a BA and an MD. After completing a long career as a surgeon, he is now the editor of the *Surgical Index*, a publication he originated that summarizes each month the best articles from thirty surgical journals. The *Index* is distributed online by its sponsor, the American College of Surgeons, to its members in the United States and other countries.

Joe was also a top-flight tennis player, in college but particularly as a senior. He had wins over Bobby Riggs, a former Wimbledon champion and number-one ranked player in the world, and Tom Brown, a Wimbledon finalist.

It is a shame he never got around to those vocational courses, but he did the best he could with what he had to work with.

Some Major Events

The Great Depression

No one who grew up during the Great Depression of the 1930s can ever be the same again. It was an impressionable time for me, between my tenth and twentieth years, and many of my habits can be traced to that far-off period.

My family was better off than most because we had enough money for food and the basic necessities and lived in a comfortable house. Luxuries such as our live-in maid became fond memories. A nephew of my father, struggling to make a go of it, moved into the maid's room and stayed there for a couple of years until his situation improved. Next door, in-laws of the Russell family crowded into the main house and the small shelter, called "the Shack," attached to the garage.

In the United States, one of every four workers was unemployed, and in Europe millions lost their jobs. The mass unemployment and economic stagnation led to totalitarian governments in Europe and extremist movements in the United States. The capitalist engine seemed to have run out of gas. In California and elsewhere in the country, there was a growing interest in cooperatives, socialistic schemes, novel approaches such as the Townsend Plan (a precursor to Social Security that promised $50 every week to those over sixty), and even communism with its enticing appeal of "to each according to his need and from each according to his ability."

My interest in government began when I was twelve, when Franklin D. Roosevelt became president, telling everybody that the only thing to fear was fear itself. In contrast to his predecessor, Herbert Hoover, Roosevelt was an activist willing to experiment with new ideas to get the economy off dead center. I remember thinking that his proposal for a vast Tennessee Valley Authority was a great concept because it would bring electric power to people without it and stimulate demand for washers, dryers, toasters, and all the other things people wanted and needed once they could afford them. Through government intervention (and the approaching war clouds), the economy began to recover. Seeing what Roosevelt and the bright young men around him had accomplished made me want to serve in the government someday.

My father always turned out lights in the house to lower his electric bill. I do the same thing today. I look at the grocery ads, as my mother did, to see who is offering the best prices on lamb chops or chicken, even though I have no need to economize. My socks with holes are darned, not discarded. The bus filled with working people is a friendlier place for me than an expensive taxicab. Habits learned in the Depression persist in a time of affluence.

My children have none of these Depression era hang-ups. They leave lights on all over the house even when the sun is shining brightly. They'd rather buy an expensive latté at Starbucks than drink warmed-over coffee at their parents' house. They are intent on enjoying life today because they haven't known the anxiety of an uncertain tomorrow.

I would never want to see again a time like the Great Depression when so many needed jobs and hope. Despite the pain, it had some redeeming features. People looked out for one another more than they do today. Scarcity seemed to encourage sharing. Wealth seems to have the opposite effect. In the United States and, more important, in the world at large there is a need to narrow the wide gap between the richest and the poorest people so that all can live with confidence in democratic societies. There are lessons from the Depression years that all of us should remember.

Human Rights

There were three great human rights achievements in my lifetime: the Universal Declaration of Human Rights in 1948; the emancipation of women; and the attainment of civil rights by black Americans.

The 1948 Declaration. It was not until the twentieth century that agreement was reached that all human beings were entitled to certain fundamental rights. Before then, primary attention was paid to property rights. The declaration of human rights by the United Nations occurred after Allied victory in World War II. That war, I believe, truly pitted good against evil and put an end to Nazi barbarities and Japanese militarism. Few of us who fought in the war gave very much thought to the need for a bold assertion of universal rights. We were glad the war was over and wanted to get on with our lives. The establishment of the United Nations offered the prospect of avoiding future wars. The declaration of human rights offered hope for those who longed for a life in freedom.

Women's Rights. I first learned about women's emancipation as a young boy when my mother told me about one of her heroines, Emmeline Pankhurst, the militant English suffragette who championed voting rights for women. In England, women earned the right to vote in 1918, followed almost three years later by women in the United States.

My economics professor at the Harvard Business School, Sumner Slichter, in a seemingly offhand comment in 1946, put the women's issue at the forefront of national interests. He was discussing some arcane subject such as whether corporations shifted their tax burdens to consumers when something seemed to remind him of brainpower. Brainpower, he said, was the most precious ingredient of the whole human enterprise: "God distributed brainpower randomly. He didn't do it by gender or by social position or by the jobs people held. He did it randomly. A lot of this precious commodity is in the heads of women, and we had better find a way to use it or the country will be the worse for it."

Slichter was no "women's libber." (I don't think the term had been invented yet.) His passing comment summed up the whole issue, I thought. There were no women students in the class to applaud him because the business school was an all-male academy at that time. One of the specious reasons it gave for excluding women was that very few of them occupied high positions in business. When HBS opened its doors more widely, its women graduates began to fill the top jobs along with their male classmates.

Civil Rights. Civil rights for black Americans should have concerned me more than it did when I was growing up. Perhaps it was because there were no Negroes, as they were called then, in my school and none living in Glendale. I learned later, to my surprise, that they were not allowed to live there. At the University of Southern California, where I went to college, there were no blacks on the athletic teams, but across town at the state university, UCLA, black stars such as Kenny Washington and Jackie Robinson began to appear. When World War II ended in the Pacific and my aircraft carrier was converted temporarily to a troopship, the senior officers feared that mixing the returning black and white soldiers might lead to violence. (It didn't.)

I never thought very much about the unequal treatment of black Americans, I suppose, because the problem seldom confronted me directly. There were many others like me. It took the civil rights movement in the late 1950s and 1960s to open our eyes. We accepted the

instances of segregation up until events such as Rosa Parks's courageous refusal to move to the black section of the bus made us realize
that things had to change. I had learned about the effectiveness of nonviolent protests from studying Mahatma Gandhi's successful efforts in
India. I was not surprised that Martin Luther King Jr.'s espousal of non-
violence was equally successful. I admired the courage of the thousands
of college students—including the Freedom Riders—who boldly confronted the issue of segregated accommodations in the South.

We were living in Washington, a segregated city, when Martin
Luther King led the massive march on the nation's capital in 1963. It
helped to bring about the Civil Rights Act of 1964, the most far-
reaching effort in U.S. history to assure equal rights for all Americans.
I was proud to be serving in the administration of a president who did
so much to facilitate passage of the legislation. It was President Johnson's finest hour, the achievement that will assure his place in history.

Vietnam and the Cold War

The Vietnam War is best understood when it is viewed as a part of the
larger effort of the Cold War, the forty-year struggle to contain the
Soviet Union and the advancement of Communism. We won the Cold
War when the Soviet Union became Russia once again, but we lost the
Vietnam War for reasons that will remain controversial for the rest of
my life and probably for the lives of my children.

The Cold War began, by my reckoning, with Winston Churchill's
"Iron Curtain" speech at Fulton, Missouri, in March 1946. "From
Stettin in the Baltic," Britain's great wartime leader said, "to Trieste in
the Adriatic, an iron curtain has descended across the continent."
Joseph Stalin, old "Uncle Joe" when England, the United States, and
the Soviet Union joined together to defeat Hitler, became the new
menace, determined to keep his Eastern European allies from contact
with the West. The United States and its allies were equally determined to prevent Communist parties from coming to power in the
Western democracies.

Harry S. Truman, initially thought to be a second-rater, proved to be the decisive leader of the Cold War effort. The Marshall Plan was inaugurated during his administration to rebuild the war-torn economies of Western Europe. A related program was launched to shore up Greece and Turkey. The national security apparatus of the United States was overhauled with the establishment of the Department of Defense, the Central Intelligence Agency, and the National Security Council, a coordinating mechanism at the White House level.

There was plenty for the new agencies to do as the Soviet Union increased the pressure in Europe. When Moscow attempted to blockade the Western-held sector of West Berlin, the United States responded with a massive airlift that thwarted the effort. To counter the formidable Soviet armies so that they would not attempt to overrun Western Europe, the United States and its allies formed the North Atlantic Treaty Organization (NATO) in 1949. The confrontation between East and West became more ominous in the same year when the Soviet Union detonated its first atomic weapon, ending the U.S. monopoly. In China in 1949, the Communists took control and established the People's Republic.

The Cold War was fought on many fronts—economic, political, ideological, and covert. While the main focus was Europe, the Cold War battlefields also included Central and South America and, to an increasing extent, the Far East. When Communist North Korea invaded South Korea in 1950, President Truman led a United Nations effort to prevent the takeover of the South by the North. The French, anxious to retain their colonies in Indochina, fought and lost a war to the Communist forces of North Vietnam. President Eisenhower, Truman's successor, refused to intervene militarily after the French defeat, but through his secretary of state, John Foster Dulles, he gave full support to the government of South Vietnam. In his transitional meeting with the newly elected president, John F. Kennedy, Eisenhower warned that the neighboring countries would fall like dominoes if the South Vietnamese were defeated by Communist forces.

I have come to believe that the struggle between North and South Vietnam was essentially a civil war among the Vietnamese. We intervened in the conflict because we regarded it as a Cold War battlefield. Domestic considerations also affected our decision to assist the South Vietnamese. President Kennedy, a Democrat, was keenly aware of the Republican charge that the Democrats had "lost" China.

As a member of the Kennedy administration, I was fully in accord with the decision to provide military assistance to the struggling South Vietnamese. So was most of the country, with strong endorsement from the Congress and in the nation's editorial pages. In an earlier chapter, I explained my growing concern as the U.S. effort shifted from assistance to the Vietnamese to a U.S. takeover of the war effort, with massive deployments of U.S. ground, naval, and air forces. A different outcome might have been achieved if we had pursued from the start the strategy of General Abrams of protecting the South Vietnamese populace instead of counting the bodies of the enemy, which included civilians as well as North Vietnamese and Viet Cong troops.

As the war dragged on with growing numbers of U.S. casualties, opinion in the country shifted from broad support to nagging doubts. My own household mirrored the disquiet of the nation. My wife, always intensely loyal to me, kept her views to herself but agonized over a war she thought was wrong and would never end. My son David was the editorial page editor of the Harvard *Crimson* in 1971 and wrote probing articles criticizing the United States for killing people who wanted their independence from colonial masters. When students marched on Washington that year to protest the war effort, David was one of the hundreds rounded up by the police and released.

Across the country at Stanford University, Sarah lived in Columbae House, a student housing cooperative devoted to "social change through nonviolent action," and demonstrated against the war. When Columbae students organized a civil disobedience action for which they expected to be arrested, Sarah decided not to join them, but later regretted her reluctance. Sarah regarded me as a person bound by high moral standards and couldn't understand why I was a part of the war effort.

Amy, a high school student, joined protests in downtown Washington. She was less interested in opposing the war than in opposing parental influence. Demonstrating against a war policy that her father supported was one of the ways she chose to break away and establish her own identity.

Adi, the youngest of our four children, preferred baseball to politics, but on the way home from the softball field he wandered into a student demonstration at nearby American University as the police were breaking it up with tear gas. Adi stumbled into the house, announcing dramatically that he had been "gassed."

Though my wife and our children opposed the war and were troubled by my involvement with it, there was enough solidarity in the family to keep us from breaking apart. I encouraged the kids to develop their own views on controversial matters, as my father had done with me. I was proud of them for speaking out against policies they thought were wrong. They grew up to be responsible citizens because they were willing to express their views on critical issues. To me, that was more important than whether they agreed with me or with official policy.

My eight Pentagon years were the highlight of my working career. With the growing consensus that Vietnam was a foreign policy mistake, "the most costly and tragic national blunder in American history," as Telford Taylor concludes in *Vietnam and Nuremburg*, I sometimes feel diminished by my public service rather than fulfilled by it. Then I think how important it was to oppose the ideology of communism and the military threat of the Soviet Union, and to bring the Cold War to an end without direct military conflict between the two superpowers, each armed with nuclear weapons. In that context, taking a stand in Vietnam made sense to me then and it still does today. Perhaps I can sum up my views on Vietnam by saying that, if we did the wrong thing, it was for the right reason.

The Piano Players

My mother's Bechstein piano is now in my son David's living room. His daughter, Elisa, sits on my mother's old piano bench studying for her next recital. The piano is over a hundred years old. It has "piano legs," the squatty kind that are wide at the top and narrow at the bottom. The bench is just as old and is covered in a faded green needlepoint. There is a place to store music in the bench, on shelves behind a door with a metal handle. The piano keys are the original ivory ones except for one or two that have been replaced with a synthetic material. They are whiter than the ivory ones and look like crowned teeth next to yellowing molars.

On the piano there is a photograph of my mother, who was also named Elisa, sitting on the same bench playing the same piano. She is wearing a long skirt, perhaps of brown velvet, and looks up with a pleasant expression at whomever it was who took the picture. I can't tell from the furniture or the look of the room or her appearance whether the picture was taken in Manchester, England, before my grandfather moved his family to California in 1911, or in the large house he built in his new homeland.

But it really doesn't matter whether the photo was taken in the Old World or the New, because my mother looks so self-assured and happy playing the piano. What is important is that the Elisa in the photograph and her great-granddaughter Elisa are together around a piano, a bench, and a shared love of music.

My mother was never a traditionally religious person. Neither she nor my father were regular churchgoers. Though not a conventional worshipper, she was nevertheless a deeply religious person. She saw God's work in trees, wildflowers, the mountains and sea, and even in the little wisps of fern that she would bend over and pick on walks in the woods. Music, painting, and poetry connected her to a mystical world of nature that to her was the divine creation—the gospel according to Wordsworth, as it were.

When I went aboard ship in the Navy in World War II, my mother copied in her careful handwriting the words of the Twenty-third Psalm. I folded the stationery on which it had been written and carried it in my wallet during our months at sea. I would take it out and read it from time to time, and always it was the link to my mother and my family that gave me comfort, more than the beautiful and reassuring words of the psalm itself.

Because I was not a regular churchgoer and did not pray as a matter of habit, I thought it was somehow dishonest to seek God's help in combat when I had not sought his help in normal circumstances. It would be hypocritical to ask for divine intervention when the chips were down when I had not paid my dues in the years before.

I have something of the same feeling when I recite the words of the Nicene Creed on occasional Sunday mornings at Washington National Cathedral. I say some of the words in a clear voice and with conviction. For example, I do believe in God and speak the creed's reference to this belief in sincere tones. But I tend to lower my voice or slur my words when we come to the part about Christ rising from his tomb after three days and ascending into heaven. Did this really happen or did Mary Magdalene imagine it, as she stood weeping and looking into the tomb and then turned to encounter the Christ risen into this world?

But then I think of my mother in the photo on the piano while her great-granddaughter Elisa plays. Did my mother ascend into heaven? I feel close to her when I visit her grave on a hillside in Glendale. I try to reach her when I am troubled, or preparing myself for something difficult like surgery. When I close my eyes and concentrate hard, I can sometimes sense a totality in which my mother and I and the universe coexist, floating in endless space.

My mother has influenced my life and made me a better person. I am glad that her presence continues in my son's living room. I can't think of anything that would have given her more pleasure than knowing that there was a great-granddaughter Elisa playing her piano.

Although I can't accept the literal meaning of Christ rising from the tomb and ascending into heaven, I can accept it fully as a way of telling us that a person's life persists after death, and that one's presence can be felt long after one is gone. That is what I know to be true when I see my mother's photograph on the piano and listen to young Elisa struggling to master a new piece of music.

A Note on Sources
and Bibliography

A Note on Sources

I have depended on my memory for much of what I have written. I have also, of course, made use of books and articles, personal files, letters, newspaper accounts, and other source materials. The bibliography lists the books. I have quoted directly from many of them. From others I have gained perspective and additional facts relating to events in which I was personally involved. Examples would be Paul H. Nitze's account of the 1961 Berlin crisis in his *From Hiroshima to Glasnost,* and Robert S. McNamara's writings on the Cuban Missile Crisis.

My *Encyclopedia Britannica* was a handy place to check facts and to refresh my memory on a variety of subjects, such as Gen. Billy Mitchell's court-martial and the development of the Nazi V-2 weapon. For details on the Battle of Leyte Gulf that involved ships or actions beyond those of my immediate carrier group, I have relied on Samuel Eliot Morison's official history of the epic battle.

Personal files have been a valuable source of information. During the years when I served as an assistant secretary of defense, I prepared detailed notes for my weekly meetings with the secretary. These notes were declassified at the end of my Pentagon years and made available to me. My files from the Washington Post Company and the Air Transport Association have also been helpful, particularly those on the illegal strike of the air traffic controllers. Copies of Harbridge House publications aided me in writing about that phase of my life.

In an earlier day, people wrote letters, and I have many of them to and from members of my family. I have quoted from these letters at several places in the book.

Newspaper articles on events that involved me were collected by administrative aides in my government and nongovernment activities. In many instances, as, for example, in Robert McNamara's remarks at the launching of the aircraft carrier *John F. Kennedy,* newspaper articles provided details that supplemented my own recollections. The newspaper files and, indeed, my papers in general have been deposited with the University of Southern California.

I have included two chapters (slightly modified) from my earlier memoir, *Now I Know in Part.* The first, which opens this book, is the account of my naval duty in World War II. The second, which brings the book to a close, is a memory of my mother.

Bibliography

U.S. Navy, World War II

Morison, Samuel Eliot. *Leyte.* Boston: Little, Brown, 1958.

Stewart, Adrian. *The Battle of Leyte Gulf.* New York: Charles Scribner's Sons, 1979.

Woodward, C. Vann. *The Battle for Leyte Gulf.* New York: Ballantine Books, 1947.

Y'Blood, William T. *The Little Giants: U.S. Escort Carriers against Japan.* Annapolis, Md.: Naval Institute Press, 1978.

Motion Pictures

Milne, Tom. *Rouben Mamoulian.* Bloomington: Indiana University Press, 1969.

Warner, Jack L. *My First Hundred Years in Hollywood.* New York: Random House, 1984.

National Security Issues

Clifford, Clark. *Counsel to the President.* New York: Random House, 1991.

Colby, William. *Lost Victory: A Firsthand Account of America's Sixteen-Year Involvement in Vietnam.* Chicago: Contemporary Books, 1989.

Coletta, Paolo E. *American Secretaries of the Navy*. Vol. 2. Annapolis, Md.: Naval Institute Press, 1980.

Enthoven, Alain C., and K. Wayne Smith. *How Much Is Enough? Shaping the Defense Program, 1961–1969*. New York: Harper & Row, 1971.

Fallows, James. *National Defense*. New York: Random House, 1981.

FitzGerald, Frances. *Fire in the Lake: The Vietnamese and the Americans in Vietnam*. New York: Random House, 1972.

Halberstam, David. *The Best and Brightest*. New York: Random House, 1969.

Haught, Robert L. *Giants in Management*. Washington, D.C.: National Academy of Public Administration, 1985.

Hewes, James E., Jr. *From Root to McNamara*. Washington, D.C.: U.S. Army Center of Military History, 1975.

Langguth, A. J. *Our Vietnam: The War, 1954–1975*. New York: Simon & Schuster, 2000.

McNamara, Robert S. *In Retrospect: The Tragedy and Lessons of Vietnam*. New York: Random House, 1995.

McNamara, Robert S., James G. Blight, Robert K. Brigham, Thomas J. Biersteker, and Herbert Y. Schandler. *Argument without End: In Search of Answers to the Vietnam Tragedy*. New York: Public Affairs, 1999.

Nitze, Paul H. *From Hiroshima to Glasnost: At the Center of Decision*. New York: Weidenfeld & Nicholson, 1989.

Palmer, Bruce, Jr. *The 25-Year War: America's Military Role in Vietnam*. Lexington: University of Kentucky Press, 1984.

Schumacher, F. Carl, Jr., and George C. Wilson. *Bridge of No Return: The Ordeal of the U.S.S. Pueblo*. New York: Harcourt, Brace, Jovanovich, 1971.

Shapley, Deborah. *Promise and Power: The Life and Times of Robert McNamara*. Boston: Little, Brown, 1983.

Sheehan, Neil. *The Arnheiter Affair*. New York: Random House, 1971.

———. *A Bright and Shining Lie: John Paul Vann and America in Vietnam*. New York: Random House, 1988.

Shillito, Barry J. *A Memoir*. San Diego: Shillito Publications, 1997.

Sorley, Lewis. *A Better War: The Unexamined Victories and Final Tragedy of America's Last Years in Vietnam*. New York: Harcourt Brace & Company, 1999.

———. *Thunderbolt: General Creighton Abrams and the Army of His Time*. New York: Simon & Schuster, 1992.

Taylor, Gen. Maxwell D. *The Uncertain Trumpet*. New York: Harper & Brothers, 1959.

Taylor, Telford. *Nuremberg and Vietnam: An American Tragedy.* New York: Bantam Books, 1971.

Tregaskis, Richard. *Southeast Asia: Building the Bases.* Washington, D.C.: Government Printing Office, 1974.

Zumwalt, Admiral Elmo, Jr. *On Watch.* New York: Quadrangle, 1976.

The Press

Bradlee, Ben. *A Good Life.* New York: Simon & Schuster, 1995.

Davis, Deborah. *Katharine the Great: Katherine Graham and the Washington Post.* New York: Harcourt, Brace, Jovanovich, 1979.

Graham, Katharine. *Personal History.* New York: Alfred A. Knopf, 1997.

Tifft, Susan E., and Alex S. Jones. *The Trust: The Powerful and Private Family behind the* New York Times. Boston: Little, Brown, 1999.

Airlines

Breyer, Stephen. *Regulation and Its Reform.* Cambridge: Harvard University Press, 1982.

Life Magazine. "Skyjacking." August 11, 1972.

Meyer, John R., and Clinton V. Oster Jr. *Deregulation and the Future of Intercity Passenger Travel.* Cambridge, Mass.: MIT Press, 1987.

Morrison, Steven A., and Clifford Winston. *The Evolution of the Airline Industry.* Washington, D.C.: Brookings Institution, 1995.

Sherrill, Robert. *The Oil Follies of 1970–1980: How the Petroleum Industry Stole the Show (and Much More Besides).* New York: Anchor Press, 1983.

Time Magazine. "TWA 847 Hijacked by Islamic Jihad." June 24, 1985.

Yergin, Daniel. *The Prize: The Epic Quest for Oil, Money, and Power.* New York: Simon & Schuster, 1991.

Armenian Issues

Alexander, Edward. *A Crime of Vengeance: An Armenian Struggle for Justice.* New York: Free Press, 1991.

Arlen, Michael J. *Exiles.* New York: Farrar, Straus & Giroux, 1970.

———. *Passage to Ararat.* New York: Farrar, Straus & Giroux, 1975.

Balakian, Peter. *Black Dog of Fate: A Memoir.* New York: Basic Books, 1997.

Bryce, Viscount. *The Treatment of the Armenians in the Ottoman Empire, 1915–16.* London: His Majesty's Stationery Office, 1916.

Chahin, M. *The Kingdom of Armenia.* New York: Dorset Press, 1987.

Chalabian, Antranig. *General Andranik and the Armenian Revolutionary Movement*. Southfield, Mich.: Antranig Chalabian, 1988.

Fromkin, David. *A Peace to End All Peace: Creating the Modern Middle East, 1914–1922*. New York: Henry Holt, 1989.

George, Joan. *Merchants in Exile: The Armenians of Manchester, England, 1835–1935*. London: Gomidas Institute, 2002.

Hourani, Albert. *A History of the Arab Peoples*. Cambridge: Harvard University Press, Belknap Press, 1991.

Hovannisian, Richard G. *The Armenian Genocide: History, Politics, Ethics*. New York: St. Martin's Press, 1992.

Krikorian, Mesrob K. *Armenians in the Service of the Ottoman Empire, 1860–1908*. London: Routledge & Kegan Paul, 1972.

Lynch, H. B. *Armenia*. In two vols. London: Longmans, Green and Co., 1901.

Morgenthau, Henry. *Ambassador Morgenthau's Story*. New York: Doubleday, Page & Company, 1918.

Nalbandian, Louise. *The Armenian Revolutionary Movement: The Development of Armenian Political Parties through the Nineteenth Century*. Berkeley: University of California Press, 1963.

Riggs, Henry H. *Days of Tragedy in Armenia, 1915–1917*. Ann Arbor: Gomidas Institute, 1957.

Saroyan, Aram. *Meet Uncle Aram*. Boston: H. H. Toumayan, 1970.

About the Author

PAUL R. IGNATIUS, a native of Los Angeles, California, served as a lieutenant in the U.S. Navy during World War II aboard an aircraft carrier and on assignments in Washington, D.C. An honors graduate from the University of Southern California, he received a master's degree in Business Administration from Harvard University after the war and served on the staff of the Harvard Business School from 1947–50 as a research assistant and instructor. He later cofounded Harbridge House, Inc., a management consulting firm, with two Harvard Business School associates and served as its vice president and director.

Mr. Ignatius served for eight years in the administrations of presidents Kennedy and Johnson, first as an Assistant Secretary of the Army and later as Under Secretary of the Army. He was appointed Assistant Secretary of Defense in 1965 and was named Secretary of the Navy in 1967.

Following his government service, Mr. Ignatius served as president of the *Washington Post* for two years and president of Air Transport Association for fifteen years.

Mr. Ignatius is the recipient of the Army Distinguished Civilian Service Award, the Navy Distinguished Public Service Award, and the Department of Defense Distinguished Public Service Award.

Mr. Ignatius resides in Washington, D.C., with his wife, the former Nancy Sharpless Weiser. They have four children.

U.S. Naval Institute Press is the book-publishing arm of the U.S. Naval Institute, a private, nonprofit membership society for sea service professionals and others who share an interest in naval and maritime affairs. Established in 1873 at the U.S. Naval Academy in Annapolis, Maryland, where its offices remain today, the Naval Institute has members worldwide.

Members of the Naval Institute support the education programs of the society and receive the influential monthly magazine *Proceedings* and discounts on fine nautical prints and on ship and aircraft photos. They also have access to the transcripts of the Institute's Oral History Program and get discounted admission to any of the Institute-sponsored seminars offered around the country. Discounts are also available to the colorful bimonthly magazine *Naval History.*

The Naval Institute's book-publishing program, begun in 1898 with basic guides to naval practices, has broadened its scope to include books of more general interest. Now the Naval Institute Press publishes about one hundred titles each year, ranging from how-to books on boating and navigation to battle histories, biographies, ship and aircraft guides, and novels. Institute members receive significant discounts on the Press's more than eight hundred books in print.

Full-time students are eligible for special half-price membership rates. Life memberships are also available.

For a free catalog describing Naval Institute Press books currently available, and for further information about joining the U.S. Naval Institute, please write to:

Customer Service
U.S. Naval Institute
291 Wood Road
Annapolis, MD 21402-5034
Telephone: (800) 233-8764
Fax: (410) 269-7940
Web address: www.navalinstitute.org